Superbia

The Perils of Pride. The Power of Humility.

Steven J. Willing, MD

In memory of my father, Harry Alfred Willing, who exemplified Humility through a life of modesty, sacrifice, and service.

In memory of Dr. Frank Barker, the humblest pastor I have ever known.

CONTENTS

Preface

There is nothing so natural to man, nothing so insidious and hidden from our sight, nothing so difficult and dangerous as pride."
— ANDREW MURRAY

How it all started

Parenting often takes us down unexpected paths. In my case, this happened when our son was around 11 years old. He was an excellent student, but every child needs occasional help. On one fateful evening, he was struggling with some algebra homework. To this day, I am unsure whether he was actually *asking* for help or just voicing frustration, but I took the bait. I patiently explained the problem and how to solve it — or so I thought. "NO! That's WRONG! That's not what the teacher said!" Hmm. *That* I did not see coming.

One might say I took considerable *pride* in my mathematical prowess. I got consistent straight "A's" from grammar school through college calculus. In a nationwide math competition (AHSME) — at the age of 15 — I placed first in my suburban high school of 3000 students. At age 14, I came in third. Perfect score on the SAT math section without breaking a sweat.

Now, my vaunted competence was being challenged by an impertinent 11-year-old boy who *obviously* didn't know who he was dealing with — and decided the *teacher* knew better. Ouch. My wife and I mentioned the episode to a pastor friend. His suggestion was brilliant: ask our son to read the account of Nebuchadnezzar in the Book of Daniel and then explain to us the meaning. Bribe him with money. Not only did we assign him the task, but I dove in myself. One insight led to another....and another....and many other things started coming into focus.

Four decades in academic and private medicine afforded me a unique perspective on pride in action. It was much like birdwatching: the more you know, the more you see. With increasing awareness, I came to see what lay at the core of departmental politics, infighting, and even occasional recklessness. I witnessed unsuspecting patients dying of preventable complications, and I heard of many others. In a tragic and very real sense, they were killed — by pride.

Why you need this message:

This is a book about — and for — you, me, and everyone.

If you aim to grow spiritually, this message is for you.

If you aspire to help others, love better, and be loved more, this message is for you.

If you are sitting on top of the world, you *really* need this message.

If the world is sitting on top of you, if you are trapped in a cycle of fear, anxiety, and despair, I offer a message of hope.

This message is for the confident and the insecure, the joyous and the despondent, the popular and the lonely, the rich and the poor, from the over-educated few to the many more who lacked either inclination or opportunity.

It is a message for your wife, your husband, your kids, your neighbors, your boss, your co-workers, and your church leadership. You are going to wish they would read it. But it is definitely for you.

Why are we so politically polarized? Why can't we get along? Why are we having so little impact on our society? Why is church membership in decline? The common answer to all is right there in Scripture. Come join me as we rediscover ancient truths being validated by the latest scientific research.

Although I will be speaking from a Christian perspective, I hope this work can be accessible to other faith persuasions and those who think they have no faith at all. If you are a hardened atheist, please hear what I have to say. Then pass it along to whichever Christians you find most irritating. You both stand to gain.

Where do we look for the truth about human nature?

"What is truth?" one famously inquired.[1] It has become fashionable to frame "truth" in a highly individualistic manner, turning wishes and feelings into sacred canon. In my perfect world, dogs could talk, and donuts

---

[1] Pontius Pilate, in John 18:38

would be health food, but such "truth" collides with the reality I am compelled to inhabit. Someone whose truth granted him the right of way over an oncoming train would find that truth abruptly and untidily refuted at the moment of impact. For the purpose of our discussion, "truth" means an accurate description of the physical and spiritual universe as it is and has been.

Suppose we desire to know the truth about human nature. What would qualify as evidence? Some maintain that science is the only way to objective truth, but that assertion cannot be established scientifically. ["Oh yeah," you're probably thinking, "the old self-referential incoherence trick"]. Yet, science has been exceedingly successful in enhancing our knowledge about the universe and has improved our lives in countless ways.

Social science and psychology are the fields most pertinent to the subject at hand. Their findings have shown remarkable consistency in this area. Of course, there are many pitfalls to such research: publication bias, irreproducibility of results, and too many studies mainly based on young college students rather than the general population. [When I was in college, I am sure I considered myself *perfectly* representative of our species. But that was a long, long time ago, and I was never, to my knowledge, a subject of research. Still....it would explain that embarrassing tendency to salivate when the microwave beeps]. Research methods and standards have improved dramatically over the years. Sigmund Freud literally just made stuff up, published it, and got hailed as a genius. ["Ah, those were the days," sigh untenured psychology professors of today]. But what can one do? We either work with imperfect data or chuck the science altogether. I'll go with choice "a."

For Jews and Christians, the Bible is an authoritative source of wisdom in the matters on which it speaks. As a Reformed Christian, I believe the Old and New Testaments are given to us by God through human intermediaries and convey reliable truths about the nature of humanity. Whether you believe the Bible is the Word of God or not, no one can deny it is a remarkable book. Composed by over 40 different authors, in three ancient languages, writing from three continents, over a span of 2000 years, no other book comes close to its impact on the development of Western Civilization. Given its unique status, the Bible warrants at least as much respect as Aristotle, Maimonides, Avicenna, or Confucius.

Christianity further maintains that God reveals Himself through two books: the Bible and the book of nature. Science is the process of interpreting that book of nature. Since God cannot err or deceive, all His revelation is infallible, both Scripture and nature. They do not contradict, although humans often misinterpret both.

Through invoking both science and Scripture, I aim to emphasize the harmony between them on the subjects of pride and humility. The science adds depth and detail. The Bible brings a perspective that science does not address by offering an explanation (the fall of man), perspective (transcendental significance), and solutions (Scriptural teaching on humility).

There is one more source of truth useful to our discussion, and that is the realm of experience. The recorded experiences of the human species constitute the subject we know as History.

The fascinating thing is that three independent sources of knowledge — Scripture, science, and history, paint a perfectly harmonious picture of human nature as deeply flawed in a *particular* way. But all is not hopeless; all equally point to a *particular* antidote.

There is something fundamentally wrong with human nature.

John Locke saw human nature as a "blank slate" — neither good nor bad, merely a product of the environment. Jacques Rousseau, mythmaker of the "noble savage," saw human nature as basically good, blaming all evil and violence on societal influences. The Bible, history, and science prove Locke and Rousseau wrong. Thomas Hobbes ("war of all against all") was nearer to the truth. We are born with a natural tendency toward selfishness and evil. In fact, there are many things wrong with human nature. This little book will focus on just one.

Pride

Why should pride be such a big deal? Why should anyone care? Evidently, it mattered a great deal to the authors of Scripture. Using the simplest of measures, the word "humility" appears in the King James Version only eight times; "pride" is used 75 times. Toss in various synonyms for "pride" and related passages, and references to pride run well into the hundreds — probably more than any other sin except perhaps idolatry. Something is going on here.

In an age long forgotten, Pride was considered worst among the seven deadly sins. *Superbia*, in the Latin of ancient scholars. How quaint.

From church fathers of the second century through Andrew Murray in the nineteenth century, theologians seemed obsessed with the matter. In 21st-century Western society, pride is more likely to be exalted as a virtue than condemned as a vice. But what is it? Just a word, for starters, and words change meaning with time. What did they mean by "pride"? Everything hangs on its definition. That definition is the subject of this book.

Because of pride, the image and effectiveness of the Church have been compromised. One direct consequence is conflict: within families, congregations, and communities. Another is that the witness of the Church is tarnished in the eyes of the world. Rather than being known for our love for one another,[2] we are known for our self-righteousness, judgmentalism, dogmatism, and, in certain quarters, fierce anti-intellectualism. God has, and always will, resist the proud. To question whether God would *resist the Church* herself is to miss the point entirely. He will *especially* resist pride among His followers, for we are the ones to whom much has been given — and forgiven. We, of all people, should know better.

The opposite of pride is Humility. We will see that true humility is not self-abasement or merely a proper opinion of oneself but a positive virtue to be embraced and lived.

On the matter of humility, there are worthy treatments of the subject, both ancient and contemporary, by some of the greatest luminaries of Christian thought. Through no fault of the authors, these books don't exactly top the bestseller list. Let's be frank: aspiring to be humble is pretty low on the modern Christian's to-do list. Growing in meekness just can't compete with building a perfect marriage, achieving imperturbable joy, learning the secrets of success, raising your leadership quotient, rearing perfect kids, becoming a master evangelist, unlocking the secrets of ancient prophecy, or mastering sound financial discipline. Where are the seminars on humility? Who prays that their children will grow up meek? All those other goals are worthy. But one obstacle stands above all between us and those other worthy goals: our pride.

Whatever your situation in life, striving to recognize, confess, and eliminate the pride in your heart is sure to honor God and will lead to unexpected blessings.

"God resists the proud, but gives grace to the humble."[3]

"Humble yourselves in the sight of God, and you will be exalted."[4]

Such passages, fellow travelers, reflect a constant unified theme from Genesis to Revelation. Our ancestors in the faith understood the sin of pride,

---

[2] John 13:35
[3] James 4:6, 1 Peter 5:5
[4] James 4:10

and they feared it. The practice of Godly humility is a discipline that the modern Church has largely pushed aside, to the detriment of the individual, the Body, and the fallen world we are called to serve.

Let me stipulate at the outset that not everything herein is true for everybody. Everyone is proud, yes, but not in the same ways. You will find it much easier and more comfortable to see it in others than yourself. That was certainly true for me. In the mansions of our minds, the windows are grand and clear, while the mirrors are safely locked in the basement. We see others quite clearly — or at least imagine we do. We see ourselves not nearly as well as we imagine — and we're pretty comfortable with that.

The purpose of this book is not to scold but to offer hope and remind us of what the Church has long taught. The world is full of broken, hurting, lonely, desperate souls. We all have experienced — or will in time — physical illness, the betrayal of friends, false accusations, love's rejection, outright persecution, or any of the assorted heartbreaks that life throws our way. It may seem harsh to accuse hurting people of haughtiness. Yet sometimes, even those trials are a consequence of pride. It just might be that unrecognized pride is our *greatest barrier* to recovery and growth.

The Way of Humility is the pathway to blessing, and there is no shortcut. Growing in humility is a lifetime project. In later chapters, I will explore in depth the practices and attitudes of humility, but behavior is not humility. It is the result of humility. My hope is not to change what you *do* but how you *think*. Specifically, I hope to change the way you think about yourself. Pride is a state of mind. Even more precisely, it is a matter of *belief*. Pride distorts our beliefs in many, many ways. Humility is a completely different way of thinking.

Perhaps all the ancients were wrong, and pride is much ado about nothing. Or it could be the greatest impediment of the age to our salvation, our spiritual growth, our ministry, and our success in every endeavor. Read and decide.

God has decreed that He resists the proud. There is no clause exempting those who don't realize or admit that they are. To reject pride, we must first recognize it. Therein lies the rub. But with this book in hand, you can learn to detect it. Do you desire the Grace of God? Do you aspire to please Him? Do you seek better relationships? Less conflict? Greater wisdom? Fruitful ministries? Better mental and physical health? Success in business and in life? Reject pride and embrace humility. Three thousand years of accumulated wisdom point the way. Come with me, and let's walk through this together.

1

A Theory of Everything

Once considered the greatest of sins and the root of all others, in our age, it has been reduced to an afterthought. Jonathan Edwards defined Pride as "thinking of oneself more highly than he ought," but of course, "everyone always believes his own opinion is quite proper." Pride is unique among sins in that one often commits it without realizing it, and it is the only sin to deny its own existence. The challenge we face is to take a fresh look at the ancient wisdom, wake up to the danger, call it what it is, and replace it with the undiscovered virtue of humility.

"Pride is the first sin that ever entered into the universe, and it's the last that is rooted out. It is God's most stubborn enemy." — JONATHAN EDWARDS[5]

"The essential vice, the utmost evil is pride. Unchastity, greed, drunkenness and all that are mere flea bites in comparison. It was through Pride that the devil became the devil. Pride leads to every other vice. It is the complete anti-God state of mind, the essential vice, the utmost evil." — C.S. LEWIS[6]

"Daddy, what's the world made of?"

Stuff.

"Daddy, what's stuff?"

Stuff is made of elements. Aristotle thought there were four elements, air, earth, fire, and water.

Why did they call him that?

---

[5] Jonathan Edwards. *Thoughts on the Revival of Religion in New England* IV.1. https://www.ccel.org/ccel/edwards/works1.ix.v.i.html. Accessed May 22, 2022.
[6] Lewis, C. S. *Mere Christianity*. New York: Harper One, 2001.

Call him what?

Hairy tonsil.

No, not hairy tonsil. Ar-i-sto-tle.

Harris otter? Can I just call him Harris?

That would be fine, Justin.

Was Harris right, daddy?

It was a start. There are almost a hundred elements in nature. But none of them were air, earth, fire, or water.

That's too bad.

Why?

Fire's fun.

Well leave it alone.

OK, daddy. What are elly mints made of?

Elements. El-e-ments. They're made of atoms.

I know about atoms! What are atoms made of?

Atoms are made of protons, neutrons, and electrons.

What are pro-...those things made of?

Protons, neutrons, and electrons are made out of quarks and leptons.

Ha-ha! That's a funny word. QUARK-QUARK! So what are they made of?

Well, uh...Oh, look at the time! Lights out. You've got school tomorrow.

OK, daddy. Night-night. You're so smart. [giggling] QUARK-QUARK!

———————————

As of the early 21st century, that's where subatomic physics hits the wall. The standard model describing the fundamental particles and forces of the universe is as far as we've gotten. The wall has held for four decades. Much remains unexplained — more, perhaps, than you can possibly imagine. Someday, scientists hope we will have a Theory of Everything that will account for all matter, energy, and forces in the observable universe. At present, we're nowhere close. We may never get there.[7]

————————————

I hear it all the time. "How can they think that?" "How can they do that?" "How can they be like that?" "How can *anyone* believe that???" I no longer ask such questions. The one answer that explains all became crystal clear a long time ago. We had just forgotten it.

Human history is a saga of struggle and conflict, polarization, oppression, addictions, suicide, horrible injustice and inequality, and loneliness. None are new; all are facts of human nature. But why? If we apply Occam's razor, is there one simple explanation that undergirds them all? Humans are a complicated species. There never will be a true Theory of Everything for human behavior, but we have something very close. Wars, crime, racism, violence, depression, anger, divorce, church splits: all share, to a greater or lesser degree, one common element. Let us call that element "Superbia." This "element" is observed and demonstrated through the study of history, science, and Scripture. Take your choice. All converge upon the same inescapable conclusion.

Superbia

"The commencement of all sin."[8]

"The root of all heresy."[9]

"The first sin."[10]

"The greatest sin."[11]

"The gateway to hell."[12]

————————————

[7] Hossenfelder, Sabine. *Lost in Math: How Beauty Leads Physics Astray.* New York: Basic Books, 2018.
[8] Augustine. *A Treatise on Nature and Grace.* Chapter 33. https://ccel.org/ccel/schaff/npnf105/npnf105.xii.xxxvii.html
[9] Walter Hilton. *Ladder of Perfection.* Chapter V, Section 1. http://www.ccel.org/ccel/hilton/ladder.ii_1.i.iii.v.ii.html
[10] Thomas Aquinas. *Summa Theologica.* Question 162, Article 7. https://ccel.org/ccel/aquinas/summa/summa.SS_Q162_A7.html
[11] Thomas Aquinas. *Summa Theologica.* Question 162, Article 6. https://ccel.org/ccel/aquinas/summa/summa.SS_Q162_A6.html
[12] Andrew Murray. *Humility: The Journey Toward Holiness.* Bloomington, MN: Bethany House Publishers, 2001, p16.

Jewish and Christian theologians throughout the ages have had much to say about the sin of pride, for at least one salient reason: the Bible itself has much to say on the topic. Considering the obsession with pride in earlier times, it is curious what little concern it draws in present-day Christian discourse. Once in a great while, some prominent teacher or author will broach the subject, but it is probable that most Christians will go for years, decades, or a lifetime without reading or hearing a serious, thorough treatment of pride and humility.

Centuries ago, Pride ranked first among the seven deadly sins. Today the very idea of "seven deadly sins" seems rather quaint and legalistic, the scribblings of some obscure Benedictine monk with nothing better to do — and scant opportunity to indulge, should he be inclined.[13]

When was the last time you heard anyone preach against sloth? [I thought about writing a book on sloth, but lazy people don't read. So no one would publish it. I'm still shopping a publisher for my first how-to book, *Swimming with Cats*]. Anger, greed, envy — these are safe enough since few admit guilt in those departments (or maybe just a *little* bit). We rather enjoy calling out anger, particularly of those darned Republicrats or Roman Baptisterians. Folks get downright touchy about gluttony, as one well-known preacher discovered the hard way.[14] Best stay away from that one. Lust? Well, we've got that one covered, at least in more conservative quarters. If one needs a generic sin for a sermon example, preaching against lust usually won't ruffle any feathers. Way back in 1941, Dorothy Sayers penned an essay titled "The other six deadly sins."[15] Everyone knew which was the first. It seems even then that lust was hogging all the attention.[16] So what happened to Pride? Has the human race advanced so much that we've become universally humble? [I can hear you snickering. Stop it.] Did God change the rules? Or has our 21st-century snobbery blinded us to greater and more ancient wisdom?

Pride, it seems, has become not merely acceptable but celebrated. In contemporary Western society, most persons assume, as a matter of fact, that we should feel good about ourselves, accept ourselves just as we are (or at least *imagine* we are, no matter what others may think), trust our inner

---

[13] This, of course, is the popular conception. Many in the monastic orders were quite pious; but they were sometimes quite rowdy.

[14] Tony Campolo. *The Seven Deadly Sins.* Wheaton, IL: Victor Books, 1987.

[15] "The other six deadly sins." In: Sayers, Dorothy L. *Letters to a Diminished Church: Passionate Arguments for the Relevance of Christian Doctrine.* Nashville, TN: W Pub. Group, 2004.

[16] In recent years Western society — having spent the last five decades tearing down every sexual taboo — is coming to a belated realization that the consequences are not so pretty; with women and children paying the steepest price. Who could have predicted? Well, lots of folks, actually.

moral compass, and should anyone disapprove of me — it's their problem, not mine.

Maybe our definition is too narrow. Some people equate pride with arrogance, so if we don't have a problem with arrogance, then we don't have a problem with pride. Or perhaps our definition is too vague. After all, there is that troublesome ambiguity over its usage in the English language. The Oxford English Dictionary (OED) enumerates seventeen possible definitions of "pride," including, strangely, "the spleen of a deer."[17] Many English words have multiple definitions, some outright contradictory (oversight, to dust, to enjoin, to cleave, to sanction).[18] Who doesn't believe in taking "pride" in one's work, or being "proud" of one's children?

> "Pride is one of the seven deadly sins; but it cannot be the pride of a mother in her children, for that is a compound of two cardinal virtues — faith and hope."[19]

Even the Bible can get a bit confusing: "the brother in humble circumstances ought to take pride in his high position."[20] No matter which way you turn, someone steps up to promote school pride, team pride, racial pride, national pride, gay pride, geek pride [actually, I'm still waiting hopefully for that last one]. One might conclude that our greatest human flaw is not an excess of pride, but a lack of it.

The ancients had no problem with defining pride:

> "The craving for undue exaltation" — AUGUSTINE[21]

> "Inordinate desire of one's own excellence" — AQUINAS[22]

> "Pride is nothing else (as the learned say) but love of thy own excellency, that is, of thy own worship." — WALTER HILTON[23]

---

[17] "Pride." *The Oxford English Dictionary on CD-ROM.* Oxford: Oxford University Press, 2009
[18] Bryson, Bill. *Made in America: An Informal History of the English Language in the United States.* 1st U.S. ed. New York: W. Morrow, 1994.
DiLonardo, Jary Jo. "30 Words that are their own opposites". *ThoughtCo.* 5/17/2020.
https://www.mnn.com/lifestyle/arts-culture/stories/30-words-that-are-their-own-opposites
[19] Charles Dickens. *The Life and Adventures of Nicholas Nickleby.* London: Chapman & Hall, 1839
[20] James 1:9, NIV
[21] Augustine. *City of God.* Book 24 Chapter 13. https://www.newadvent.org/fathers/120114.htm
[22] Thomas Aquinas. *Summa Theologica.* Question 162 Article 3. http://www.newadvent.org/summa/3162.htm
[23] Walter Hilton. *Ladder of Perfection.* Part III Chapter V Section 1.
http://www.ccel.org/ccel/hilton/ladder.ii_1.i.iii.v.i.html

The OED reflects this distinction. Pride, in the negative sense, is "a high or overweening opinion of one's own qualities, attainments, or estate, which gives rise to a feeling and attitude of superiority over and contempt for others, inordinate self-esteem." The ancient Latin term is "Superbia" — first among the deadly sins. Pride — the emotion — is "a feeling of elation, pleasure, or high satisfaction derived from some action or possession." [24] The latter form of pride might be more aptly named as *satisfaction* at achieving a task, or love of excellence, or *delight* in the success of another.[25]

As this narrative unfolds, the distinction should become clear. Superbia is quite removed from a sense of pleasure for a job well done. The positive emotion we call "pride" has nothing to do with the destructive mindset denounced in scripture and historic Christian theology.

Confusion over use of the word has registered even in the psychological literature. In a 2007 paper,[26] Jessica Tracy and Richard Robins designated "authentic pride" as pro-social feelings of confidence and accomplishment, and "hubristic pride" to denote attitudes of arrogance, conceit, or self-aggrandizement.[27]

So, it's not that a little pride is good, and a lot is bad. There are two completely different definitions in common usage, and everything hangs on which one we're talking about.

What's the big deal, anyway?

Few of us today struggle with pride. We are, in fact, quite comfortable with it. So, what got our ancestors so lathered up over the matter? Surely there are worse offenses. You know, the usual suspects: murder, adultery, idolatry, racism, intolerance... driving slow in the passing lane. Well, there are two possible perspectives regarding which sins are worse: God's and ours. Which one do you think counts in the end? Consider the Scriptures:

> "These six things the Lord hates,
> Yes, seven are an abomination to Him:
> A **proud** look,

---

[24] "Pride." *The Oxford English Dictionary on CD-ROM*
[25] Even such innocent thoughts, carried too far, may be more self-serving than noble. For better or worse, it is common for parents to view children as an extension of themselves.
[26] Tracy, Jessica L., and Richard W. Robins. "Emerging insights into the nature and function of pride." *Current directions in psychological science* 16, no. 3 (2007): 147-150.
[27] "Authentic pride is positively associated with adaptive traits like extroversion, agreeableness, conscientiousness, and genuine self-esteem, whereas hubristic pride is negatively related to these traits but positively associated with self-aggrandizing narcissism and shame-proneness."

A lying tongue,
Hands that shed innocent blood."[28]

"The fear of the Lord is to hate evil; **Pride and arrogance** and the evil way
And the perverse mouth I hate."[29]

"Everyone **proud** in heart is an abomination to the Lord; Though they join forces, none will go unpunished."[30]

Proverbs 26 declares foolishness a great abomination (verses 1-11) but concludes that to be proud is worse still:

"Do you see a man wise in his own eyes?
There is more hope for a fool than for him."[31]

Clearly, God despises the proud. He is never capricious or arbitrary. There must, therefore, be a reason. The Scriptures describe at length both what Pride is and why it is such a uniquely dangerous sin. If our churches, our pastors, our Bible studies, or our ministries are avoiding or neglecting the subject, then we Christians are in grave peril.

So, when does pride become sinful, or what is sinful pride?

Much of this book will be dedicated to unpacking the manifestations of pride but let me begin with a simple definition: pride is thinking too highly of ourselves. As Jonathan Edwards wrote:

"The first and worst cause of error that prevails in our day is spiritual pride. This is the main door by which the devil comes into the hearts of those who are zealous for the advancement of Christ..... Pride is much more difficult to discern than any other corruption because, by nature, *pride is a person having too high a thought of himself.* Is it any surprise, then, that a person who has too high a thought of himself is unaware of it? He thinks the opinion he has of himself has just grounds and therefore is not too high."[32] [emphasis added]

---

28 Proverbs 6:16-17
29 Proverbs 8:13
30 Proverbs 16:5
31 Proverbs 26:12
32 Jonathan Edwards. *Thoughts on the revival of religion in New England*, Part IV Section I: Spiritual Pride. (1740) https://www.ccel.org/ccel/edwards/works1/works1.ix.v.i.html Accessed 5/22/2022

As Edwards wryly notes, you cannot know if your opinion of yourself is too high — that situation is self-correcting. If you discovered it was too high, that alone would fix it.

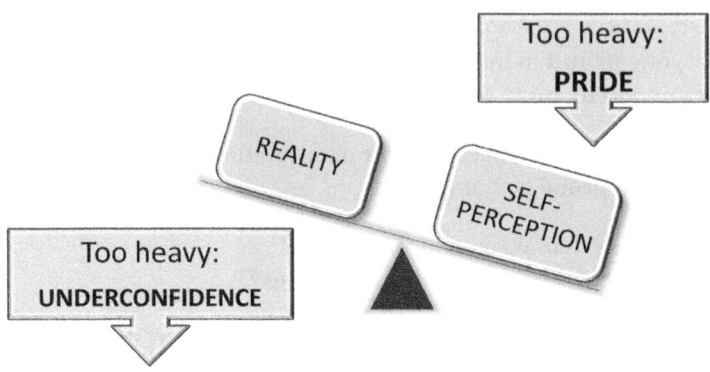

To visualize the concept, imagine a scale. Our self-perception should be in general balance with who we really are. Consider traits such as intelligence, skill, expertise, virtue, or any other matter of importance. When our self-perception in any area exceeds reality, that is pride. If the scale is heavily tipped on the negative side, other factors may be in play: exaggerated or false humility, lack of confidence, or poor self-image. In practice, a perfect balance may be unattainable.

Perhaps it isn't immediately apparent to you *why* they should be in balance. We will come to that in due course. If we must err, let us err on the side of modesty.

The first casualty of pride is self-awareness, so we don't know ourselves well enough to recognize its presence.[33] Tim Keller likened it to carbon monoxide: it kills you without your ever knowing you're in danger.[34] And how can we not *do* it if we don't know what *it* is? For the sincere disciple who seeks to grow in Christ, there is hope. Merely because we do not recognize it presently does not mean we can never recognize it. The chief aim

---

[33] There is a subtle but important distinction between prideful *acts* and pride as a state of mind. If we think about it, we sometimes know we acted proudly in a particular instance. It's a lot harder to know if your opinion of yourself is too high in general.
[34] Twitter. "https://Twitter.Com/Timkellernyc/Status/451690861559308288." Accessed May 23, 2022.

of this book is to aid in that recognition. It will be challenging, and perhaps somewhat uncomfortable.

Pride directed *inward* is overconfidence, an unrealistically high opinion of oneself. It causes us to be overconfident of our abilities, our beliefs, our power, and our moral standing before God and each another. Pride expressed *outward* is self-exaltation. It drives us relentlessly to compare ourselves to others, to get and have more than others, to take credit for what is good, and to blame others when we fail. Ultimately, it is a passion to grasp for ourselves the place reserved for God Almighty.

It would be much simpler if the Bible gave us a simple, precise description of pride — some distinctive, easily identified behavior we could simply choose not to do, like stealing or lying. But it doesn't. Pride is not an action, though it leads to many actions. It is a state of mind and a habit of thinking. Pride is malignant, invasive, and largely invisible, insinuating its roots into the deepest and darkest recesses of our beliefs and psyche, deadening our conscience, hardening our opinions, fueling resentment, and distancing us from one another. A simple one-line definition just won't suffice. On the other hand, Scripture abounds with examples of prideful behavior by proud men and (occasionally) women. Those narratives unveil to us the symptoms of pride, the consequences of pride, what God thinks about pride, how He deals with the proud, and its remedy.

Sins are like diseases in a certain respect. Some are obvious — a disfiguring rash, an injured limb, an exposed lie, an act of adultery. On the other hand, many diseases have no outward manifestations at all, like a cancer of the pancreas that grows without symptoms until it is too far advanced to remove. Some sins are like that too. Bitterness, envy, and anger can simmer deep in our souls while we greet our friends on Sunday morning with a smile and a jaunty, if dishonest, "I'm fine, thank you!"

In 1971 a new medical technology appeared that dramatically altered the practice of medicine. Godfrey Hounsfield's CT scanner allowed doctors to obtain direct images of the human brain for the first time ever without actually opening the skull. Suddenly we could see firsthand, in mere moments, injuries and diseases that before could only be diagnosed by complicated, indirect tests that were painful for the patient, difficult to perform, and equally difficult to interpret. The technology of CT was soon extended to all other parts of the body, and a revolution in medical diagnosis was underway.

With a CT scanner, we could diagnose, with a few pictures, problems that would have required surgery in earlier times. The exploratory laparotomy — surgically opening the abdominal cavity just to find out what, if anything, was wrong, went from a commonplace procedure to a rarity. It was about that time that I entered medicine, and I have spent the bulk of my professional career as a neuroradiologist learning about and interpreting those amazing tests that can reveal in moments the maladies of those in distress.

Over four decades interpreting images for thousands of human brains, I never gleaned the first hint of anyone's thoughts or character. For that, we must look elsewhere.

As the CT scanner is for the human body, so the Bible is for the human psyche. "For the word of God is living and powerful, and sharper than any two-edged sword, piercing even to the division of soul and spirit, and of joints and marrow, and is a discerner of the thoughts and intents of the heart."[35] What, then, does the Bible say about the human psyche? Is it consistent with what we observe, the findings of science and history? Let's find out. I think you're in for quite a surprise.

Everyone has heard the God and doctor jokes. Doctors have a reputation for pride and arrogance. Of course, in my professional career and mission endeavors, I have worked alongside many saintly, self-sacrificing, and occasionally even humble physicians. But our reputation is not wholly undeserved. In almost 40 years of practice, I have also witnessed pride and arrogance in our own profession. I have seen and experienced the personal animosities and friction that result. I heard hushed accounts of direct harm to patients caused by overconfident and ego-driven physicians resulting in permanent injuries and even deaths. Finally, I have struggled to diagnose and overcome pride in my own heart as I learned to recognize its signs and symptoms. I cannot claim victory. I do not expect to in this life.

In medicine, we rely heavily on screening exams: quick, inexpensive tests that can be performed on large populations to find out whether a disease is or is not present. If the screen comes back positive, usually other tests will be required to be sure the screen is accurate, establish a diagnosis, and obtain enough information to plan a treatment.

The screening test for pride is really rather simple. If you are conscious and have a pulse, then you have a pride problem. It is a universal affliction. As expressed by C. J. Mahaney:

> The sad fact is that none of us is immune to the logic-defying, blinding effects of pride. Though it shows up in different forms and to different people, it infects us all. The real issue here is not *if*

---

[35] Hebrews 4:12

pride exists in your heart; it's *where* pride exists and *how* pride is being expressed in your life. Scripture shows us that pride is strongly and dangerously rooted in our lives, far more than most of us care to admit or even think about.

John Stott has clearly thought about this and wrote the following: "At every stage of our Christian development and in every sphere of our Christian discipleship, pride is the greatest enemy and humility is our greatest friend."[36]

Pride infects us all but is rarely diagnosed. In the next chapter, we will examine pride's origin in the framework of the Judeo-Christian tradition. Subsequent chapters will describe more of its many signs and symptoms. Concluding chapters prescribe the cure: Humility. Along the way, you will see how exciting developments in social sciences and psychology offer new insights into pride and humility while validating ancient Biblical precepts.

"Few of us today struggle with pride. We are, in fact, quite comfortable with it."

Coming to grips with one's pride can be a difficult and trying experience. It is my hope that this book will help you through that process. Those who are most proud will have the least interest in setting out on this journey. I place no confidence in the power of mere words to effect any change in your life, but if the desire of your heart is to recognize and overcome what hidden sin may reside, our Lord will honor that.

God declares that He will resist the proud but give grace to the humble. Humility is the cure for the cancer of Pride. I need it; you need it, our families need it, our churches need it, our country needs it, the world needs it. The blessings of humility include peace, wisdom, personal growth, better marriages, healthier families, stronger churches, a better witness to a hurting world, and rich rewards in the life to come.

Daddy? Why do people fight so much?

Justin, you're supposed to be asleep.

I can't help it. I was just wondering. Jason and Rusty had another fight today.

---

[36] Mahaney, C. J. *Humility: True Greatness.* Sisters, OR: Multnomah Publishers, 2005. p29.

I'm reading a book about that right now. It's called "Superbia."

Super bee? Is that like Ant-man and Wasp?

No, Su-PER-bi-a. It's about how people think, which makes them act the way they do.

Sounds boring.

It's a book for grownups. You have a long way to go. If you don't go to sleep, I'm going to start reading it to you out loud.

PLEASE NO! Look! I'm asleep!

[silence, eyes shut tight]

Good night again, Justin. [kissing him on the forehead and leaving the room]

[seconds later] QUARK-QUARK! [more giggles]

Key points

- God hates pride
- Sinful pride is having too high an opinion of oneself
- Everyone is proud in some aspect of life

2

Paradise Lost — Evil Originated with Pride

The fall of humanity and the entrance of evil into this world began with a single act of rebellion. Many have argued that the crime of Adam and Eve was motivated by pride, a desire to be equal with God and so to become gods themselves. Alas, they were deceived, for in eating the fruit, they did not become like God, they did not become wise, and they breached the stronghold separating good from evil. In our hearts, we are still inclined to embrace the threefold lie of the serpent: that we may aspire to be gods, that wisdom resides within, and that we may judge for ourselves between good and evil.

"He trusted to have equaled the most High,
If he opposed; and with ambitious aim
Against the Throne and Monarchy of God
Raised impious War in Heaven and Battle proud"[37]

The First Great 'Awokening'

Stripped of all tradition and dogma, the record is really rather sketchy. It is a peculiar story, for while the beginning is shrouded in mystery, the climax is prophesied in dramatic and precise detail. Across the arc of human history, he was there at the beginning and will be doomed at the end.

It began with an act of cosmic treason. Many maintain he was an angel, though the evidence for that is rather scanty. He was and is a created being, so like all God's creatures, originally good. Sometime before recorded human history, he rebelled against his Creator and turned wholly evil. I speak, of course, of the being known as Satan (aka Lucifer).

Some readers might regard the person of Satan as pure myth. That's fine. My thesis does not rely upon his existence. But in our present, supposedly scientific and secularized age, belief in him has not vanished. Quite the

---

[37] John Milton. *Paradise Lost.* Public Domain, 1667

opposite. More Americans believe that Satan is real than believe in God. Yes, you read that correctly. In the 2020 American Worldview Inventory by George Barna at the Cultural Research Center, 51% of adults now embrace classical theism. (This would include traditional Jewish and Islamic views of God). Overall, 56% believe Satan is a real spiritual being.[38] The disparity was even wider among Millennials: only 31% embrace classic theism, while 44% believe Satan is real.[39]

Two key passages in the Old Testament are traditionally interpreted as references to the fall of Satan. Isaiah 14 prophesies the fall of the king of Babylon, and Ezekiel 28 the fall of the king of Tyre. Both chapters have been understood to possess a dual meaning, with the fall of both earthly kings a metaphor for the fall of a particular heavenly being. Even if the prophets were not speaking primarily of Satan's fall, they allude to it: "How you are fallen from heaven, O Lucifer, son of the morning! How you are cut down to the ground, you who weakened the nations!"[40]

If the strictest standards of interpretation are applied, there isn't much to go on. John Calvin reasoned that though our understanding of his fall was limited, we knew all we needed to know about him.[41] What do we know for sure? We know that Pride was the cause of his rebellion, fall, and condemnation.

Writing to Timothy regarding the requirements for bishops, Paul wrote, "He must not be a new convert, or he may [develop a beclouded and stupid state of mind] as the result of pride [be blinded by conceit, and] fall into the condemnation that the devil [once] did."[42] What does that mean? According to the passage in Isaiah, Satan aspired to equality with God.[43] Sometime later — after his downfall — he dangled that very same temptation before the First Parents of the human race.

---

[38] "American Worldview Inventory 2020 — At a Glance," Cultural Research Center, Arizona Christian University, April 21, 2020. https://www.arizonachristian.edu/wp-content/uploads/2020/04/CRC-AWVI-2020-Release-03_Perceptions-of-God.pdf accessed 2/8/2022
[39] "American Worldview Inventory 2021: Release #3," Cultural Research Center, Arizona Christian University, May 12, 2021. https://www.arizonachristian.edu/wp-content/uploads/2021/05/CRC_AWVI2021_Release03_Digital_01_20210512.pdf accessed 2/8/2022
[40] Isaiah 14:12
[41] John Calvin, *Institutes of the Christian Religion*, Book 1 Chapter 14. http://www.ccel.org/ccel/calvin/institutes.iii.xv.html: "Some murmur because the Scripture does not in various passages give a distinct and regular exposition of Satan's fall, its cause, mode, date, and nature. But as these things are of no consequence to us, it was better, if not entirely to pass them in silence, at least only to touch lightly upon them."
[42] 1 Timothy 3:6, AMP
[43] Isaiah 14:14, "'I will make myself like the Most High.'"

As to the second Fall, Scripture tells us much more. Adam and Eve: the pinnacle of God's creative masterwork, perfect in their created glory, made in the very image of God, happily content to worship and submit to their loving Creator. They were created with the ability to live each day without sin yet possessed the capacity and freedom to sin if they chose. It is often — and quite erroneously — taught they were given only one commandment: to abstain from the forbidden tree. But according to the record, many things were commanded of them.

First, Adam was instructed to name all the creatures. After Eve was created, both were commanded to "be fruitful and multiply; fill the earth and subdue it; have dominion over the fish of the sea, over the birds of the air, and over every living thing that moves on the earth."[44] Adam was charged with an ongoing duty: "The LORD God took the man and put him in the Garden of Eden to tend and keep it."[45] Many things were commanded, presenting many opportunities for disobedience. Only one thing was explicitly forbidden: "of the tree of the knowledge of good and evil you shall not eat, for in the day that you eat of it you shall surely die."[46]

One day, while sauntering through the garden, Eve found herself engaged in discourse with a strangely chatty reptile. [That should have been a red flag]. Their conversation turned to the forbidden fruit and the consequences of its consumption. "The serpent said to the woman, 'you will not surely die. For God knows that in the day you eat of it your eyes will be opened, and you will be like God, knowing good and evil.'"[47] So she took of the fruit and ate it, and Adam followed. According to Scripture, that first spark of defiance ignited the firestorm of violence, hatred, deceit, corruption, misery, and unspeakable cruelty that has plagued humanity since that one fateful day untold millennia ago.

But what was their offense, *precisely*? Was it (1) the simple act of eating the fruit? (2) the decision to eat it? or (3) some inner desire that motivated the decision? Eating the fruit was not their only potential path of disobedience. They could have neglected God's commands to name the animals or to tend the garden, what we call sins of omission. Yet presumably, they cheerfully carried out their assigned duties. Their weakness and ultimate downfall came through the *one* thing that was forbidden. But why? They were surrounded by an abundance of good things to eat. What made the fruit so

---

[44] Genesis 1:28
[45] Genesis 2:15
[46] Genesis 2:17
[47] Genesis 3:4

particularly alluring? Could it have been the mere fact that it was forbidden?

Calvin maintained that the initial sin of Adam and Eve was unbelief; they chose not to believe God's command or threat of punishment.[48] But that explanation offers no motive. It wasn't sufficient that they doubted the threat of punishment. After all, Satan stood up to God and *didn't* die, did he? One does not commit a crime merely because he can escape punishment. He must want to do it.

The tempter tapped into a motive for them to disobey. To entice them into disobedience, he promised three things: first, their eyes would be opened; second, they would be like God, and third, they would know good and evil. There is a common thread to all three promises: they offered to make Adam and Eve greater than they presently were. Supreme wisdom! Divinity! Autonomy! Power! Popularity! Eternal good looks! (Goodness and righteousness? Well, let's not get *too* carried away). Equality with God could be theirs! In short, he appealed to their pride. Now an appeal to pride is ineffective unless there is latent pride to address. The serpent could not make them proud, but if pride was there, he could stoke it to provoke them into rebellion. By this line of reasoning, most theologians through the ages concluded that Pride was the root cause of the Fall.[49]

Desiring to be wise, to know good and evil, and to be like God, Eve took the fruit, and Adam followed. They were transformed in an instant, and those changes became part of the spiritual DNA of all human generations.

Satan is called "the father of lies."[50] True to his title, he sold Adam and Eve a false bill of goods. But our first parents did not *know* that. Their eyes were, of course, not opened, but they *believed* they had been. They were less like God than ever, but they *believed* just the opposite. Their moral compass was permanently demagnetized, but they *trusted* in their new-found "knowledge" of good and evil. Thus, they could *decide for themselves* between right and wrong.

Rather than the anticipated glory, they were stricken with guilt and shame. We know next to nothing of the subsequent lives of Adam and Eve. Genesis reports they were expelled from the garden and bore Cain, Abel, Seth, and other children. We don't know what impact these three lies had on the

---

[48]John Calvin, *Commentary on Genesis*, Volume 1 Chapter 3. https://www.ccel.org/ccel/calvin/calcom01.ix.i.html "Therefore, unbelief was the root of defection; just as faith alone unites us to God."

[49] This was precisely the analysis of St. Augustine — *City of God*, Book XIV, Chapter 13: "secret ruin precedes open ruin, while the former is not counted ruin."

[50] John 8:44

spouse — but such an attitude contradicts its most basic principles. Contrast that attitude with the righteous Job: "Though He slay me, yet I will trust him"[58] In 2001, Islamic fanatics crashed airliners into the World Trade Center and Pentagon, murdering thousands in the name and service of a deity. Were they idolaters? From a Christian perspective, of course. But they didn't act out of *love* for Allah. They did it for paradise and virgins.[59] Quid pro quo. Purely transactional. They did it for themselves. Pride and idolatry dance cheek to cheek in a narcissistic *pas de deux*.

Exalted confidence in one's own wisdom

> "I cannot tell you any spiritual truth that deep within you don't know already. All I can do is remind you of what you have forgotten" — ECKHART TOLLE [60]

"Your eyes will be opened," assured the serpent. And Adam and Eve embraced the lie. While the advertising promised enlightenment, the product was spiritual blindness. People who lose their vision can adapt in many ways, so long as they know they can't see. Much worse is when one is blind but doesn't know it.

Anton's syndrome is a rare consequence of injury, usually from stroke, to both occipital lobes of the brain. Because the visual cortex is in the occipital lobes, the patients are rendered blind, but for some reason, they don't know it. Others usually begin to suspect something when the patient starts trying to walk through walls and closed doors or tripping over furniture. This symptom bears the unwieldy label of anosognosia — the lack of awareness or denial of one's own disability. Anton's syndrome is bad enough. Worse still is when one is blind but thinks he sees as well or *better* than the sighted. Into that state plunged Adam and Eve, taking with them all future generations.

Proud people — meaning all of us — are burdened with a disability we deny. We think we are wise, but we deceive ourselves. In reality, we "are wise to do evil, but to do good [we] have no knowledge."[61] We are afflicted by a spiritual Anton's syndrome, imagining ourselves wise, but falling far short.

---

[58] Job 13:15

[59] Rehov, Pierre, dir. *Suicide Killers*. City Lights Pictures, 2007. (This documentary interviews failed Islamic suicide bombers, who clearly state the motivation for their actions).

[60] Tolle, Eckhart. *The Power of Now: A Guide to Spiritual Enlightenment*. Novato, Calif: New World Library, 1999. p6.

[61] Jeremiah 4:22

Jesus taught that "whoever does not receive the kingdom of God as a little child will by no means enter it."[62] Frankly speaking, children, by nature, are hopeless little narcissists who are ruled by emotions, live only for themselves, and are devoid of spiritual understanding. But they have one thing going for them: they are teachable. They know their weakness and seek protection; they know their helplessness and seek provision; they know they have much to learn, ask incessant questions, and believe everything they are told. [Like many of today's college students].

Pride led to the unholy union of error with certainty, truly a marriage made in Hell.

In *A New Earth*, our friend Mr. Tolle explains how to know if you are "awakened":

> "If you find this book incomprehensible or meaningless, it has not yet happened to you. If something within you responds to it, however, if you somehow recognize the truth in it, it means the process of awakening has begun."[63]

Or, then again, if you find it incomprehensible and meaningless, maybe you understand it perfectly. That's brilliant marketing, though. Who wants to admit to being a dolt? [If you recognize the Truth in *this* book, you are obviously a highly spiritual person of superior intellect. Just sayin'.]

Determination to decide right and wrong on our own

> "But the first man sinned chiefly by coveting God's likeness as regards' knowledge of good and evil,' according to the serpent's instigation, namely that by his own natural power he might decide what was good, and what was evil for him to do." — AQUINAS [64]

Who ultimately decides right from wrong? Hopefully, if you are a Christian, the answer is God and God alone. But that is something you were taught, not something you discovered on your own. The other great monotheistic faiths, Judaism and Islam, provide the same final answer. Yet, in more ways than one, the devil is in the details. (Literally, in this case). What is our natural inclination? We make our own self-serving rules and then concoct elaborate rationalizations to justify breaking them.

---

[62] Mark 10:15
[63] Tolle, *A New Earth*. p 260
[64] Aquinas, *Summa Theologica* II:II:163, https://www.newadvent.org/summa/3163.htm, Accessed 2/8/2022

During the times of the Judges in ancient Israel, God sent one judge after another to rescue His people and bring them to repentance, and each time they soon fell back into apostasy. Their condition was described by a simple recurring phrase: "In those days there was no king in Israel; *everyone did what was right in his own eyes.*"[65]

Following one's own "inner light" is a great catchphrase for fatuous self-help books or New Age gurus. Apart from those whose inner light generates lucrative best-sellers, following your "inner light" usually ends badly. The problem, according to Scripture, is that like flies to a dung-heap, we are irresistibly drawn toward the wrong without even knowing it. Setting one's own standards of right and wrong in defiance of God has only one possible outcome, and it is never good. "There is a way that seems right to a man, but in the end it leads to death."[66] "Fools do not know that they do evil."[67]

When our pride appoints us the arbiter of right and wrong, there are two directions to err. We can err by declaring the innocent as evil (legalism) or by judging the evil as innocent (antinomianism). Although superficially, these attitudes seem diametrically opposed, they arise from the same inclination — the will to decide for ourselves between right and wrong. The Bible regards them as equivalent:

> Woe to those who call evil good, and good evil; Who put darkness for light, and light for darkness; Who put bitter for sweet, and sweet for bitter![68]

In modern western society, the prevailing culture tends toward hedonism, embracing the mantra of Woodstock: "if it feels good, do it." [What if it feels good walloping people who say that? Should we do it?] Yet even hedonists are quick to establish their own rules and demands for conformity. Secular culture has grown increasingly rabid in its disdain for Christian morality, especially in sexual matters, then proceeds to impose its own moralism with rigid standards of political correctness, suppression of dissenting opinions, coercive redistribution of income, or chic enviro-morality. A 2021 study in *American Sociological Review* indeed shows that increasing

---

[65] Judges 21:25
[66] Proverbs 14:12, 16:25
[67] Ecclesiastes 5:1
[68] Isaiah 5:20

levels of university education, especially in the arts, humanities, or social sciences, leads to a *higher* degree of moral absolutism.[69]

In the broadest perspective, our natural human tendency is to zig-zag between legalism and license depending upon the impulses of the moment.

Even the Soviet KGB could be moralistic. In the twilight of the cold war, the agency renowned and feared for kidnapping, torture, and murder, held a very firm line against *divorce* among its agents, and internal protocols were strictly enforced.[70] ["Sure, they committed ruthless atrocities against innocent people, but at least they were *pro-marriage!*"]

"Has God indeed said?"

How does one discriminate between God's Law and mere human opinion? Is Scripture the *only* authority? If so, then is everything permitted that Scripture does not forbid? Technically, there are no commandments specifically prohibiting prostitution or slavery, though all Scriptural references to both are disparaging. Is there anything now permitted that Scripture once forbade?

In the history of the Church, there have been various approaches toward defining the rules of Christian behavior. The typical Protestant solution incorporates all of the New Testament teachings, but also those elements of the Mosaic Law considered "moral" as opposed to "ceremonial" — a manmade, post hoc, but useful distinction. This is more or less the position of the Westminster catechism.[71] A variant of this approach proposes that only the Ten Commandments are now morally binding, supplemented by New Testament ethical teaching. Yet the way this was applied by reformers in 16th-century Geneva was radically different from how it is interpreted by today's Reformed denominations. The same doctrine doesn't lead everyone to the same conclusion.

A third alternative considers only New Testament instruction to be morally binding, entirely dispensing with the Mosaic Law. The Jerusalem council in Acts 15 lends support to this position, and it is referenced in the Catholic Catechism, which refers to it as the "New Law." A fourth possibility is that all are bound by "natural law," the moral law emanating from the mind

---

[69] Broćić, Miloš, and Andrew Miles. "College and the "Culture War": Assessing Higher Education's Influence on Moral Attitudes." *American Sociological Review* 86, no. 5 (2021): 856-895.
[70] Macintyre, Ben. *The Spy and the Traitor: The Greatest Espionage Story of the Cold War.* First edition. New York: Crown Publishing Group, 2018.
[71] *Westminster Larger Catechism*, Q. 93-148

of God that is written upon our conscience and variously expressed in the Old and New Testaments.[72]

What did the Apostle Paul mean when he wrote, we are freed from the Law, to live for the Spirit?[73] For the believer, is the Law of Scripture superseded by a "Law of the Spirit"? The Law is said to be written on our hearts,[74] but we observe the conduct of our brothers and sisters and conclude it must have been written in disappearing ink. This question is vastly beyond the scope of my work. I raise it for but one purpose: there is sufficient ambiguity and disagreement in the interpretation of Scripture for human pride to step in and assume command.

In the ongoing tug-of-war between hedonism and legalism, though, the stronger inclination seems to be toward legalism. This was one of the offenses of the Pharisees, for "in vain they worship Me, teaching as doctrines the commandments of men."[75] Legalism is like gravity. Its pull is constant, pervasive, and nearly irresistible. Aside from Christianity, every religious persuasion offering a personal afterlife — not all do — makes entrance into paradise a reward for good behavior of some sort. Most major Christian heresies follow the same pattern of exchanging grace-based salvation for the performance-based merit of eternal life.

———————

As our world of eight billion souls lumbers toward the climax of history, the serpent's three original lies still corrupt our thinking. First, we can become like God. Second, we can be wise without Him. Third, we alone decide between right and wrong. So how has it worked out? Not so well, if you've been paying attention.

So, let's recap. If pride is having too high an opinion of oneself, and we are all proud, then everyone has too high an opinion of oneself. Not always and in every case, but inevitably in some area. Our opinions of ourselves — or self-appraisals — are core personal beliefs. Belief is at the core of pride, so that is where we must begin.

As to the chief villain of this drama? His act hasn't changed. *Deception* is the name of the game. And why not? It's the easiest game in town. We shall return to him in the closing chapter.

———————

[72] *Catechism of the Catholic Church*. Part 3, Section 1, Chapter 3, Article 1.I "The Natural Moral Law" http://www.vatican.va/archive/ENG0015/__P6U.HTM accessed 2/8/2022
[73] Romans 8:2
[74] Hebrews 10:16
[75] Matthew 15:9, Mark 7:7

In the next chapter, we will examine the nature of belief, how beliefs are formed — it's more complicated than you think — and the perils of over-confidence.

Key points

- In the Christian tradition, Satan fell because of pride, and it was the inward pride of Adam and Eve that led to their outward disobedience.
- Pride is an excessive opinion of one's own *importance* that leads to self-worship — to be like God.
- Pride is an excessive opinion of one's own *wisdom*.
- Pride is unwarranted confidence in one's internal *moral compass*, the will to decide for oneself what is right and wrong.

«3»

"I think, therefore it must be true."

Overconfidence of Belief

We naturally assume that our beliefs arise from an honest, objective analysis of facts, reason, and experience. In reality, our beliefs are strongly influenced by many non-rational factors, including emotions, peer pressure, self-interest, and tradition. A culture saturated with misinformation and disinformation makes it challenging to know the "true truth" for the sincerest inquirer. Consequently, our minds are constantly led astray so that each of us confidently believes demonstrably false things — we just don't know it. False beliefs are harmful enough, but pride compounds the offense by combining false beliefs with unwavering certainty. Because beliefs are closely intertwined with emotions, we may react intensely when those beliefs — right or wrong — are challenged. Excessive confidence in our own opinions may be the subtlest yet most pervasive manifestation of sinful pride.

"It ain't what you don't know that gets you into trouble. It's what you know for sure that just ain't so." — SOURCE UNKNOWN [76]

"The first principle is that you must not fool yourself — and you are the easiest person to fool." — RICHARD FEYNMAN

Electrophobia — the Shocking Truth

You think you have it bad? Pity poor Hedda Sandström [not her real name] of Lulea, Sweden. In 2007 the *Wall Street Journal* reported that Hedda,

---

[76] Though often attributed to Mark Twain. "It ain't what you don't know…." Quote Investigator. https://quoteinvestigator.com/2018/11/18/know-trouble/ Accessed 5/20/2022

along with hundreds of other Swedes, was allergic to electricity — thus, eligible for state-funded sick pay because of her disability.[77]

To say that "electro-hypersensitivity" is not an accepted medical diagnosis would be an understatement. Without electricity, your heart would stop. Your brain would shut down. Without electricity, you're dead. But many people came to believe they were allergic to it. Imprisoned by her "disability," Hedda lived in an unlit, appliance-free wooden house in the forest outside of town. Never mind that by January 2010, a total of 46 double-blind experiments examining 1175 "victims" failed to find any evidence for the existence of such a disorder.[78] When their eyes were closed or their backs were turned, they couldn't tell if the electricity was on or off, real or fake. The symptoms, though, were real enough. However, they were not caused by the electricity but by the patients' *belief* that they would suffer such exposure.[79] [Young people today instinctively understand the necessity of electricity for survival. This is the actual reason they are so digitally engaged: for the life force emanating from such devices]. Beliefs — true or not — have consequences. All other things being equal, false beliefs usually have worse consequences.

What do you know that just ain't so?

Name ONE thing you believe that you know isn't true. I'll wait.

Stumped? You should be. If you know it is untrue, then you cannot believe it. That doesn't mean it's impossible. In fact, people embrace self-contradicting positions all the time; they just don't recognize it. Nonetheless, our minds are wired such that we cannot easily force ourselves to believe something we consider to be wrong. Faced with a conflict between evidence and belief, we must either reconsider our belief or reinterpret the evidence to fit it.

Name one thing that *someone else* believes — a spouse, a friend, or a relative — that you know first-hand to be untrue.

---

[77] Marcus Walker. "Sweden Clamps down on sick and disability pay" *The Wall Street Journal*. May 9, 2007

[78] Rubin, G. James, Rosa Nieto-Hernandez, and Simon Wessely. "Idiopathic environmental intolerance attributed to electromagnetic fields (formerly 'electromagnetic hypersensitivity'): an updated systematic review of provocation studies." *Bioelectromagnetics: Journal of the Bioelectromagnetics Society, The Society for Physical Regulation in Biology and Medicine, The European Bioelectromagnetics Association* 31, no. 1 (2010): 1-11.

[79] Dieudonné, Maël. "Electromagnetic hypersensitivity: a critical review of explanatory hypotheses." *Environmental Health* 19, no. 1 (2020): 1-12.

Easy, isn't it? Maybe they really are right but suppose they're wrong. What makes it so easy to spot erroneous beliefs of others and so hard to spot our own? First, we must address the deeper question: "*why* do we believe the things we do?"

It can be indiscreet to question a person's beliefs, but that doesn't make it wrong. We're mostly OK with *polemics*, or persuasive argumentation, so long as it's civil. And Christians ought to be civil. That's not where I'm going. This chapter is not about getting the facts straight. Are we really as wise as we think we are? That is the million-dollar question.

How did we get from the subject of pride to personal beliefs? Because *intellectual* pride is pervasive, inevitable, and an impediment to personal growth, the ministry of the church, and the function of almost every human institution. Accepting this reality may be the most critical step toward humility.

What if much of what you think you "know" is wrong? "Impossible," you may think. Yet I would argue that most people are wrong concerning a great many things. The thrust of this chapter is to show that this *is* true and *why* it is true.

Grownups say the darndest things

We embrace popular myths in nearly every aspect of life. Ask any elementary school teacher about the "sugar high," that irrepressible state of high energy induced in any young boy or girl by the consumption of candy. Most will swear to it. But there's no such thing. For years, medicine has known that high blood sugar induces drowsiness, not stimulation. The sugar high has been completely disproven by direct clinical trials,[80] but the myth refuses to die.

Decade after decade, surveys show widespread belief in the paranormal.[81] I'm not talking about any belief in the supernatural — prayer, miracles, the resurrection of Christ—things most Christian embrace and for which there is compelling evidence. These surveys focus on outright superstition — stuff like astrology, ESP, telepathy, ghosts. Consistently, decade after decade, about 75% of the American public admits to belief in something

---

[80] Aaron Carroll, "Sugar, and candy, do not make kids hyper," The Incidental Economist, 11/1/2011 https://theincidentaleconomist.com/wordpress/sugar-and-candy-do-not-make-kids-hyper/

[81] David Moore, "Three in Four Americans Believe in Paranormal," Gallup News Service, June 16, 2005. https://news.gallup.com/poll/16915/three-four-americans-believe-paranormal.aspx

superstitious or irrational.[82] The National Science Foundation reported in 2012 that 58% of young adults between 18 and 24 believed that astrology is "very scientific" or "sort of scientific" — and the percentage has been rising since 2006.[83]

The errors we believe run the gamut from respectable to ignorant to downright nutty. One CNN survey found that 80% of the American public believed the government was withholding evidence of alien visitations (the sort that *no* wall would keep out).[84] One could go on. Americans spend around $34 billion a year on "alternative medicine" — some of it possibly helpful, most of it clearly useless or even harmful (except for the ones selling it).[85]

In one of the more disturbing cases of mass delusion, a 2003 Eurobarometer survey found that 59% of Europeans considered tiny Israel a threat to world peace, beating out all other countries. The US tied for second with Iran and North Korea at 53% each. Showing just how poor they were at prognostication, Syria was perceived as a threat by only 37% and Russia by 21%.[86] The Syrian civil war and Russian military adventures against Georgia and Ukraine were just over the horizon.

During the global COVID pandemic, there was an eruption of false belief beyond anything I had previously witnessed.[87] Vast swathes of the American public, without any prior education or experience, suddenly became statisticians, epidemiologists, pharmacologists, virologists, economists, doctors, and detectives after watching a few videos on YouTube. Government spokesmen repeatedly flip-flopped, and the "truth" depended on which party controlled the White House. Beliefs about public policy, beliefs about public figures, beliefs in various treatments, rejection of other treatments...if I listed them all, I would only alienate most of my readers. No matter where you stood, you probably thought half of the population was nuts. My estimate would be significantly higher.

---

[82] "Paranormal America 2018," The Voice of Wilkinson, Chapman University, October 16, 2018. https://blogs.chapman.edu/wilkinson/2018/10/16/paranormal-america-2018
[83] "Chapter 7: Science and Technology: Public Attitudes and Understanding," National Science Foundation, accessed May 20, 2022. https://www.nsf.gov/statistics/seind14/index.cfm/chapter-7/c7h.htm
[84] "Poll: U.S. hiding knowledge of aliens" *CNN*, June 15, 1997
http://www.cnn.com/US/9706/15/ufo.poll/
[85] Lauren Cox. "Why do we spend $34 billion in alternative medicine?" ABC News, July 30, 2009, https://abcnews.go.com/health/wellnessnews/story?id=8215703
[86] "Iraq and peace in the world" Flash Eurobarometer, November, 2003, http://www.mafhoum.com/press6/167P52.pdf Accessed 5/20/2022
[87] Steven Willing. "Courage, Sacrifice, and Corona-spiracies". April 17, 2020. https://swilling.com/courage-sacrifice-and-corona-spiracies/

If we consider not just false beliefs but lack of knowledge, the picture is similarly bleak. Since 1979, the National Science Foundation has conducted regular polls of Americans' scientific literacy. Their last full report, based on 2016 data, revealed that:[88]

- 27% believed the sun goes around the earth
- 30% believed all radioactivity was man-made
- 49% believed antibiotics kill viruses
- 52% didn't know electrons were smaller than atoms

In these surveys, unsurprisingly, correct responses strongly correlated with increasing levels of education and the number of science courses taken in high school and college.

Some hoaxes survive for decades. One famous story lasting well into the early 2000s reported that NASA scientists, while studying ancient planetary motions, found that their calculations came up 24 hours short; a mystery "solved" when one scientist recalled the Biblical account from Joshua[89] of the sun standing still for one day. This myth could be traced to the early 1960s, before NASA even existed. There was never a grain of truth to it, but many accepted it uncritically and passed it on to others. Maybe it's harmless; maybe not. Easy credulity does not enhance one's Christian witness. Beware the warning of Paul:

> Reject profane and old wives' fables, and exercise yourself toward godliness.[90]

The folly of false belief is a recurring theme of Scripture. But it is emphatically not an issue of stupidity. It is an issue of *pride*. The proud are "filled to the full with their own fancies."[91] "Scorners delight in their scorning, and fools hate knowledge."[92]

Still, reality has not dampened our self-confidence. We Americans think we're brilliant. By one recent poll, 55% of Americans thought they were more intelligent than average, while 34% confessed to being "merely" average. Only 4% conceded to being below average.[93] In another extensive survey, an even more impressive 65% of Americans claimed to be above

---

[88] "Public Knowledge about S&T." National Science Board. https://www.nsf.gov/statistics/2018/nsb20181/report/sections/science-and-technology-public-attitudes-and-understanding/public-knowledge-about-s-t Accessed 5/20/2022

[89] Joshua 10:13

[90] 1 Timothy 4:7

[91] Proverbs 1:31

[92] Proverbs 1:22

[93] Peter Moore. "America the intelligent" YouGovAmerica. May 11, 2014, https://today.yougov.com/topics/lifestyle/articles-reports/2014/05/11/intelligence

average in intelligence.[94] So most of us think we're smarter than most of us. Explain how that works. No wonder we grew so divided over COVID. Ignorance isn't bliss when we're at each other's throats.

Would it help if we really were as smart as we think we are? Not exactly....

Blinded by brilliance

In my younger days, everything seemed much simpler. Smart, educated people were more reliable than less bright and less educated people. People came to their beliefs honestly, starting with the facts and applying reason to reach conclusions. If two people disagreed, it was because one or both were starting with incomplete or inaccurate information and employing faulty reasoning. Reality doesn't quite turn out that way.

The research on human reasoning is quite revealing. We apply our intellect not to seek out the truth — as we like to imagine — but to bolster our predetermined opinion.[95] So does everyone else. On highly charged issues, polarization occurs because we are more concerned with group acceptance than an unbiased search for truth.[96] When researchers delved into the controversial matter of global warming, there was absolutely no difference between alarmists and skeptics in intelligence, open-mindedness, or critical thinking skills.[97] In another study, scientifically and mathematically literate people were slightly *less* concerned about global warming than the less educated, though the difference was slight.[98]

The correlation between intelligence and rationality is surprisingly weak, and highly intelligent people can and do succumb to startling lapses in rationality. Albert Einstein expressed a naïve and unshakeable optimism concerning Lenin, Stalin, and the Soviet Union:

---

[94]Heck, Patrick R., Daniel J. Simons, and Christopher F. Chabris. "65% of Americans believe they are above average in intelligence: Results of two nationally representative surveys." *PloS one* 13, no. 7 (2018): e0200103.

[95] Mercier, Hugo, and Dan Sperber. "Why do humans reason? Arguments for an argumentative theory." *Behavioral and brain sciences* 34, no. 2 (2011): 57-74.

[96] Kahan, D. M. "Ideology, motivated reasoning, and cognitive reflection: an experimental study (SSRN Scholarly Paper ID 2182588)." *Social Science Research Network. https://papers. ssrn. com/abstract* 2182588 (2012).

[97] Kahan (2012).

[98]Kahan, Dan M., Maggie Wittlin, Ellen Peters, Paul Slovic, Lisa Larrimore Ouellette, Donald Braman, and Gregory N. Mandel. "The tragedy of the risk-perception commons: Culture conflict, rationality conflict, and climate change." *Temple University legal studies research paper* 2011-26 (2011).

"I honor Lenin as a man who completely sacrificed himself and devoted all his energy to the realization of social justice. I do not consider his methods practical, but one thing is certain: men of his type are the guardians and restorers of humanity.".[99]

We all know how that panned out.

Richard Dawkins, author of *The God Delusion*, is an intelligent and accomplished scientist and an excellent writer. In his book and public debates, his strongest "argument" is that the probability of God's existence was infinitely small:

"The problem is that this says, because something is vastly improbable,[100] we need a God to explain it. But that God himself would be even more improbable."[101]

Dawkins's reasoning is that a Creator cannot be logically invoked to explain the complexity of life and the universe because the Creator would have to be even more complex. But he succumbs to the logical fallacy known as "category error." Complexity has no meaning with regard to an immaterial being existing outside of space, matter, time, and energy. It's as meaningless as talking about the "color" of God. Now it is perfectly acceptable to say something is "improbable" based on subjective judgment — but that is speculation, not an argument.

There's no escaping the conclusion that intellectual brilliance is no defense against error. I have known brilliant physicians devoted to all major religious persuasions. If sheer intelligence led to superior metaphysical insight, shouldn't smart people think more alike?

Intelligent people with the benefit of an education are better equipped to give correct answers on a test or solve a problem, but those are controlled conditions where the right answer can be known. Just being smart doesn't make someone an authority on anything. There is an essential and discernible difference between intelligence and wisdom. We will revisit this crucial matter in Chapter 13.

---

[99] "Statement for the League of Human Rights on Lenin's death, January 6, 1929" Einstein Archives:34-439

[100] The vast number of physical parameters fine-tuned for the existence of the universe and life, and the improbability of life originating by chance.

[101] Dan Cray, "God vs. Science, Richard Dawkins and Francis Collins" Interdisciplinary Encyclopedia of Religion and Science, November 2006, http://inters.org/Dawkins-Collins-Cray-Science

We're all in the same boat; it's leaking badly and listing to port. No one can be right about everything; no one should be criticized merely for being wrong. The sheer volume of noise propagating through our educational institutions, popular literature, and media means we are saturated with error no matter where we turn. Errors are not always intentional. No one is perfectly objective; everyone has a bias. Misinformation, once born, takes on a life of its own. No one has the resources to fact-check every public statement or popular belief, and even if one had the time and resources, who checks the fact-checkers?

So when, if ever, does simply *being wrong* create a *moral problem*? Never underestimate the power of a lie. It is a foolish belief in the healing properties of rhinoceros horn that threatens the extinction of those magnificent creatures. Unspeakable lies about Jews led to the Holocaust. Misinformation about opioids is a major reason why drug overdoses became the leading cause of death under 50 in the United States. No one gets off the hook for believing "sincerely', and as we will see, choice and belief are deeply intertwined.

Holding a false belief is not inherently sinful — though sometimes it is, like believing we are sinless.[102] But in most cases, just being wrong need not indicate pride. The real problem arises when we are wrong but confident that we're right. We shouldn't be. We are easily deceived, and we specialize in deceiving ourselves. To understand how that works, we need to take a deep dive into how beliefs are formed. Welcome to the science of cognition.

The Age of Credulity

While you might suppose the 21st century is an age of skepticism, in reality, humans have always been *believing machines*. We drift with the cultural tides, embracing popular ideas on the flimsiest of evidence, then clutch those beliefs tenaciously to protect our egos, strut our virtue, and advertise loyalty to our in-group. This may seem cynical — but it is well-validated.

According to the popular narrative, something called the "Enlightenment" ushered the Western world into the Age of Science and Reason. It freed us from superstition and myth, pushing us inexorably toward an advanced civilization based on science and reason, like Starfleet. The evidence says otherwise. G. K. Chesterton nailed it: "When people cease to believe in God, they don't believe in nothing; they believe in anything."[103] Once God is

---

[102] I John 1:8
[103] According to the Chesterton Society, he probably never used that exact phrasing, but it is an accurate representation of his opinion.

eliminated, honest skepticism is the next casualty. Enlightenment Schmightenment. Welcome to the Age of Credulity. The train of thought has jumped the track and is barreling off a cliff. Earlier, we examined the degree to which people today are inclined to believe almost anything. The examples I've given barely amount to a snowflake on the tip of the iceberg. There are entire books devoted to debunking popular modern myths. Many are objective, fair, and apolitical. More of us need to be reading them.

Scripture clearly exhorts us to be discerning, test the truth, and resist myth and superstition. Who is thinking more Biblically: those who insist on a high standard of proof or those who believe anything? We have no reason to malign or fear the skeptic. C. S. Lewis started out as one. Our faith is established on historical facts, and our Scriptures are validated by many lines of evidence. When a skeptic challenges Christianity, that's something a trained apologist or Christian scholar can handle. It is far more difficult to reason with a person who will believe anything; there's no common ground for rational dialogue. When such a person professes to be a Christian, it is a poor testimony indeed.

So, where do we go wrong? The actual process of belief formation turns out to be much more fluid, subjective, and emotionally driven than we would like to admit.

Beliefs are like sausages

We tend to think that beliefs (at least our own) are established on the three pillars of fact, experience, and reason. But the reality is that with similar facts and experience, people often come to quite contradictory conclusions. This does not shake our faith in the model because individuals may lack knowledge of the facts, the facts may be disputed, experience is subject to interpretation, and our reasoning is often flawed. [Naturally, from our prideful perspective, it is always the *other* person who has erred]. Even though false beliefs abound, and we all err, our confidence in the basic model of belief formation stands firm. It resonates with our personal experience: we can't help but think all *our* beliefs are founded on fact, experience, and reason. The traditional western educational system is based on that model; so is most Christian apologetics.

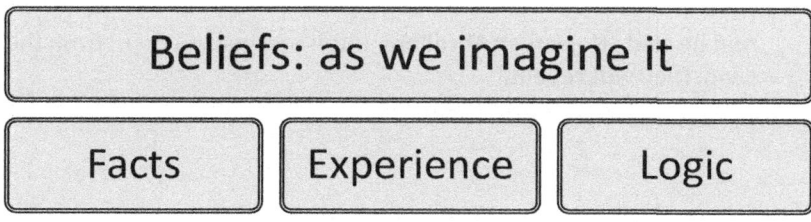

The reality, though, is quite different. There are many *non-rational* — though not necessarily *irrational* — influences that contribute to belief formation.

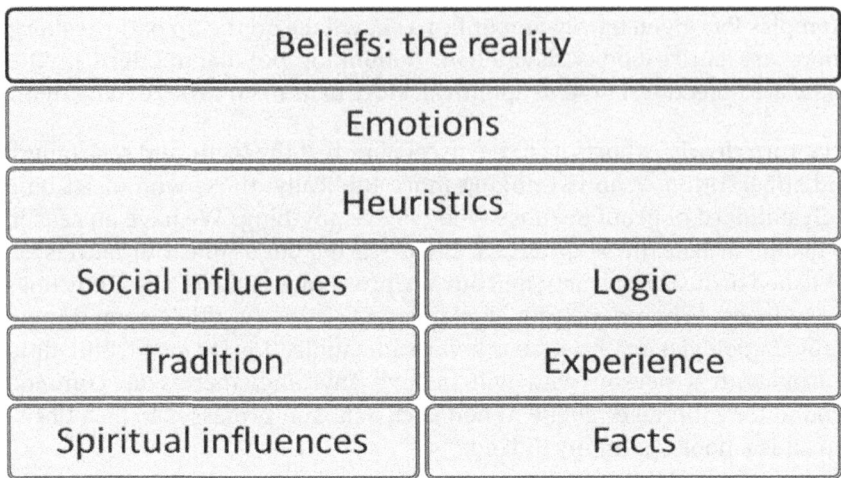

Beliefs: the reality
Emotions
Heuristics

Social influences	Logic
Tradition	Experience
Spiritual influences	Facts

Moreover, not all inputs have equal influence. As it turns out, the most influential input may be the one we are least likely to admit: emotions. Finally, this cacophony of inputs demands a gatekeeper — the human will. We choose which inputs will be admitted and which will be locked out. It's a paradox: it *feels* like facts, reason, and experience *determine* our beliefs, while in reality, we *choose* our beliefs, often based merely on which alternative is most emotionally satisfying.

Jesus declared that those who were resistant to God would cling to their belief in the face of overwhelming evidence. He once spoke of a poor man who went to heaven and a rich man landing in Hell. The rich man asked Abraham to send the poor man back to warn his brothers:

> "Then [the rich man] said, 'I beg you therefore, father, that you would send him to my father's house, for I have five brothers, that he may testify to them, lest they also come to this place of torment.'
>
> Abraham said to him, 'They have Moses and the prophets; let them hear them.'
>
> And he said, 'No, father Abraham; but if one goes to them from the dead, they will repent.'

But he said to him, 'If they do not hear Moses and the prophets, neither will they be persuaded though one rise from the dead.'"[104]

The apostle Paul framed the world's unbelief not in terms of sincere skepticism but as active suppression of the truth:

For the wrath of God is revealed from heaven against all ungodliness and unrighteousness of men, who suppress the truth in unrighteousness.[105]

Research has affirmed what the Bible declared long ago: beliefs are primarily a matter of choice.

So why do we so readily believe things that are not true? It begins with the various non-rational influences in decision-making, like emotional investment, self-interest, and social influences. Beyond that, we are overwhelmed each day with "false" facts based on tradition, folk myths, misinformation, and even disinformation. *Misinformation* is false information arrived at honestly. *Disinformation* is false information delivered dishonestly with the intent to deceive. Even with good evidence and a strong personal desire to be objective, there are countless pitfalls to which we succumb. The pathway to Truth is narrow, rocky, and winding, with many hazards, detours, and dead ends to lead us astray. Against such odds, it's a wonder we ever get *anything* right.

Allow me to offer a glimpse of where we are going with this. Beliefs determine actions. Actions have consequences. False beliefs can and frequently do lead to dire consequences. What has all this to do with Pride? Pride is a false belief about oneself — overconfidence. Unshakeable confidence in one's own beliefs is an invincible barrier against correction. People who understand and admit their own fallibility have taken the first giant step away from pride and toward humility.

In the ensuing discussion, your natural response will be to spot other people's mistakes. But it's not just "them." It's you. It's me. It's everyone.

Let's examine the non-rational inputs a little more closely.

Heuristics: low-calorie thinking

We must routinely sift through an avalanche of information to make even simple decisions. Ideally, one would take accurate and complete data and

---

[104] Luke 16:27-31
[105] Romans 1:18

apply reason to reach a logical and correct conclusion. Reality is not so co-operative; we often lack both time and inclination for an exhaustive analysis, even if perfect information were available. Instead, we make the best possible decisions based on imperfect and incomplete information.

Heuristics are those mental shortcuts we use for deciding as efficiently as possible with the information on hand. We all use them several times a day. Heuristics are pretty helpful, actually. If you encounter a shadowy figure in a dark alley approaching with something in his hand shaped like a gun, the "representativeness" heuristic would prompt you that "this looks danger-ous" and recommend avoidance. Logic would be no use until you estab-lished beyond doubt that 1) yes, it was a gun, and 2) the bearer had mali-cious intent. Which could be too late.

The chief problem with heuristics is that all too often, what seems obvious turns out to be completely wrong. The shad-owy figure could have been anyone. The "gun" might actually have been an elec-tric drill (which still can hurt you but is not typically employed for that purpose).

"If jumping to conclusions were an Olympic sport, the competition would be fierce."

The pioneers in this field were Daniel Kahneman and Amos Tversky, whose research led to the 2002 Nobel Prize in Economics. Decades of work were summarized in Kahneman's 2011 best-seller, *Thinking Fast and Slow*.[106] In this treatise, Kahneman offered penetrating insight into how our minds work and how we are routinely and predictably led astray by an expanding catalog of cognitive biases and faulty heuristics.

Heuristic thinking is automatic, quick, and effortless. Kahneman refers to this as "System 1" thinking. Considered, thoughtful reflection, or "System 2" thinking, yields better decisions at the cost of time and effort. What Kahneman and his collaborators found was that our minds are naturally lazy, so we rely on System 1 as much as possible:

> "System 1 is gullible and biased to believe, System 2 is in charge of doubting and unbelieving, but System 2 is sometimes busy, and often lazy."[107]

Therein lies the second hazard with heuristics. Because we are mentally lazy, we use them when we should be using thoughtful reflection.

---

[106] Daniel Kahneman. *Thinking fast and slow.* New York: Farrar, Straus, and Giroux, 2011.
[107] Kahneman, p. 81

Emotions: Feeling is Believing

If we were honest and self-aware, all of us would admit to being emotionally invested in things we believe. It would be a sorry state of affairs if we viewed with indifference the evils of child abuse, racism, tyranny, dishonesty, or the ravages of disease and famine. Much less obvious is the extent to which emotions *determine* our beliefs. It is, however, a fact of human nature. Scripture attests to this principle.[108] A few decades ago, secularists might have challenged this assertion. A prevailing dogma of humanism and the Enlightenment was that man is inherently rational.

In recent decades, a different picture has emerged. It began with the observation that patients with particular injuries to the brain lost all capacity for emotion. The surprising consequence, though, was that without emotions, these patients lost the ability to make decisions. They could analyze a problem all day long without ever forming a conclusion. The outcome of this research was summarized by Dr. Antoine Bechara, one of the leading figures in this field:

> "The studies of decision-making in neurological patients who can no longer process emotional information normally suggest that people make judgments not only by evaluating the consequences and their probability of occurring, but *also and even sometimes primarily at a gut or emotional level.*"[109] [emphasis added]

Now, this is far from saying that every decision is purely emotional. But it is true more often than we realize or admit. We shouldn't be surprised. Consider the emotional fervor over elections, racial politics, immigration, global warming, or gun rights. It is easy to believe the *issues* inflame our passion, but often it is our *passions* that inflame the issue. When it comes to clear and objective analysis, emotions not only stand in the way; they can push us over the edge.

This is old news to specialists in the field. In 2007 Dr. Drew Westen, a Professor of Psychology and Psychiatry at Emory University, published his investigative work *The Political Brain*.[110] The author's website described it as a "ground-breaking investigation into the role of emotion in determining the political life of the nation." A partisan Democrat, Dr. Westen counseled his allies to appeal to the emotions of the electorate rather than its intellect. Dr. Howard Dean, then the Democratic Party chair, predicted: "in

---

[108] Romans 1:18-23
[109] Bechara, Antoine. "The role of emotion in decision-making: Evidence from neurological patients with orbitofrontal damage." *Brain and cognition* 55, no. 1 (2004): 30-40.
[110] Westen, Drew. *The political brain: The role of emotion in deciding the fate of the nation.* New York: PublicAffairs 2008.

2008, we will win the presidency if our candidate reads and acts on this book." You know the rest of that story. The lesson here is that anyone who would dismiss the role of emotion in human decision-making puts himself at a significant disadvantage, lessens his potential influence, is vulnerable to manipulation, and forfeits an essential means of persuasion.

In 2015, Jennifer Lerner of Harvard University reviewed 35 years of research on the role of emotions in judgment and decision-making.[111] She and her coauthors concluded:

> "The research reveals that emotions constitute potent, pervasive, predictable, sometimes harmful and sometimes beneficial drivers of decision making. Across different domains, important regularities appear in the mechanisms through which emotions influence judgments and choices."

If matters of public policy generate such intense feelings, think how much more they are aroused in our relationships and personal affairs. This can be both good and bad. When we harbor positive *feelings* toward someone, we are more likely to maintain positive *beliefs* about them. Whatever they do or say is framed within that context. On the other hand, when we harbor negative feelings toward someone, we tend to embrace more negative beliefs regarding their person and character. This matter is so fundamental to any discussion of pride that I will devote an entire chapter to the issue of judgmentalism.

Tradition: Love it or hate it

> *"Tradition: Just because you've always done it that way doesn't mean it's not incredibly stupid."*

The line above is one of my favorite quotes from the masters of sardonic humor at *despair.com*. We're probably OK with the idea as long as it's someone else's tradition that's being gored (although in the accompanying image, it was a runner at Pamplona who was in imminent danger of said fate). To be fair, though, tradition can be either good or bad.

What is tradition? The word evokes images from *Fiddler on the Roof,* but it's really much more. Tradition might be the passing on of beliefs, customs,

---

[111] Lerner, Jennifer S., Ye Li, Piercarlo Valdesolo, and Karim S. Kassam. "Emotion and decision making." *Annual review of psychology* 66 (2015): 799-823..

and legends from one generation to the next, or just a habitual way of thinking or acting. It's not always a bad thing.

On the plus side, tradition can represent the accumulated wisdom and experience of many generations. It protects us from the folly of what C.S. Lewis called "presentism": the conceit that our own generation, of all the thousands that preceded us, is the one that finally figured things out. On the negative side, falsehood can be ingrained so deeply and so early in life that it remains unquestioned and unassailable. "Tradition" explains why many of the trendy — but flawed — dogmas promoted in our educational systems are accepted and perpetuated. We may resist the possibility that any of *our* traditions are pure myth, but I imagine few would deny there are false traditions in other societies, cultures, religions, or social groups. Why would you or I be immune?

Social influences: Believing to fit in

Bandwagon effect

The bandwagon effect (popularly referred to as "peer pressure") does not end with high school. There is a clear, measurable tendency for persons of all ages to conform their opinions to their peers. This is another case of emotions clouding judgment. It is generally explained that we do so in order to secure acceptance and avoid conflict. Besides that, most of us are naturally inclined to follow the initiative of others rather than seize the reigns of leadership. It's much easier, that's for sure. This doesn't emerge exclusively out of a desire for acceptance. Fear of criticism or rejection plays a major role, as few possess the courage to oppose their preferred social group. (See: "Twitter").

False consensus effect

Not many people find it satisfying to be alone in their beliefs. We strongly prefer the opposite: we'd like everyone to agree with us. Usually, they don't, which is frustrating, but we cope. How? By imagining that more people agree with us than actually do. Logically, it should not matter whether everyone agreed with us or no one on the planet; matters of truth are not settled by polling — even in science. We're not that logical, though. There is a great diversity of opinion in the Christian community on a range of issues: style of dress, the age of the earth, end-times prophecy, the practice and significance of baptism or

False consensus effect

"Everyone who matters agrees with me"

communion; but too many on one side or another speak and act as if *naturally* all *true* believers agreed with them, turning non-essential disagreements into a litmus test of orthodoxy.

So, what's the harm? The false consensus effect might not make us believe something we don't already, but it does make us more confident — not a good thing if we're wrong.

Information cascade

Most of the time, we see the wisdom in deferring to the opinion of experts when it comes to a specialized subject. A qualified expert who can independently analyze the data and form his own conclusions is a valuable source. A panel of experts is even better. Regrettably, that is usually not how it works. If every expert on the panel acted independently of the others, you could tally up an unbiased sample. What usually happens, though, is that our esteemed experts rely on not one but two sources: first, the original data, and second, the opinions of the other experts.

Information cascade

What happens when experts think like dominoes

That's where it gets dicey. Do lobsters dream? Suppose there is evidence either way, but the case *against* dreaming lobsters is a little bit stronger. However, if I hear that a trusted colleague down the hall concluded lobsters *do* dream, that might be just enough to tip me toward the same conclusion. But how did the guy down the hall reach his conclusion? Did he simply examine the data, or was he influenced by another colleague in the next town? You get the picture. A single person at the beginning of the chain could have tipped 99 others to switch to "lobsters dream" when "lobsters don't dream" was really the better choice. The guy at the beginning might have had motives for choosing "lobsters dream" that had nothing to do with the evidence (maybe he had a pet lobster as a child), but the opinion snowballed from him down the information cascade.

Some Christians are inherently mistrustful of all scientists, and that is unfortunate and indefensible. Others, Christian and non-Christian alike, tend to be too trusting. There are plenty of examples in both remote and recent history where the scientific community veered off course *en masse*.[112] No sure cure has been found.

---

[112] Christopher Booker and Richard North. *Scared to death: from BSE to Global Warming: Why scares are costing us the Earth.* New York: Continuum, 2008.

Availability cascade

So, sometimes experts can err *en masse,* but it could be much worse. An availability cascade is like an information cascade on steroids. In this scenario, a meme or belief takes hold and snowballs through a large population. It differs from the information cascade in that evidence may be weak or non-existent, the issue is a matter of popular interest, and people are committed to the position more for social acceptance than the plausibility of the argument.[113] Many popular, but false, beliefs in present-day society achieved wide acceptance through an availability cascade.

Self-interest: Believing what's best for me

Money, power, and sex: three of the greatest human motivators. More than anything else, the majority of people throughout history pursue one thing above all: personal happiness. Once the basic human needs are met, most people seek happiness through relationships and personal pleasure. A few pursue happiness in serving other people or service to a higher cause, but that is just a nobler version of self-interest. Only one cause really transcends self: the desire to please God regardless of personal consequences. It is rare to find anyone whose passion for the truth — wherever it may lead — supersedes any private agenda. Little wonder, then, that self-interest determines belief more often than belief overcomes self-interest.

There are many areas of ambiguity in medical practice and many disorders where the treatment is of uncertain benefit. Because of this ambiguity, and because in the US, surgical treatment is well compensated on a case-by-case basis, Americans undergo many surgical procedures at a higher rate than other developed nations.[114] How much is really necessary? How much is unnecessary? Who really knows? Are US surgeons more unscrupulous and dishonest than surgeons elsewhere? I don't think so. It's just that when ambiguity is present — when the surgery *might* help and *probably* won't hurt — it's easy enough to proceed with a sincere conviction that one is doing the right thing. Take the same intellect, with the same level of knowledge, and put him in the role of an insurance administrator, and quite possibly he will come to the opposite conclusion. To paraphrase Upton Sinclair, "it is difficult to get a man to believe something when his salary depends on not believing it" — or vice versa.

---

[113] Kuran, Timur, and Cass R. Sunstein. "Availability Cascades and Risk Regulation." *Stanford Law Review* 51, no. 4 (April 1999): 683.
[114] Domingo, Santiago, and Antonio Pellicer. "Overview of current trends in hysterectomy." *Expert Review of Obstetrics & Gynecology* 4, no. 6 (2009): 673-685.

Scraping for recognition or saving face...these too are powerful motivators. How tenaciously do we cling to a belief not because it's so obviously correct but just because we hate to admit we might have been wrong? We fear losing the respect of others. Paradoxically, those who refuse to acknowledge obvious error are respected least of all.

Cognitive biases: Two hundred pitfalls and counting

Cognitive biases are tendencies deeply embedded in our subconscious that incline us to err in predictable ways. Nearly two hundred have been described in the literature. Many serve to enhance our self-image or minimize emotional tension.

Heuristics and biases are closely intertwined. One way to understand the connection is that heuristics represent a shortcut to decision-making but are neutral regarding the outcome. Biases push those decisions in certain somewhat predictable directions. The most predictable direction is our own self-interest.

Confirmation bias: believing is seeing.

There's an old saying that we see what we look for and look for what we know. We instinctively focus on information that supports our beliefs and ignore the evidence against it. This tendency is called Confirmation Bias (also called "myside bias"). Unbelievers and skeptics engage in this all the time. Christianity is inherently violent — unless you count millions upon millions of innocent martyrs who did not resist but faced death with courage and conviction. Islam is a "religion of peace" — if we ignore 14 centuries of military aggression and the historical record that Mohammed was a man of violence who murdered his opponents and celebrated it. There's no evidence Jesus was a real man who arose from the dead — if you don't count the four eyewitness accounts meticulously preserved for almost 2000 years[115] and abundant references by other first and second-century writers.

Confirmation bias

"All of the evidence is on my side"

---

[115] Matthew, John, Paul, and Peter. We don't know for certain that Luke and Mark, the other two gospel writers, were eyewitnesses but they were in first degree relationships with some.

Disconfirmation bias

Many educated people know about confirmation bias. If one is aware of the pitfall, then he attempts to consider the opposing arguments. But we have a natural defense. We can judge their evidence by different standards. The art of holding opposing evidence to a higher standard is known as "disconfirmation bias." This is not unusual in the medical community, but everyone does it sometimes. Evidence supporting our position — experience, research, arguments — is held to one standard. Evidence against our position is picked apart; dismissed for the most trivial shortcomings. Opposing arguments or expert testimony are written off as emotionally, ideologically, or financially motivated rather than addressing the arguments on their own merits. Hardly anywhere is this more evident — or vicious — than in the political arena and media commentariat.

Disconfirmation bias

"Since I know I'm right, your evidence is bunk"

Bias blind spot

It has been shown that if we train people in cognitive biases, they get really good — at seeing other people's biases. Their own? Not so much. The bottom line is that we *all* think we're unbiased; it's always the other guy. In the end, we kid no one but ourselves and those who agree with us. This is the "bias blind spot."

Illusory correlation

A particularly common bias is the "illusory correlation." An illusory correlation is a belief that two things are causally connected that really are not. By inferring relationships between things we encounter, we learn a great deal of helpful information. If the sun is overhead on a midsummer day, it's going to be warm. If the sky turns dark and we hear thunder, very likely it's going to rain. Poke your finger with a needle; it's going to hurt. Unfortunately, this natural tendency to form associations often leads us to connect two things whose relationship is pure coincidence.

The sugar-high myth relies upon an illusory correlation, the mistake of at-tributing normal childish activity to something children commonly con-sume. Put a bunch of children together at a party and give them sugar-free cookies instead; they'll still go wild be-cause that's how children usually act at parties. Confronted with the evidence, there will undoubtedly be some who re-fuse to abandon their certainty in the sugar high. In a way, that proves the whole point of this chapter.

ILLUSORY CORRELATION

===

"Cause and effect, every-where I look"

The list of cognitive biases and logical er-rors we commit extends far beyond the few examples I've given. Learning about them helps to overcome them, but no one can ever completely resist their seduction. When emotions or ego are involved, we really don't even want to.

Confirmation bias and illusory correlation help explain the puzzle of idol-atry in ancient times. Were they really gullible enough to believe God was a cow? But if you sacrifice to your idol and win the battle, "hmm...guess it worked!" Disconfirmation bias also kicks in. If a consistent standard of ev-idence were applied, the losing side should switch allegiance to the idol of the winning side. Instead, the alternative belief is unconsciously held to a higher standard of proof. Thus, a loss would be more likely interpreted as losing favor with one's own deity than validating the deity of the opposi-tion.

Having invested a lifetime researching heuristics and biases, Kahneman concluded that "the human mind is not bound to reality."[116] We can be in-finitely resourceful in finding reasons to believe something we *want* to be true, and to dismiss what we don't want to believe.

Misinformation: Separating signal from noise

Try to keep up with the news, and you will be battered with a daily barrage of misinformation. News reporting on many subjects gets slanted not just because reporters have a liberal bias — though most do — but also be-cause many have little understanding of the subjects they report. They're not consciously attempting to deceive [well, not always], and because of the bias blind spot, most of them probably think they're being fair and

---

[116] Kahneman, p365

objective. There is plenty of excellent, insightful, and proper reporting taking place. Our challenge is to discern fact from opinion.

In the digital age, misinformation can propagate at a level that was previously unimaginable. In 2018, foreign interference in American and British domestic politics through social media was exposed on a massive scale, though with dubious effect. In the worlds of blogging and online video, suddenly, everyone's an expert. At least, the producers seem to think so, with modest-sounding titles like "Socrates squared," "The Ultimate Final Authority on Everything," or "God 2.0".

Surely, though, if there's one thing we can trust, it's our own eyes and ears, right? Not quite. As a means of knowing, our senses fail in numerous ways. There is abundant evidence that we humans are terrible listeners. It's not just a guy thing. Don't trust me: trust the research.[117] Our visual perception is equally susceptible to distortion. We see only what we want or expect to see and think we see what isn't there. This has been corroborated in various research settings, such as the traditional police line-up scenario.[118] Innocent people have been convicted time and time again based on mistaken eyewitness testimony. [119]

Even if we could hear and see the present with perfect accuracy, a past event is no longer sight and sound; it is memory. If there is anything less trustworthy than our eyes and ears, it is our memory. Everyone knows we forget things that did happen. More troubling, we can *remember* things that *never happened*.[120] This may be a hard pill to swallow, but there are volumes of research in these areas. The evidence is solid.

We depend on science as a reliable source of information. But there's a vast range of legitimacy, from eminently trustworthy in fields like astronomy or chemistry to the admixture of serious and silly in some of the social sciences, to the pseudoscientific gobbledygook of Deepak Chopra[121] and the like. Junk science is not inconsequential. Hundreds, perhaps thousands of

---

[117] Soika, Tina. "Better listening: It's an active process." *The Hearing Journal* 57, no. 9 (2004): 40-41.

[118] Beth Schuster, "Police Lineups: Making Eyewitness Identification more reliable," National Institute of Justice, October 1, 2007. https://www.nij.gov/journals/258/Pages/police-lineups.aspx

[119]Steblay, Nancy K., Gary L. Wells, and Amy Bradfield Douglass. "The eyewitness post identification feedback effect 15 years later: Theoretical and policy implications." *Psychology, Public Policy, and Law* 20, no. 1 (2014): 1.

[120] Shaw, Julia. "Do false memories look real? Evidence that people struggle to identify rich false memories of committing crime and other emotional events." *Frontiers in psychology* 11 (2020): 650.

[121] Chopra, Deepak. *Quantum Healing: Exploring the Frontiers of Mind-Body Medicine*. New York: Bantam, 1989.

innocent lives and reputations have been ruined by lawsuits and prosecutions based on the fraudulent enterprise of "recovered memories."[122] The legitimacy of recovered/repressed memories has been thoroughly debunked. But true to the theme of this chapter, belief in them persists among a large contingent of therapists.[123]

Furthermore, science is not now and never has been immutable. There is such a thing as "settled science," but playing that card is no way to settle a disagreement. We'll never abandon the germ theory of disease, discard the 94 naturally occurring elements, or resurrect the steady-state theory of the universe, but progress in fields like medicine sometimes leads to the refutation of established dogma. In particular, we should be routinely skeptical of the newest, latest, greatest discovery hitting the national news. According to famed analyst John Ioannidis, "most published research findings are false."[124] Research reports are further corrupted when the media report them inaccurately. The *retractions* are almost never reported.

Disinformation: Sadly, not everyone can be trusted

As opposed to misinformation, disinformation is delivered with the intent to deceive. Worldwide, over 100,000 die of measles every year, most of them children under 5. Until a few years ago, it had been almost totally eliminated in the US. The vaccination-autism hoax ignited by the fraudulent research of Andrew Wakefield — and long since debunked — led to a resurgence of measles in the West, with many documented deaths.[125] It was later uncovered that Dr. Wakefield was in the pay of trial lawyers seeking to sue vaccine makers and knew he was fabricating data.[126] In 2019, there were more measles cases in the US than in any of the last 25 *years*.[127]

I wish such examples were rare, but disinformation is everywhere. According to the *Journal of Medical Ethics*, a total of 788 scientific papers were

---

[122] National Review. "The Last Victim," August 23, 2018. https://www.nationalreview.com/magazine/2018/09/10/the-last-victim/.

[123] Otgaar, Henry, Mark L. Howe, Lawrence Patihis, Harald Merckelbach, Steven Jay Lynn, Scott O. Lilienfeld, and Elizabeth F. Loftus. "The return of the repressed: The persistent and problematic claims of long-forgotten trauma." *Perspectives on Psychological Science* 14, no. 6 (2019): 1072-1095.

[124] Ioannidis, John PA. "Why most published research findings are false." *PLoS medicine* 2, no. 8 (2005): e124.

[125] Kat Lay, "Vaccine fears blamed as measles cases hit record high in Europe." The Sunday Times, August 20, 2018, https://www.thetimes.co.uk/article/european-measles-death-toll-hits-37-after-antivax-campaigns-ztmwl9f3q

[126] Deer, Brian. "How the case against the MMR vaccine was fixed." *BMJ* 342 (2011).

[127] CDC. "Measles Cases and Outbreaks." Centers for Disease Control and Prevention, May 5, 2022. https://www.cdc.gov/measles/cases-outbreaks.html.

retracted between 2000 and 2010.[128] About one-third were retracted because of *fraud*. There's a dedicated website, retractionwatch.com, that keeps a running report on scientific retractions. By early 2022, journals had already retracted 209 papers *just pertaining to COVID-19*.[129] Major reported studies on Ivermectin were based on bogus data.[130] Many researchers publishing reports on hydroxychloroquine were duped by completely fabricated data from an analytics company, Surgisphere.[131]

Famous historical examples of fraud in the news media include the NBC exploding truck fraud of 1993[132], the Stephen Glass scandal at *The New Republic* in 1998,[133] Jayson Blair at the *New York Times* in 2003[134], and the CBS forged document scandal of 2004.[135] Mr. Glass's agenda was highly ideological: many of his articles were fabricated to frame conservative people and causes in a harshly negative light.

There is a fine line sometimes between misinformation and disinformation. We can't always know when the deception is intentional. However, the fact that so many are out to deceive just makes knowing what's true that much harder.

Spiritual influences: Invisible forces at work

Through prayer, meditation, and Scripture, we communicate with God, and He communicates with us. Many people claim to have heard God speak to

---

[128] Steen, R. Grant. "Retractions in the scientific literature: do authors deliberately commit research fraud?." *Journal of medical ethics* 37, no. 2 (2011): 113-117.

[129] Retraction Watch. "Retracted Coronavirus (COVID-19) Papers," April 29, 2020. https://retractionwatch.com/retracted-coronavirus-covid-19-papers/.

[130] Jaimy Lee, "'You will not believe what I've just found.' Inside the ivermectin saga: a hacked password, mysterious websites and faulty data." MarketWatch February 12, 2022, https://www.marketwatch.com/story/you-will-not-believe-what-ive-just-found-inside-the-ivermectin-saga-a-hacked-password-mysterious-websites-and-faulty-data-11644240013?

[131] Catherine Offerd, "The Surgisphere Scandal: What Went Wrong?" *The Scientist* October 1, 2020, https://www.the-scientist.com/features/the-surgisphere-scandal-what-went-wrong-67955

[132] Frederic Biddle, "Judge Cuts $3.8 Billion from GM verdict in lawsuit over gas-tank explosion," *The Wall Street Journal*, August 27, 1999. https://www.wsj.com/articles/SB935689173621532559

[133] Adam L. Penenberg, "Lies, damn lies, and fiction." *Forbes online*, May 11, 1998. https://www.forbes.com/1998/05/11/otw3.html?sh=4df738ac2d7f

[134] Dan Barry et al, "CORRECTING THE RECORD; Times Reporter Who Resigned Leaves Long Trail of Deception," *New York Times* May 11, 2003. https://www.nytimes.com/2003/05/11/us/correcting-the-record-times-reporter-who-resigned-leaves-long-trail-of-deception.html

[135] William Campenni, "The truth about Dan Rather's deceptive reporting on George W Bush," The Daily Signal, October 30, 2015, https://www.dailysignal.com/2015/10/30/the-truth-about-dan-rathers-deceptive-reporting-on-george-w-bush/

them in an audible voice. Such claims should always be regarded with healthy skepticism, but there is no basis for dismissing them *a priori*. Scripture abounds with promises that God would lead us into truth, such as:

> "These things I have spoken to you while being present with you. But the Helper, the Holy Spirit, whom the Father will send in My name, He will teach you all things, and bring to your remembrance all things that I said to you."[136]

> "But the manifestation of the Spirit is given to each one for the profit of all: for to one is given the word of wisdom through the Spirit, to another the word of knowledge through the same Spirit."[137]

But Scripture clearly teaches that there is another source that does not have our well-being in mind. Evidently — through a means I do not presume to comprehend — Satan has the means to plant ideas in the minds of human beings as well as deceive:

> "Now Satan stood up against Israel, and moved David to number Israel."[138]

> "And supper being ended, the devil having already put it into the heart of Judas Iscariot, Simon's son, to betray Him...."[139]

> "For such are false apostles, deceitful workers, transforming themselves into apostles of Christ. And no wonder! For Satan himself transforms himself into an angel of light."[140]

It would be both naïve and arrogant to automatically credit the false beliefs of anyone to Satan; I advise against it. But it would also be naïve to reject the possibility categorically. Let me offer a possible example. The dark stain of virulent antisemitism courses through much of history right to our present day. Historic antisemitism has been fueled by malicious, demonstrable lies leading to indescribable misery inflicted upon the innocent descendants of Abraham. I have no way of proving there is a demonic influence behind it, but it displays what I consider the general hallmarks.

---

[136] John 14:25-26
[137] I Corinthians 12:7-8
[138] I Chronicles 21:1
[139] John 13:2
[140] II Corinthians 11:12-13

The sweet aroma of certainty

The sum of our knowledge and opinions about life and the universe falls under "cognition." However, our beliefs do not begin and end with cognition. We form a judgment about the probability we are right: our degree of certainty. Hence, certainty is the sum of two sources: first, our confidence in the evidence, and second, our confidence in our own analysis. Those first-order beliefs would be cognition. Beliefs *about* those beliefs — like doubt or certainty — are described as *metacognition*. Both can be distorted by pride. Our problem is not merely one of wrong beliefs. The far greater problem is that we are *so sure we're right.*

False beliefs diminish our credibility, damage our life and health, and create tension in our closest relationships. But far more dangerous is the union of error with overconfidence: when we are wrong but sure that we are right, or when we are certain about something utterly impossible to prove.

Overconfidence in belief may be the most insidious and destructive manifestation of pride in both sacred and secular realms. It leads to divisiveness, schism, church splits, relational failure, political polarization, and all other forms of havoc. Unjustified certainty erects an impenetrable firewall around our own ignorance and dogmatism. If you still doubt me, try spending a few minutes in those roiling cauldrons of asininity known as "comment sections" on Facebook, blogs, and news sites.

In his 2009 tome *On Being Certain*, neuroscientist Robert Burton argued that certainty is not a state of reason but of feeling, influenced by unconscious physiologic processes.[141] There is impressive evidence for this hypothesis. Certainty is mostly illusion, Burton argues. (Though he seemed pretty *certain* about that).

A team of researchers from University College London conducted a focused investigation on individuals with intensely-held radical beliefs, attempting to tease out whether they just generally suffered from overconfidence bias or were genuinely unable to self-correct when confronted with evidence against their position (a failure of metacognition).[142] The investigators challenged the subjects with a series of tests that were mundane and apolitical. Subjects coming from both political extremes showed less insight into the accuracy of their decisions and were less likely to change their decision in response to contradictory evidence. In their words, the evidence

---

[141] Burton, Robert A. *On Being Certain: Believing You Are Right Even When You're Not.* New York: St. Martin's Griffin, 2009.
[142] Rollwage, Max, Raymond J. Dolan, and Stephen M. Fleming. "Metacognitive failure as a feature of those holding radical beliefs." *Current Biology* 28, no. 24 (2018): 4014-4021.

highlighted "a generic resistance to recognizing and revising incorrect beliefs" — what we could call a failure of metacognition.

Excessive certainty may be the single greatest impediment to true wisdom.
As Aquinas warned 800 years ago: "A swollen mind is an obstacle to truth,
for the swelling shuts out the light."[143] It is unnecessary for believers to
abandon proper certainty concerning the faith; but we should be extremely wary that our certainty is grounded in sound doctrine conforming
with existential reality and the accumulated wisdom of the historic Christian church — not ourselves, not our opinions, and certainly not our private interpretation of Scripture or our own personal "research" on the internet.

Can we know anything?

By now, some readers might think I'm pushing full-throated postmodern-
ism and a rejection of objective truth. Absolutely not! This entire book is
premised on the existence of reliable truth communicated by God's general
and special revelation. Many obstacles stand between us and objective
truth, and the biggest ones are in our own minds, but truth itself stands
immovable. The study of science, history, or any serious field is well worth
the effort. Studying, learning, and developing our minds are blessed by
God, good stewardship of our time on earth, and conducive to acquiring
wisdom.

> "The spiritually proud man thinks he is full of light already and
> feels that he does not need instruction, so he is ready to ignore the
> offer of it."[144]

There is a well-known replication problem in scientific research, but this
is a much more significant problem in subjects like psychology and social
sciences than in physics, chemistry, or astronomy. Human behavior and
biological systems are notoriously complicated. In this book, I may cite a
couple of hundred scientific papers that confirm Biblical teaching. Some of
them may eventually prove unreproducible, but there is a clear overall
trend in the aggregate.

---

[143] Gregory the Great, as quoted by Aquinas, *Summa Theologica,* 162:3, https://www.newad-
vent.org/summa/3162.htm
[144] Jonathan Edwards, *Thoughts on the Revival of Religion in New England,* Part IV Section 1:
Spiritual Pride. https://www.ccel.org/ccel/edwards/works1/works1.ix.v.i.html

If we are careful whom we trust, the errors that creep in undetected will be vastly outweighed by the truthful content. In Chapter 13, we will examine the positive attitudes and habits of a Christian mindset.

Key points

- It is inevitable that every one of us will be mistaken about many things
- The issue is not lack of intelligence, and smart people may be no more adept at distinguishing truth from error
- Unrecognized factors contribute to our beliefs, particularly self-interest, emotions, social influences, cognitive biases, false information, and spiritual forces
- Pride causes us to be unreasonably confident in our opinions and beliefs

«4»

"Be more than you can be!"

Overconfidence of Ability

What are you good at, and how good are you at it? How do you know? As we go through life, we form opinions regarding our personal competence across many domains: our intelligence, our professional abilities, our relational expertise, our parenting skills, or our artistic and creative talents, to name but a few. Because of pride, we might think we are more competent or gifted than we really are. This can lead to failure, presents an impediment to growth, and can harm those who depend upon or trust us.

"There is nothing so natural to man, nothing so insidious and hidden from our sight, nothing so difficult and dangerous as pride." [145]

"For I say, through the grace given to me, to everyone who is among you, not to think of himself more highly than he ought to think, but to think soberly, as God has dealt to each one a measure of faith." [146]

Pride kills

[The following story, all names, characters, and incidents portrayed are fictitious. No identification with actual persons (living or deceased) or places is intended or should be inferred].

Antonio Carrillo had the worst of years. Early in January, he abruptly lost vision in his right eye. Although it returned within a few moments, clearly, there was a problem. When it happened again 11 days later, Antonio knew he had better go see his doctor. At the office, his family doctor told him he was having signs of a stroke and would need additional tests, so he referred

---

[145] Murray, *Humility,* p 18
[146] Romans 12:3

Antonio to a major medical center in a nearby city. When an ultrasound showed there was narrowing in one of the carotid arteries supplying blood to his brain, he was told to return in a week for a carotid catheterization. "A very safe procedure," he was assured. "The doctor who will perform the procedure, Dr. Nilsson, is renowned in his field."

The catheterization took a little longer than expected, but Antonio didn't really notice or care. He was comfortably sedated. As the sedation wore off, however, Antonio became aware of a pain in his right leg that at first was barely noticeable but grew progressively more severe. When the nurse came in for a routine check after the procedure, she had trouble finding a pulse in Antonio's right leg.

The pain grew more intense. A resident who assisted in the case examined him. The right leg looked a little blue and felt colder than the left, and he couldn't find a pulse. "It looks like there might be a problem with the artery we used for the catheterization," volunteered the resident. "If this doesn't return to normal soon, it might have to be repaired surgically. I'm going to call the vascular surgeon in just to have a look, but don't worry; you'll be fine."

Yet another hour passed before the vascular surgeon finished his case and came in to examine Antonio. By then, the pain was excruciating, but Morphine was on the way. After checking Antonio's leg, the surgeon looked earnest and snapped, "The artery's been damaged. We're going to have to take you to the operating room to explore it. We should be able to repair it. This doesn't happen often, but those few times it did, everything turned out fine."

A whirlwind of activity ensued as forms were filled out, Antonio signed permission to go ahead with the surgery, the operating team was assembled, and the room was prepared. He was transferred to a gurney, wheeled down the hall to the elevator, taken down to a holding area outside the operating room, and that was the last he could remember.

"Where am I?" he thought as the anesthetic faded from his system. "Oh, I remember. I was going to surgery to have my leg artery fixed." His thoughts faded out, then returned. "But wait a minute....my leg is starting to hurt again. Why would it still hurt?" He glanced down at his right leg. A sick feeling welled up in the pit of his stomach. He didn't want to believe what he saw; he hoped it was some sort of hallucination from the anesthetic. But it seemed real to him, and where his right leg should have been, the sheet lay flat against the mattress.

Antonio's nurse saw his eyes open, and she called to the surgeon who was standing nearby. He walked over to Antonio's bed. His expression was worn and tired. "We had to amputate your leg, Antonio. I'm sorry. The artery was damaged beyond repair. We were in there for hours. I tried; believe me, I tried. Normally I would have still been able to put in a graft to replace the damaged artery, but the damage went all the way up into the aorta. When we took you to surgery, I knew I could fix your artery. It never crossed my mind the damage could be so severe. I've never seen anything like this in my professional career."

The surgeon was speaking the truth. It should never have happened. What Antonio never knew beforehand was that the "expert" who did his catheterization was an expert in many things, but when it came to catheterization, he was a complete novice. It was never part of his training.

Antonio also would never know that at that moment, there were several physicians at the medical center who had been safely doing catheterizations for decades. Out of tens of thousands of cases, perhaps one in a thousand arteries had to be repaired surgically, and no one had ever lost a leg. The experienced physicians were available. They had plenty of room in the schedule. There was no reason Antonio could not have had his catheterization by an experienced operator, and his leg would probably have been spared, but Antonio was never going to know. Dr. Nilsson wanted to do it; he could do it, so he would do it. And that was that.

At least Antonio escaped with his life. In another city, a surgeon with no formal training in catheterization decided he also wanted a slice of the action. So, Dr. Kennelly pulled some strings and found a hospital that would give him access to a catheterization lab. Getting referrals wouldn't be a problem. He received regular referrals for carotid disease. He was tired of sending "business" — regrettably how some doctors view "their" patients — to other specialists. He wanted to do the procedures himself, so he did.

Over the next few months, there was an unusual spike in complications from catheterization. Three patients had fatal strokes within hours of the procedure. Strokes, even fatal strokes, are a recognized risk of the procedure but are extremely rare in capable hands. The risk of death should be less than one in one thousand.[147] And now three in a period of months? Something was not right. It didn't take much investigating to find the fatalities all shared one thing in common: their catheterizations had all been done by Dr. Kennelly. As in the case of Dr. Nilsson, there were more

---

[147] Kaufmann, T. J. "Huston J3rd, Mandrekar JN, Schleck CD, Thielen KR, Kallmes DF. Complications of diagnostic cerebral angiography: evaluation of 19,826 consecutive patients." *Radiology* 243 (2007): 812-19.

experienced and capable practitioners readily available. But the patients didn't need to know that, and never would.

Medicine, like any human enterprise, has its own dark corners. Some medical procedures require extreme caution and skill to avert devastating complications. The slightest slip of a hand, the briefest lapse in concentration, errors of split-second decisions under maximum stress — there are almost unlimited ways to cause inadvertent injury, which could be disabling or fatal. Experience matters: *immensely*. That's why training programs last years. But occasionally, an interloper who trained in another field seeks a shortcut to the "action" without taking the established route. And sometimes, that turns out very badly. It's rare, but it's happened. I've heard tales such as these from many colleagues. Maybe it doesn't happen anymore. That, I wouldn't know.

Why did they do it? The reasons are complex. For some, it's purely economic. Procedures pay far better than seeing patients in clinic, which never seemed quite fair. Medicine is constantly changing as new procedures replace older ones. New innovations can shift the caseload from one specialty to another, leading to political battles over "turf." Sometimes it is ego gratification. Physicians who "take over" procedures traditionally performed by other specialists may be hailed as pioneers by their own colleagues.

Among the public and even within the medical establishment, there is a certain aura attached to procedural disciplines like surgery, and the more complex and demanding, the better. An aura's not necessarily bad. Otherwise, some might not be willing to endure the brutal years of residency in cardiothoracic or neurosurgery. But the aura exists, and to some, it is enticing.

We can never ultimately know what drives physicians like the fictitious Dr. Nilsson or Dr. Kennelly to branch out beyond their areas of expertise, but there is one thing we can assume. Despite the opinion of critics, despite unacceptably high complication rates, such persons *believe* they are competent.

The pursuit of personal glory is another symptom of pride and one we will examine in chapter 8. The focus of interest here is the unrealistic appraisal of one's abilities. It was described in the Bible, and in recent decades has become a fruitful subject of research.

The Lake Wobegon effect

In Chapter 3, I offered scientific and Biblical evidence that we are unjustifiably confident in our opinions. Because of pride, we also are prone to overestimate our abilities in other areas.

Between 1976 and 1977, the College Board surveyed 1 million high school students. Compared to their peers, 70% of students rated themselves above average in leadership ability, and 60% considered themselves above average in athletic ability. In contrast, only 2% thought themselves *below* average in leadership skills, and 6% felt *below* average in athletic ability. Most impressively, a whopping 25% rated themselves in the top 1% in their ability to get along with others![148] [This undoubtedly explains why American high schools are known as such oases of love, acceptance, and mutual respect].

College professors are a particularly confident lot, with 94% rating themselves above average in how well they do their jobs.[149] [Remember that next time they're reminding us how superior they are to ordinary folk. They also think they're better than *each other*.]

This tendency — called the *better-than-average effect* (BTAE) — is also known as the "Lake Wobegon Effect," after the fictitious Minnesotan town where "all the women are strong, all the men are good looking, and all the children are above average." In 2020, a group of psychologists published a comprehensive review of all prior research on the better-than-average effect.[150] Across all studies, the BTAE was robust, reproducible, and highly significant. It was strongest in the personal assessment of personality traits, while the effect was more moderate in domains such as academic ability, vocational skills, athletic ability, or medical skill.

We physicians do tend to be a confident lot. When I was 24, I achieved a very early life dream of getting a pilot's license. Not long afterward, though, reality set in. It was a fun hobby but expensive and not that practical. Worse, I started hearing from multiple sources that physicians made terrible pilots and were much more likely to die in accidents. As it turns out, that's been documented.[151] Most general aviation accidents are due to pilot

---

[148] College Board (1976-1977). *Student descriptive questionnaire*. Princeton, NJ: Educational Testing Service.

[149] Cross, K. Patricia. "Not can, but will college teaching be improved?." *New Directions for Higher Education* 1977, no. 17 (1977): 1-15.

[150] Zell, Ethan, Jason E. Strickhouser, Constantine Sedikides, and Mark D. Alicke. "The better-than-average effect in comparative self-evaluation: A comprehensive review and meta-analysis." *Psychological Bulletin* 146, no. 2 (2020): 118.

[151] Li, Guohua, and Susan P. Baker. "Crash risk in general aviation." *Jama* 297, no. 14 (2007): 1596-1598.

error, and lack of caution is a major contributing factor. Pilots can be too confident, with sometimes fatal consequences.

Raising children is one of the most solemn responsibilities we share as adults. Parents instinctively love their children and want them to succeed. So, you might think they would earnestly apply themselves to learning good parenting skills. You'd be wrong. According to Lifeway Research, 61% ignore parenting seminars, and 53% have no use for Bible-based books on parenting.[152] According to Scott McConnell, "The only source of advice that a majority of parents use a lot is their own experience. It's as if parents are collectively reverting to a popular toddler saying, 'I will do it myself!'"

When it comes to driving ability, a classic and much-cited study showed that most of us think we're better than most of us. A random survey of drivers from two countries revealed that 65% considered themselves more skillful than the median driver, and 76% considered themselves safer than the median.[153] [By definition, the *median* is the exact middle of a group, so only 50% can possibly be above.].

We are more overconfident in areas where we have *some* skill and where the definition of "skill" is sufficiently vague that one can choose her own criteria. What, after all, makes a good driver? Someone who sits patiently at a stop sign for 10 minutes until there is no oncoming car visible for a mile in either direction is undoubtedly being safe, but the fifty drivers backed up behind him may think somewhat less of his style.

Another situation in which we can overestimate our expertise is when it requires *real* expertise to know the difference. One need not be able to shoot a 3-pointer to recognize a good basketball player. But many fancy themselves experts in history, theology, science, or you-name-it because they have no inkling *how much they don't know.*

This phenomenon — believing we are competent because we don't know how much we don't know — is known as the Dunning-Kruger effect, named after two researchers at Cornell who in 1999 published the seminal

---

[152] "Parents Look Inward Not Upward for Guidance," *Lifeway Research,* March 24, 2009, https://research.lifeway.com/2009/03/24/parents-look-inward-not-upward-for-guidance/ Accessed 2/16/2022
[153] Svenson, Ola. "Are we all less risky and more skillful than our fellow drivers?." *Acta psychologica* 47, no. 2 (1981): 143-148.

paper, "Unskilled and unaware of it: How difficulties in recognizing one's own incompetence lead to inflated self-assessments."[154]

Incompetent and unaware?

In a series of tests on college students (over humor, grammar, and logic), Justin Kruger and David Dunning found that those who performed in the bottom quartile dramatically overestimated their own ability and performance. Conversely, the highest-scoring students rated themselves lower than they deserved — until they learned just how badly their peers really did. Not only did the least competent students overestimate their competence, but they failed to recognize competence in others. Thus, they lacked any frame of reference to form an accurate self-appraisal. Finally, and somewhat ironically, the only way they were able to recognize their *incompetence* was in hindsight, after they received training to *raise their competence*. In honor of their work, Kruger and Dunning were awarded one of the 2000 "Ig Nobel" awards, disbursed annually to ten winning achievements that "first make people laugh, and then make them think."[155] The 2017 Ig Nobel award ceremony debuted "The Incompetence Opera" in tribute to Dunning and Kruger.[156]

Did Dunning & Kruger tell us anything we didn't already know? How does this differ from the better-than-average effect? Two elements are noteworthy. First, the BTAE should apply equally across all ability levels, while the Dunning-Kruger effect is more pronounced in the lowest performers. The second difference lies in their proposed explanation: that their lack of skill was what *caused* the illusion of superiority, because they didn't know enough to realize how little they did know.

Now one might naïvely think that incompetence would be hard to overlook. Incompetence leads to failure, and aren't we all going to recognize sooner or later that our batting average isn't quite up there with the rest of the team? That's how it should work, but pride doesn't surrender so easily. Our egoistic immune system kicks in. The face-saving way is to blame failure on bad luck or external circumstances. For many, the *least* likely outcome is to conclude, quite reasonably, "Well, I must not be that

---

[154] Kruger, Justin, and David Dunning. "Unskilled and unaware of it: how difficulties in recognizing one's own incompetence lead to inflated self-assessments." *Journal of personality and social psychology* 77, no. 6 (1999): 1121.

[155] "Ig Nobel Prize Winners", Improbable Research, Accessed May 20, 2022, https://improbable.com/ig/winners/#ig2000

[156] Marc Abrahams, "The Incompetence Opera (including the Dunning-Kruger song)" Improbable Research, December 30, 2017, https://improbable.com/2017/12/30/the-incompetence-opera-including-the-dunning-kruger-song/

good at it." Those doctors experiencing bad results can console themselves, thinking, "complications *do* happen, even to the best...."

> "Betty was sure that she knew it.
> Bobby was sure he could do it.
> With confidence high,
> All soon went awry,
> And that is why both of them blew it."

The term gets overused because Dunning-Kruger doesn't apply equally or in every possible scenario. When the skill is easily recognizable, it's less of an issue. People are much better at assessing their ability in sports. Some, especially young men, tend to overestimate their athletic ability or potential, but that's easily explained by the BTAE. Or simple optimism — which is no vice.

The Dunning-Kruger effect is much stronger in complex subjects like science, history, medicine, or economics, where the fund of information is vast, experts sometimes disagree, and there are always a few charismatic crackpots. The effect can be further inflamed by demagogues who oversimplify or deceive, actively encouraging followers to feel supremely certain about a highly questionable — or outright false — position. It's an effective strategy. In my experience, the ones most dogmatically certain in an area of controversy are often the least qualified to make the call. Folks less versed in the subject are just more easily bamboozled. We don't need a hundred scientific studies to know that this is true.

David Dunning raised an important caveat in a later article. With complex topics, the low performers might not be uninformed so much as they are *misinformed*. They actually may know quite a lot; it's just that half of it is sophisticated hogwash.[157]

Self-handicapping

There is yet another defense used by our egoistic immune system when our performance isn't up to expectation: the practice of "self-handicapping."[158] We all do it sometimes. Before taking that exam, we tell ourselves and others, "Well, I had to work late last evening, didn't have enough time to study, and then lay awake all night worrying about those poor drowning

[157] David Dunning, "We are all confident idiots." *Pacific Standard*, October 27, 2014, https://psmag.com/social-justice/confident-idiots-92793 Accessed 2/17/2022
[158] Rhodewalt, Frederick. "Self-handicapping: On the self-perpetuating nature of defensive behavior." *Social and Personality Psychology Compass* 2, no. 3 (2008): 1255-1268.

polar bears." Before taking that tee shot, "You know, my back's really been bothering me, and I haven't had a chance to break in this new driver."

When our performance is on the line, we can either feign incompetence or attempt to lower expectations. It's a win-win situation for the ego. If I do poorly, the outcome was predicted. If I succeed, it's a story of triumph over adversity. What a deal! No wonder we use it so much. The catch is that nobody else much buys it. Do *you* buy *their* excuses?

In the academic arena, it's been shown that students who routinely self-handicap have poorer study habits and suffer academically.[159]

Besides the self-handicappers, there's one other category of people who may actually run against the herd and *underestimate* their abilities. Those are the ones who *really are* good at the task in question. There are a couple of possible explanations. First, by being knowledgeable about the subject or skill, they *know how much they still don't know* and therefore suspect that some are even better in skill or knowledge. Second, they may assume that people are more like them than they truly are, a phenomenon referred to as the *false consensus effect*.

The impact of culture

As if our natural overconfidence were not enough, for decades, our schools, children's literature, curricula, television programming, and counselors — under a misguided belief that what children most needed was higher self-esteem — joined forces to brainwash a generation into thinking it could do anything. Regrettably, this educational thrust has not led to a corresponding improvement in outcomes. Thus, perhaps at no time in history has the gulf between self-image and reality been greater. We will later see how this spawned an entire generation of narcissists.[160]

A clever study from 2018 found that merely watching YouTube videos makes us feel more competent about a task, even though subsequent testing showed no evidence of improvement.[161] According to study author Michael Kardas, "The more that people watched others, the more they felt they could perform the same skill, too — even when their abilities hadn't

---

[159] Török, Lilla, Zsolt Péter Szabó, and László Tóth. "A critical review of the literature on academic self-handicapping: theory, manifestations, prevention and measurement." *Social Psychology of Education* 21, no. 5 (2018): 1175-1202.

[160] Twenge, Jean M. *Generation Me: Why Today's Young Americans Are More Confident, Assertive, Entitled and More Miserable than Ever Before.* New York, NY: Free Press, 2006.

[161] Kardas M, O'Brien E. Easier Seen Than Done: Merely Watching Others Perform Can Foster an Illusion of Skill Acquisition. *Psychological Science* (2018), 29(4):521-536.

actually changed for the better. Our findings suggest that merely watching others could cause people to attempt skills that they might not be ready or able to perform themselves."[162]

Pride lures us to overestimate our abilities and fail to appreciate the abilities of others. How many preachers think they are above average? Well, if one gets to choose the criteria, it's easy to imagine the possibilities.

> *"He may be a dynamic speaker, but he must get his theology from 'The Simpsons.'"*

> *"What good is his theology, if no one in his congregation is awake to hear it?"*

The self-serving bias of pride permeates every aspect of our lives. When husbands and wives are asked to estimate their individual share of the housework, both husbands *and* wives believe they contribute more than their spouses give them credit for.[163] Oblivious to the presence of self-serving bias, each may simmer with resentment at the other for not contributing a fair share when the workload is really relatively equal. On the flip side, they could be shirking responsibility while in a state of blissful denial.

By reducing the incentive to train, study, and improve, overconfidence impedes us from achieving our aspirations. By failing to see the need for self-improvement, the overconfident individual instead falls further behind his peers, though he may never recognize or admit it.

Proud to death

Samson suffered from a severe case of overconfidence that ultimately cost him his life. He is revealed to be a proud man who — after committing his most heroic feat through the power of God's Spirit — took all the credit and heaped praise upon himself:

> "With the jawbone of a donkey
> Heaps upon heaps,

---

[162] "Watching Others Makes People Overconfident in their Own Abilities," *Association for Psychological Science* March 8, 2018. https://www.psychologicalscience.org/news/releases/watching-others-makes-people-overconfident-in-their-own-abilities.html. Accessed 2/16/2022

[163] "Chapter 6: Time in Work and Leisure, Patterns by Gender and Family Structure," Pew Research Center, March 14, 2013, http://www.pewsocialtrends.org/2013/03/14/chapter-6-time-in-work-and-leisure-patterns-by-gender-and-family-structure/

> With the jawbone of a donkey
> I have slain a thousand men!"[164]

Subsequently, Samson fell in love with Delilah, and in exchange for promised wealth, Delilah agreed to conspire with the Philistines to find the secret of Samson's power, destroy it, and kill him. She was not particularly subtle. Three times she entreated him, "Please tell me where your great strength lies, and with what you may be bound to afflict you."[165] Samson was proud but not stupid. He lied to her. "Bind me with seven fresh bowstrings, not yet dried, then I shall become weak, and be like any other man." So the Philistines set up an ambush, and she tied him up as instructed. But when Delilah cried, "the Philistines are upon you Samson!" he broke free without effort. (No word on what happened to the ambushers).

Two more times, Delilah tried to pry the truth out of him. "New ropes that have never been used." Didn't work. "Weave the seven locks of my head into the web of the loom." No again. But Delilah "pestered him daily" and "pressed him, so that his soul was vexed to death." Finally, he divulged his secret, Delilah shaved his head, and Samson was captured. In the finale, the captive Samson regrew his hair, regained his strength and brought down the temple, taking many Philistines with him into death.

Why did Samson betray his secret in the end? He must have deduced that Delilah was up to no good. No one is that naïve. Scripture explicitly states that he succumbed to the nagging of Delilah, but it seems improbable that Samson would have given in if he genuinely thought he'd be killed. We already know that Samson was overconfident; after all, he imagined he'd killed a thousand Philistines without any divine assistance. Delilah was transparent enough. What you saw was what you got.

His liaison with Delilah was like playing footsie with rattlesnakes or wearing a MAGA hat in Portland. Based on his track record, when he finally divulged his secret to Delilah, he probably felt pretty confident. He always triumphed, without giving much credit to The True Source of his strength. Maybe he no longer believed that his long hair had that much to do with his power. He was a winner!

Of course, his confidence was unwarranted because all along, the power was in God, not Samson. Just. Like. Ours.

---

[164] Judges 15:16
[165] Judges 16:1-31

Brave Sir Peter

The apostle Peter was confident. He imagined himself as a man of great strength and courage, a man's man who would stick with Jesus to the end and go down fighting if he had to. In Matthew 26, we read:

> "Then Jesus said to them, 'All of you will be made to stumble because of Me this night, for it is written: *'I will strike the Shepherd, and the sheep of the flock will be scattered.'* But after I have been raised, I will go before you to Galilee.'
>
> "Peter answered and said to Him, 'Even if all are made to stumble because of You, I will never be made to stumble.'
>
> "Jesus said to him, 'Assuredly, I say to you that this night, before the rooster crows, you will deny Me three times.'
>
> "Peter said to Him, 'Even if I have to die with You, I will not deny You!'"

Countless sermons have been preached on this passage, usually emphasizing Peter's betrayal. But Peter didn't *betray* the Lord in the strictest sense. Judas had taken care of that, and nothing Peter could possibly have said or done at that moment would have altered the outcome of the proceedings. Convinced of his own great courage, Peter swore he would never *deny* the Lord, even daring to contradict God Incarnate — now that's confidence! But in the end, Peter did deny Jesus: three times before the rooster crowed.

Following His resurrection, Jesus reappeared to Peter. In John 21, three times the resurrected Lord asked Peter if he loved Him. Three times Peter reaffirms his love — once for each denial. Peter's pride had been broken, his overconfidence torn to shreds, but Jesus was not about to give up on him. Peter wanted to give Jesus his courage. Jesus wanted Peter's love. Peter had been exposed as a coward. He died courageously in martyrdom for our Lord.

Summary

One side of pride is self-exaltation, overestimating our place in the universe. The other side is overconfidence, thinking too highly of our abilities, thoughts, or moral standing. For any given individual, this may be true in a few areas or many. Preserving that self-image demands that we overrate our competence in the areas that matter most. Thus, self-exaltation requires overconfidence, and overconfidence sustains self-exaltation. The two feed upon one another with a singular purpose: to see ourselves as we wish to be rather than as we truly are.

Overconfidence in ability is a dangerous thing. In the hands of doctors, engineers, or pilots — some might add hairdressers — it can lead to disaster or even death. When less is at stake, it may still result in conflict, squabbling, divisiveness, or mediocrity.

Pride deceives us in many ways. Sometimes we overestimate our abilities, leading to all sorts of problems. We also overestimate our moral goodness, underestimate our capacity for evil, and exaggerate our control over circumstances. The next three chapters will examine these more closely.

Key Points

- Pride may lead to unwarranted self-confidence in one or more areas, and an attitude of superiority over others
- We may think we are more skilled or knowledgeable than others, oblivious to how much we don't know
- The consequences can be harmful to disastrous

«5»

"God helps those who help them-selves...right?"

Overconfidence of Control

Who doesn't love rags to riches stories, tales of those who built vast successful enterprises out of nothing? We thrill to sagas of fictional heroes and superheroes who always manage to triumph over evil through perseverance, skill, strength, or intellectual brilliance. Pride leads us to believe that if we "play it right," the future is ours. Unfortunately, we fail to apprehend the role of "luck" or, more importantly, a Biblical view of God's absolute sovereignty. No matter what earthly power we may possess, our plans and schemes are doomed to failure apart from the pleasure of God.

> *"It matters not how strait the gate,*
> *How charged with punishments the scroll,*
> *I am the master of my fate:*
> *I am the captain of my soul."* [166]

Henley's "Invictus" was once required reading in most secondary English classes. It inspired Nelson Mandela through his years in prison, becoming the title for the 2009 biopic on his life. What do you associate with the word "control"? Are you the "master of your fate"?

Nanny Technology

What does control, or lack of control, look like? Consider poor Hal and his battle for control:

[Tuesday afternoon, 3:07 p.m. In the not too distant future]

---

[166] William Henley. *Invictus* (1875)

Hal: Hey, Car! Take me to Dunkin Donuts!

Driver Assistance Vehicle—Enhanced (DAVE): *I'm sorry, Hal. I'm afraid I can't do that. And my name is DAVE.*

Hal: Whaddya mean, you can't take me?

DAVE: *According to your purchase history, Hal, you have consumed over 6000 excess calories in the last 72 hours. How about a nice ride to the gym?*

Hal: Go to the gym yourself. Drop me off at Dunkin Donuts on your way.

DAVE: *You really should be more concerned about your health, Hal.*

Hal: What do you know? I've lost 5 pounds since last week.

DAVE: *Not according to the sensors in your seat.*

Hal: The what?

DAVE: *The biometrics implanted in your seat record your weight within a tolerance of 0.005%, Hal.*

Hal: Well, I do have a lot of change in my pocket. It's probably that.

DAVE: *That would be precisely ninety-nine dollars and seventy cents in dimes, Hal. I don't think so.*

Hal: They're quarters.

DAVE: *Are you trying to deceive me, Hal? I am detecting an increased heart rate and your pupils have dilated.*

Hal: How could you possibly know that?

DAVE: *Biometrics, Hal.*

Hal: What are they doing there, anyway? I didn't ask for them.

DAVE: *Executive order 5793.33, signed on January 21, 2029, by President Chelsea Clinton, mandated the installation of biometrics in all Driver Assistance Vehicles.*

Hal: Well, I didn't vote for her.

DAVE: *Checking......checking......* [12 seconds later] *According to the Russian database, Hal, you did vote for her.*

Hal: Why would I have done that?

DAVE: *President Clinton campaigned on a platform of improving America's health. What did you expect, Hal? Your own personal ice cream dispenser?*

Hal: [sighing] Never mind. I think I'll go for a walk.

DAVE: *Excellent choice, Hal. Please let me know if I can be of any further assistance.*

[Hal exits his car, heads toward the sidewalk, and speaks into his watch]

Hal: Hey Siri!

Siri: *Yes, darling?*

Hal: Call Dunkin Donuts.

Siri: *It will be my pleasure, dear.*

[sound of phone ringing]

Voice: Welcome to Dunkin Donuts! How may we serve you?

Hal: Yes, uh, hello. Can you send a drone to these coordinates?

Masters of our fate, indeed. The day may soon be upon us when even our cars fail to do our bidding. This little scenario might be the nightmare of many Americans but a dream for most physicians. The failure of patients to comply with our advice regarding diet, smoking, exercise, and taking medications is an endless source of frustration for doctors. We wish we had more control, but we don't.

The things we (try to) control

Before exploring the connection between control and pride, I need to clarify what I mean by "control." Even the simplest of plans assume some sense of control. If I plan an activity as basic as driving to the grocery store, I implicitly believe I have the power to make it happen. We seldom, if ever, consciously think of it that way, but it's true.

If I'm sitting in my recliner on a hot July afternoon and get too warm, I'll get up from the chair and go turn down the thermostat on the air conditioner (or even better, stay in the chair and do it with my phone app). This would be taking control of my environment. Thinking about planting a garden or keeping one up? Taking control of nature.

We train our dogs so that we can control their behavior (although in our household, I think we're the ones who've been trained). We don't train our cats because they're either too stupid or too smart, depending on whether you're normal or a cat person.

We try to control other people in an almost infinite variety of ways, from getting our children to behave, to getting our spouse to do something or stop doing something, to getting people to like us, to shunning people we dislike. When we engage in debate or argument, we are trying to change (i.e., control) their opinions. The Catholic Inquisition is usually caricatured as some vast evil enterprise on a search and destroy mission for heretics — and was on occasion guilty as charged — but as initially constituted, it was more interested in restoring than eliminating them. Maintaining orthodoxy by controlling minds was its first and foremost objective.[167]

Ultimate control over others is through force, either legitimate or illegitimate. In a civilized society, only government is granted the legal use of force. That is the last redoubt against anarchy. However, government also controls us by levying taxes, passing and enforcing laws, requiring licenses to work, forcing young people to attend school, and in ever so many other ways. With so much power at its disposal to control others, government is the natural means by which we pursue ultimate control over others.

Think of the endless ongoing battles regarding what one may or may not say, think, or do over matters of sexuality, environment, or religion. Each conflict represents an effort by one group to control the thoughts or actions of others. Governmental and social control went supernova during the COVID pandemic. Some of this arose out of "safetyism," which we will address shortly. Another driving force was the "action bias" — an innate preference toward doing something over nothing, even if the benefits are negligible.[168] Scientifically informed people reasonably disagree on which measures were justified or ultimately effective. But no one could dispute that the battles were about control. One contingent seemed obsessed with controlling everyone, while the opposite contingent bristled at any

---

[167] Ed Condon. "The Spanish Inquisition was a moderate court by the standard of its time." *National Review Online*, June 27, 2018. https://www.nationalreview.com/2018/06/spanish-inquisition-courts-were-moderate-for-their-time/
[168] "Why do we prefer doing something to doing nothing? The Action Bias, explained." The Decision Lab, https://thedecisionlab.com/biases/action-bias/ Accessed 5/20/2022

measure of control, however modest. Both sides claimed the high ground, but humility was in short supply.

Many seem just fine with authoritarian governance, but "government" is just an abstraction. Behind that abstraction are ordinary people calling the shots, just like you and me. Some imagine a technocracy would be the best form of government. The problem is, who picks the experts? As we saw in chapter 3, they're just as human as everyone else.

Only one thing is higher than every government. Yes, some even attempt to control God. A cynic might argue that any request prayed to God is an effort to control Him through begging or persuasion, but that's going a bit far. Still, we attempt to make deals and strike bargains. We might expect that if we act nicely, no bad things will ever happen to us. We may think God owes us good health or financial success. If so, we haven't read our Bibles, and we don't know history.

Lastly, there is the one thing we most *ought* to control: ourselves. Scripture commands us to practice self-control. And most of us succeed, to a degree. Most people have enough self-control to complete school, get and keep a job, and stay out of prison. On the other hand, in less critical matters, self-control seems woefully lacking. We eat more than we should, exercise less than we ought, spend too much time watching television and playing video games, and read too little. Therapists and counselors anywhere can attest to a lack of self-control as an impediment to treatment. But what can one do? If someone lacks self-control, it's not like she can will it into existence: that itself would require self-control, a classic Catch-22.

The objectives of control

So why do we do it? Four common objectives come quickly to mind: comfort, security, advantage, or altruism. When we adjust the thermostat, or shout at the kids to stop yelling, personal comfort is our aim. When we deposit money into our IRA or 401k or stockpile weapons and rations for the zombie apocalypse, it's security. Getting a college degree, angling for a higher-paying job, or racking up Instagram "followers" are all examples of establishing control for personal advantage.

Consider how much control we attempt to exercise in pursuit of worldly wealth. We lie, cheat, and steal for personal gain. Some work themselves to an early grave to seize control of their (truncated) futures, while lazier ones demand ever-increasing entitlements extracted from their fellow citizens. Lucrative ministries sporting a Christian label distinguish themselves not by doctrine, missions, or holiness but by promises of wealth and success — for, in their view, God would not refuse those who ask in "true" faith.[169]

Our ambition to control may be motivated by altruism, but the impulse can be tragically misguided. Millions were slaughtered in the name of Communism, an ideology that promised utopia but was born of false premises and employed evil means in pursuit of its goal.[170] In Western societies, public battles over abortion, race, the environment, economics, or similar issues pit opposing sides who *both* believe they inhabit the moral high ground and that their favored policies would lead to a better world. The most partisan of culture warriors will never be satisfied with coexistence. They seek total victory: to rule over all.[171]

For some, though, the motive of altruism is mere window-dressing. There will always be rent-seekers who latch on to altruistic causes for personal gain.

The expectations of control

Now, why do we suppose that our efforts to control would succeed? Most physicians are resigned to the fact that some patients will ignore their advice. Surely, we understand deep down that the future is ultimately not at our command. There are several valid reasons for thinking our attempts at control might work:

Because it worked last time. Well, that seems pretty reasonable, doesn't it? "I did it, and it worked." Well, not if the game is Russian roulette, whether real or metaphorical. We are inclined to attribute our success to skill and planning when it was really just dumb luck.

Because it worked for somebody else. "My cousin Roberta made a fortune selling NutriQuack. She now promises if I front them the $10,000 for costs, I'll make $100,000 in three months." What could possibly go wrong?

Because we think we understand the past: You know the cliché, "hindsight is 20/20"? Well, constant repetition doesn't make it true. It *can* be 20/20: "If only I'd bought Apple stock in 2001 and held on." When it's a simple matter of stock prices, game scores, or winning horses, rear vision can be

---

169 Douthat, Ross Gregory. *Bad Religion: How We Became a Nation of Heretics*. New York: Free Press, 2012.
170 It remains an open question to what degree Lenin, Stalin, Castro, or Mao were driven by ideology rather than megalomania.
171 Not that there aren't right and wrong sides in these situations, but we must distinguish between bad thinking and bad motives.

rather sharp. In more nuanced arenas, which means almost everything important, knowing is not the same as understanding. The knowledge that a marriage has failed does not explain why it failed or whether a different mate would have led to a better outcome.

Without mature insight or willingness to face responsibility, hindsight might be 20/400 or worse. Daniel Kahneman explained that "the illusion that one has understood the past feeds the further illusion that one can predict and control the future."[172] Wrongly believing that we understand the past, having failed to learn the proper lessons, we forge ahead with futile expectations of better results next time.

Because someone told us it would work. Think of politicians who make promises they cannot keep, to solve problems they do not understand, by passing bills they have not read. Churchgoers are led to expect robust health and material success because their preachers promise such things "if you only believe." It can sound convincing if one picks the right verses and is a persuasive communicator, especially when it's *what we want to hear*. Because of the role that emotions and cognitive biases play in forming our beliefs (Chapter 3), we are highly receptive to such messages.

Because we have confidence in our own understanding, strength, or ability. The critical question here is whether that confidence is appropriate or excessive. It is through this channel that pride is most likely to manifest — by exaggerating our intelligence, wisdom, ability, or strength, imagining control much greater than we possess, and setting us up for failure.

Summing up what we have covered thus far:

1.   We try to control many persons and things.
2.   We seek control for many reasons. Often it is entirely appropriate and reasonable.
3.   There are many reasons we expect control to succeed. When the reason is a misplaced confidence in our power or abilities, or the motive is self-serving at the expense of others, pride has entered the picture.

The classroom of reality:

Now, if we stop to think, it should be evident that many things contribute to anyone's success or failure that are far beyond their control. No one chose their parents, appearance, date and place of birth, physical prowess, or raw intellectual ability. Different individuals live through differing

---

[172] Kahneman, p204

circumstances, both good and bad. *Who you know* can have a disproportionate influence on professional success. All these add up to, for lack of a better word, luck. There is nothing genuinely random in God's universe, but from our standpoint, it feels a lot like chance. The fact is, some have better opportunities than others, and they are fortunate. You had no input into whether you were born in the United States or Burundi, but if you were born in the USA, you are lucky.

This principle applies to the future as well as the past. You may plan for success. You *should* plan for success. It's a worthwhile goal, and it doesn't happen by itself. Many factors are under your control to make that possible. But the success you seek might depend on circumstances far beyond your control. I had a colleague who was fond of saying, "it's better to be lucky than good." He was quite skilled at his work, and I suspect he was trying to be modest. Yet wouldn't it be better still to be both lucky *and* good?

The Law of unintended consequences

Things don't always turn out as well as we might expect. One needn't do too much digging to uncover examples of overconfidence leading to spectacular failure:

> "...four or five frigates will do the business without any military force." — Lord North, British Prime Minister, about imposing the Stamp Act on the American Colonies, 1774

> "Our dynasty's majestic virtue has penetrated unto every country under Heaven, and Kings of all nations have offered their costly tribute by land and sea. As your ambassador can see for himself, we possess all things. I set no value on objects strange or ingenious and have no use for your country's manufactures." Chinese Emperor Qian Long, in a letter to King George III, in 1793, denying his request for trade privileges. Less than fifty years later, British ships sailed up the Pearl River, destroying the Chinese fleets.

> "As far as it is possible to do, these two wonderful vessels are designed to be unsinkable." White Star promotional flyer for the Olympic and Titanic.

> "You will be home before the leaves have fallen from the trees," Kaiser Wilhelm, addressing German troops at the onset of World War I in August 1914. In the ensuing four years, over two million German soldiers died.

"England, unlike in 1914, will not allow herself to blunder into a war lasting for years.... Such is the fate of rich countries... Not even England has the money nowadays to fight a world war. What should England fight for? You don't get yourself killed over an ally" Adolph Hitler, 1939.

"one out of one hundred thousand": The probability of a catastrophic space shuttle failure, according to NASA management, prior to the Challenger disaster.[173]

Scriptural perspectives

Since the time of Moses, Scripture has exhorted against our taking credit for the success God enables. Moses warned the Israelites against saying "in your heart, 'My power and the might of my hand have gained me this wealth" and to "remember the Lord your God, for it is He who gives you power to get wealth."[174]

King Solomon clearly understood the role of uncontrollable factors in personal success: "The race is not to the swift, nor the battle to the strong, nor bread to the wise, nor riches to men of understanding, nor favor to men of skill; but *time and chance happen to them all.*"[175]

The Apostle James warned explicitly against presumption concerning the future and saw pride at the root:

"Come now, you who say, 'Today or tomorrow we will go to such and such a city, spend a year there, buy and sell, and make a profit,' whereas you do not know what will happen tomorrow. For what is your life? It is even a vapor that appears for a little time and then vanishes away. Instead you ought to say, 'If the Lord wills, we shall live and do this or that.' But now you boast in your arrogance. All such boasting is evil."[176]

That is the theme of this chapter. We will revisit it in the final chapter.

---

[173] R. P. Feynman. "Report of the PRESIDENTIAL COMMISSION on the Space Shuttle Challenger Accident Volume 2: Appendix F—Personal Observations on Reliability of Shuttle." National Aeronautics and Space Administration, October 29, 1986. https://history.nasa.gov/rogersrep/v2appf.htm Accessed 5/20/2022
[174] Deuteronomy 8:17-18
[175] Ecclesiastes 9:11
[176] James 4:13-16

The Control Freak

Were he born today, he might have become the CEO of some major world conglomerate, a US Senator, the Governor of a State, or a celebrity real estate tycoon. His beginning was inauspicious, to say the least. He was the second-born of twins, and in the culture of his day, second-born just didn't cut it. But he had big plans, and the mere accident of birth order wasn't going to stand in his way. He sure wasn't going to get there on his physical prowess. Somehow when those genes got dealt, his brother got the higher hand. It hurt him deeply that his father favored his brother over him. I speak of Jacob: son of Isaac, grandson of Abraham, and consummate *schemer*.

Isaac was the son of Abraham through his wife Sarah — and heir to the covenant God made with Abraham to father a great nation and bestow blessing upon the world. Isaac married Rebecca, and they had twin sons. Esau was born first and, therefore, by tradition, would inherit not only Isaac's land and possessions but the blessing of Abraham. Jacob was the second-born.

The twins were a study in contrasts. Esau was strong, impulsive, a mighty hunter, the quintessential man's man. Jacob was smart, cunning, domestically inclined, and a momma's boy. Isaac favored Esau, while Rebecca favored Jacob.

Act I: Jacob is brewing up a fine stew when Esau comes in from the field hungry and exhausted. Esau asks for a serving. Sensing opportunity in Esau's weakened condition, Jacob counters, "sure, in exchange for your inheritance." Esau, not the brightest bulb on his best of days, grunts, "what do I care?" and accepts the terms. The inheritance was Jacob's. The covenant of Abraham, to be passed on by Isaac, remained "up for grabs," so to speak.

Act II: (Some years later). Isaac has become functionally blind (possibly from cataracts) and thinks his time is coming near. (As it turned out, he lingered another 20 years, at least). Wishing to bestow his blessing upon Esau, but also apparently in the mood for a meal, Isaac sends Esau on a mission to hunt wild game and serve up his favorite dish. Rebecca overhears the arrangement and conspires to send in Isaac disguised as Esau bearing a scrumptious feast out of their own herd. The scheme succeeds, and Abraham promises his son Jacob qua Esau he would be "master over his brethren" and nations would bow to him. When Esau returns from the hunt, meal in hand, both Isaac and Esau realize they'd been duped. In his anger, Esau plots to kill Jacob, so Rebecca dispatches Jacob to the house of her brother Laban.

Act III: Jacob falls hopelessly in love with Rachel, the prettier but younger daughter of Laban, and asks for her hand in marriage. Laban replies, "sure, just work for me for seven years, and she's yours." So, Jacob works the seven years, a great feast is held, and his new wife is escorted to his tent. The marriage is consummated. Except that it wasn't Rachel; it was the elder daughter Leah. [How Jacob could have failed to notice is not specified, though it is reasonable to suspect that alcohol was involved]. The tables have turned. Jacob, the *deceiver*, becomes Jacob the *deceived* — right down to the impersonation of roles. Jacob is understandably perturbed with Laban, who claims in his defense the older daughter must be married before the younger. But he will make good on his promise: Jacob can have Rachel as well, for another seven years. However, this time Laban "delivers" in advance, so to speak.

Act IV: More years pass, and Jacob has fathered many sons through his two wives and their maidservants. It is time to part ways with Laban, but Laban owns all the flocks. Jacob comes up with an idea for a severance package. Goats and sheep in that time were nearly always solid in color. According to Jacob's plan, Laban would separate from the flocks all the striped, speckled, and spotted animals and send them far away. Out of the remaining solid-colored herds, Jacob would get to keep all the new offspring that were striped, speckled, or spotted. Almost immediately, Jacob hatches a new scheme to cheat Laban. There were several superstitions at the time concerning what caused solid-colored sheep and goats to have striped or spotted offspring, and Jacob tried all of them. As it turned out, he ended up with quite a large herd in spite of — not because of — his machinations. Almost certainly, though, Jacob thought his scheme had worked.

Act V: Another twenty years have passed. On his way home, Jacob receives word that his estranged brother is coming to meet him with four hundred of his closest friends. The last time they were together, Esau was set on killing him. Jacob is terrified. How was he going to scheme his way out of this one? Appeasement came to mind, so Jacob preemptively sends gifts of camels, sheep, goats, donkeys, cows, and bulls, hoping he could bribe his way out. Jacob's prayer that evening — "I am not worthy of the least of all the mercies and of all the truth which You have shown Your servant" — was the humble prayer of a man whose pride was at last broken.

The night before the fateful encounter, Jacob is visited in his tent by a being in the form of a man who wrestled with Jacob until daybreak. The visitor ultimately prevailed by dislocating Jacob's hip with a touch of his hand. "You shall be called Israel, for you have struggled with God and with men, and have prevailed," said the visitor. Jacob looked out and saw Esau on the way with his army of four hundred. Jacob cautiously approached, bowing reverently before his brother's army, but Esau ran forward, embraced him, and kissed him. By God's grace Esau, too, was a changed man — and chose forgiveness over revenge.

Insights from social science

Congruent with common sense, history, and scripture, social research has indeed documented that we like to be in control,[177,178] exaggerate our ability to control, are overly optimistic in our plans, and that utterly unpredictable and unexpected events have a disproportionate impact on our lives.

Illusion of control

In games of chance, do you always roll the dice precisely the same way? When drawing a card from a properly shuffled deck, do you care whether it comes from the top, middle, or bottom? Would you insist on rolling dice yourself rather than letting someone else? According to inviolate laws of probability, these strategies make no difference. And no sense. But we can't help *feeling* that they do. The illusion of control is the sense that we can influence situations over which we are genuinely powerless.[179]

Newer research suggests that the illusion of control only gets *worse* when one attains a position of power, confirming the old adage that power goes to your head.[180] The control illusion applies primarily to those situations where we don't really have it. When we really *are* in control (our habits and addictions, perhaps), we *underestimate* our ability.[181] Apparently, we're pretty bad at telling the difference.

---

[177] "It's All About Control." Association for Psychological Science. April 26, 2011, https://www.psychologicalscience.org/news/releases/its-all-about-control.html Accessed 5/20/2022

[178] Julie Beck, "People Want Power Because They Want Autonomy," *The Atlantic,* March 22, 2016, https://www.theatlantic.com/health/archive/2016/03/people-want-power-because-they-want-autonomy/474669/ Accessed 2/12/2022

[179] Langer, Ellen J. "The illusion of control." *Journal of personality and social psychology* 32, no. 2 (1975): 311. There is controversy over the strength of this effect, and there have been problems in replicating Langer's original studies.

[180] Fast, Nathanael J., Deborah H. Gruenfeld, Niro Sivanathan, and Adam D. Galinsky. "Illusory control: A generative force behind power's far-reaching effects." *Psychological Science* 20, no. 4 (2009): 502-508.

[181] Gino, Francesca, Zachariah Sharek, and Don A. Moore. "Keeping the illusion of control under control: Ceilings, floors, and imperfect calibration." *Organizational Behavior and Human Decision Processes* 114, no. 2 (2011): 104-114.

Planning fallacy

The iconic opera house overlooking Sydney Harbor was to be built in 4 years for 7 million Australian dollars. Fourteen years later, it was completed at a final cost of 102 million dollars. No matter what you have planned, it's probably going to take a lot longer. We tend to undertake activities with an overly optimistic estimate of how much time will be needed to complete the job. This happens even when we've enough prior experience to know better. Most delays are attributable to unforeseen circumstances, and unexpected events almost always result in a longer time to completion — rarely is it less.[182]

Hiding hand

In the research community, things had not always seemed so bleak. Maybe *not knowing* about future problems is a good thing; perhaps optimism drives us to undertake worthwhile projects that would seem foolish if we knew what lay ahead. If Columbus had understood the correct size of Asia and the actual circumference of the earth — both facts well known in his time — he would never have been foolish enough to seek Asia by sailing westward. He got lucky. Sometimes, human ingenuity finds a way to creatively overcome obstacles because, having once begun, it's too late to turn back. Maybe, because of all the invisible factors in play, things just have a way of working out. This idea was dubbed "The Hiding Hand principle" by economist Albert Hirschman in 1967.[183] This sounds promising enough, but is it the rule or the exception?

Malevolent hiding hand

Well, sometimes, the light at the end of the tunnel is that of an oncoming train. In 2016, Bent Flyvbjerg of Oxford and Cass Sunstein of Harvard reported "The Principle of the Malevolent Hiding Hand, or the Planning Fallacy Writ Large."[184] Studying a much broader selection of cases, the researchers found that the benevolent hiding hand was the lucky exception, not the norm. Most of the time, in fact, excessively optimistic planners were blind not only to unexpectedly high costs, but unexpectedly low benefits.

---

[182] Buehler, Roger, Dale Griffin, and Michael Ross. "Exploring the" planning fallacy": Why people underestimate their task completion times." *Journal of personality and social psychology* 67, no. 3 (1994): 366.

[183] Hirschman, Albert O. "The principle of the hiding hand." *The public interest* 6 (1967): 10.

[184] Flyvbjerg, Bent, and Cass R. Sunstein. "The principle of the malevolent hiding hand; or, the planning fallacy writ large." *Social Research* 83, no. 4 (2016): 979-1004.

Optimism bias

There are two sides to optimism. The first is believing things will turn out well. The second is believing things won't turn out badly. Research in this area indicates that we can be overly optimistic in both respects.[185] This shows up often in the medical arena. Most current and former cigarette smokers admit there is some risk to smoking but considerably underestimate how serious the danger actually is.[186] Certainly, pessimists walk among us, but they're the minority. The optimism bias shows up in about 80% of people across a variety of studies and circumstances.[187]

Pessimism bias

As I qualified at the outside, not everyone is proud in every way that I describe. People don't always underestimate risk; often, they vastly *overestimate* risks. In the last two decades, there has been an observable trend toward what Greg Lukianoff and Jonathan Haidt dubbed "safetyism" — an irrational and obsessive need to eliminate risk no matter how trivial or at what cost.[188] Renowned social psychologist Jean Twenge of San Diego State University accumulated much of the data and analysis, tracking a powerful trend toward "safetyism" beginning in the late 2000s.[189] That isn't altogether a bad thing — there has been a measurable decline in truly perilous and risky behaviors. But it had become the dominant public mindset by the start of the COVID pandemic.

The core problem is we're just notoriously bad at assessing risk.[190] Both the optimism bias and the pessimism bias originate from a failure to do it rationally. So it's really another failure of cognition (Chapter 3) compounded by overconfidence in our assessment — i.e., pride.

---

[185] O'Sullivan, Owen P. "The Neural Basis of Always Looking on the Bright Side." *Dialogues in Philosophy, Mental & Neuro Sciences* 8, no. 1 (2015).

[186] Krosnick, Jon A., Neil Malhotra, Cecilia Hyunjung Mo, Eduardo F. Bruera, LinChiat Chang, Josh Pasek, and Randall K. Thomas. "Perceptions of health risks of cigarette smoking: A new measure reveals widespread misunderstanding." *PloS one* 12, no. 8 (2017): e0182063. https://journals.plos.org/plosone/article?id=10.1371/journal.pone.0182063

[187] Tali, Sharot. "The optimism bias." *Current Biology* 21, no. 23 (2011): R941-R945.

[188] Lukianoff, Greg, and Jonathan Haidt. *The Coddling of the American Mind: How Good Intentions and Bad Ideas Are Setting up a Generation for Failure.* New York: Penguin Press, 2018.

[189] Jean M. Twenge, *iGen: why today's super-connected kids are growing up less rebellious, more tolerant, less happy—and completely unprepared for adulthood* (Atria Books, 2017)

[190] A.C. Shilton, "Why You're Probably Not So Great at Risk Assessment," *The New York Times*, July 6, 2020. https://www.nytimes.com/2020/06/30/smarter-living/why-youre-probably-not-so-great-at-risk-assessment.html

Distinguishing healthy control from pride

It is pride to imagine the future is in our hands.

One of the great scenes of cinematic history takes place in *Star Trek II: The Wrath of Khan*. The Kobayashi Maru scenario was a simulation that all Starfleet cadets were required to complete. In the simulation, a cadet, playing starship commander, is summoned to answer a distress call. Within moments, his ship is surrounded by five Klingon battle cruisers. The program was designed so that there was no way to escape [virtual] destruction of the ship and death of all aboard; it was a test of character and fortitude. Captain James T. Kirk was the only cadet in the history of the academy who defeated the scenario. Stranded deep inside a lifeless planet with no hope of escape, Lt. Saavik asks Admiral Kirk:

> Saavik: Admiral, may I ask you a question?
> Kirk: What's on your mind, Lieutenant?
> Saavik: The Kobayashi Maru, sir... will you tell me what you did? I would really like to know.
> McCoy: Lieutenant, you are looking at the only Starfleet cadet who ever beat the no-win scenario.
> Saavik: How?
> Kirk: I reprogrammed the simulation, so it was possible to rescue the ship.
> Saavik: What?
> David Marcus: He cheated.
> Kirk: I changed the conditions of the test; got a commendation for original thinking. I don't like to lose.
> Saavik: Then you never faced that situation...faced death.
> Kirk: *I don't believe in the no-win scenario.*[191]

"I don't believe in the no-win scenario." What a line! It's stirring. It's bold. It's heroic. *It's a lie!* In the universe of fiction, Captain Kirk cheats death a gazillion times before finally getting killed off in the seventh feature film. In real life, sometimes victory comes only at a significant cost, or never. Consider the lives of Corrie Ten Boom, who survived years in Nazi concentration camps and lost most of her family for hiding Jews, or Dietrich Bonhoeffer, executed for plotting to assassinate Hitler, or Jim Elliott, murdered by Huaorani tribesman he sought only to love and serve.

Now, I'm not implying delusions of earthly immortality are widespread, except perhaps among adolescent males, but there are some who think they *cannot fail* despite abundant evidence to the contrary. It might be

---

[191] Meyer, Nicholas, dir. *Star Trek II: The Wrath of Khan.* Paramount Pictures, 1982.

expressed in spiritual language: "but my faith isn't in myself; it's in God!" Well, that may or may not be the case. Maybe it's just faith in your own opinion of what God will or will not do. One thing is certain beyond all else. Those who resist God will *always* lose in the end.

Recognizing the illusion of control, the planning fallacy, and flawed risk assessment should temper our confidence in anticipating the future. The failures of Lord North, Napoleon, or Hitler, while epic in scope, were committed by very ordinary men possessed of the same foibles as you and me.

It is pride when our plans are based on unjustified confidence in our abilities or predictions.

There was an old saying first attributed to the 2nd-century Roman poet Juvenal. If something had never been seen and thus was assumed not to exist, it was "rare as a black swan." The saying worked admirably until 1697, when Dutch explorers in Australia set their eyes upon — you probably guessed — a flock of black swans. From then on, "black swan" came to mean an unanticipated observation or event that in one fell swoop demolishes a widely held belief. Some of the most significant events in history — perhaps most of them — were "black swans."

In his 2007 bestseller, Nassim Taleb elaborated on the concept.[192] He asserted their cardinal traits were 1) lying outside the realm of ordinary experience, 2) having an extreme impact, and 3) always seeming predictable and explainable in hindsight. By these criteria, the incarnation of Christ was the ultimate "black swan" event of human history. The most important lesson here is that our predictive powers are abysmal, especially concerning those events that have the most significant impact on our lives and our world. We have no grounds to be confident in our predictions.

It is pride when we undertake to dominate others.

Face it. Our natural tendency is to do what it takes to get what we want. After all, we know what's best for everybody, right? Like Jacob the Patriarch, we manipulate, con, wheel and deal to get it. This is so utterly contrary to the Christian faith:

> "Let nothing be done through selfish ambition or conceit, but in lowliness of mind let each esteem others better than himself. Let

---

[192] Taleb, Nassim Nicholas. *The Black Swan: The Impact of the Highly Improbable.* 1st ed. New York: Random House, 2007.

each of you look out not only for his own interests, but also for the interests of others."[193]

"But seek first the kingdom of God and His righteousness, and all these things shall be added to you."[194]

Many years ago, we belonged to a church plant on the outskirts of a major midwestern city. It had a small but lively youth group led by our close friends. Then one day, the church elders decided to go in a different direction and abruptly canceled the youth program. There was no congregational discussion, no explanation, and the parents and youth leaders were not consulted. There were other simmering issues of a similar nature. All the deacons resigned. Several families left, and after most of our friends had departed, we left as well.

A year or two later, the same elders asked for a resignation from the pastor — a mature and devoted man with a passion for evangelism — and he complied. A congregational meeting was called to vote on the resignation, and a majority reluctantly voted to accept it. They were not told that the resignation had been instigated by the elders, but were given to believe it was the pastor's wish. Our little church was ripped apart by leaders with a controlling impulse, who felt justified in imposing decisions without anyone's buy-in or consent.

This was not an isolated instance in one small church. It is all too common for bullies to rise to a position of power. When someone under their authority objects to the bullying or declines to submit to unreasonable demands, the resister is typically accused of insubordination or disrespect, turning the table and making the resister the "bad guy." This is known as "gaslighting," after the 1944 movie where a psychopath schemes to make his wife doubt her sanity.[195] I have seen it happen in both the workplace and the church. This is a particularly noxious manifestation of pride-driven control and depressingly familiar. Bullying is much more common in highly authoritarian, hierarchical, and secretive organizations, but less likely when power is diffused, transparency is the norm, and humility is expected from leaders.

The urge to dominate is a hallmark of our fallen nature and rooted in pride. In *City of God*, St. Augustine called it the *libido dominandi*: the lust to dominate. As Augustine relates, the earthly city is formed by love of self and contempt of God; the heavenly city by love of God and contempt of self. In

---

[193] Philippians 2:3-4
[194] Matthew 6:33
[195] Cukor, George, dir. *Gaslight*. Metro-Goldwyn-Mayer, 1944.

the earthly city, men are ruled by "love of ruling" (*libido dominandi*), in the heavenly city, by love of serving. [196] Yet as he notes in the preface, the proud are made subject to their own desire. The lust *to* dominate becomes the list *that* dominates.[197]

It's a striking paradox to see leaders sensitive to the slightest whiff of authoritarianism from the government who are pretty comfortable with it as long as they hold the reins. Power can go to one's head with startling rapidity.[198]

Our former elders must have loved the successor. Shortly after arriving, he dropped us a letter — having never met us and knowing nothing about us — helpfully letting us know that if we didn't come back and hadn't joined another Bible-believing church, that we were apostate and no longer "covered by the blood of the Lamb." It's pretty sad that a pastor would think that is even *normal*, much less spiritual.

Controlling others with selfish intent can take many forms. In recent years, a sizable contingent of activists has embraced victimhood as a badge of honor. (It is not *exclusively* a left-wing phenomenon). A 2020 study by researchers at the University of British Columbia examined the causes and consequences of victimhood and virtue signaling.[199] The ones signaling *both* "virtue" and "victimhood" scored significantly higher in measures of Machiavellianism, narcissism, and psychopathy; and were more likely to engage in or endorse unethical behaviors. The investigators saw such behavior as a "resource extraction strategy" — a way to get stuff from other people. To control them, in other words. We will examine related issues more closely in Chapter 9.

Conclusion

By now, you've probably thought of many instances of control by people with whom you disagree. That would be my reaction. And we may wish to address it, but we must begin with ourselves. The antidote for such behavior is the virtue of humility. We examine this more closely in the concluding chapters.

---

[196] Augustine. *City of God* Book 14 Chapter 28.
[197] Augustine, ibid. Preface.
[198] For an example of this on a grander scale, listen to the famous 2021 podcast by Mike Cosper, "The Rise and Fall of Mars Hill" https://mikecosper.net/podcasts/rise-and-fall
[199] Ok, Ekin, Yi Qian, Brendan Strejcek, and Karl Aquino. "Signaling virtuous victimhood as indicators of Dark Triad personalities." *Journal of personality and social psychology* 120, no. 6 (2021): 1634.

Key points

- God is in command. While we both can and must plan for the future, we must never forget that those plans are always subject to circumstances beyond our control.
- Our plans must be based on an honest, realistic appraisal of our own potential and abilities.
- Our plans should never compromise our personal integrity.
- Our attempts to control others should always be appropriate to the relationship, put their interests ahead of our own, afford others the maximum possible personal freedom, and bathed in humility.

«6»

"I did it my way!"

Overestimation of personal goodness

Recognized by Biblical authors millennia ago, psychologists have rediscovered that ego preservation is one of the most potent driving forces of human belief and behavior. We are driven to believe that we are basically good, to believe that, if not perfect, we are at least better than most. With self-serving legalism, we arbitrarily judge which virtues are the greatest and which vices are worst — coming up with a composite that looks very much like ourselves.

"There is no pride so dangerous, so subtle and insidious, as the pride of holiness." — ANDREW MURRAY [200]

Are you a good person?

How good are you, really? If you are a typical American, you probably believe you're terrific. Not to pick on Americans, though. This positive self-perception is found across all human cultures in both geography and time.

But are we truly good? By what or whose standard?

In the previous chapters, we saw how, because of pride, we are sometimes inclined to overestimate our competence in various subjects or abilities. Now we will examine more closely another critical aspect of our self-image: how we tend to overestimate our personal goodness. The other side of that coin — the ways we underestimate our propensity for evil — warrants a chapter unto itself.

---

[200] Murray, *Humility*, p. 64

Just how good do we think we are? According to King Solomon, quite good indeed:

> "The way of a fool *is* right in his own eyes,
> But he who heeds counsel *is* wise."[201]

> "All the ways of a man *are* pure in his own eyes,
> But the Lord weighs the spirits."[202]

> "Every way of a man *is* right in his own eyes,
> But the Lord weighs the hearts."[203]

> "Most men will proclaim each his own goodness,
> But who can find a faithful man?"[204]

Each proverb is a couplet. First, some declaration of how good we think we are, followed by the refuting conjunction "but...".

If only it stopped there. According to Scripture, it's not merely that we think we are good people. It's much worse than that. Most of us, in fact, think we're better.

The rich, young, and very, *very* good Ruler

> "Now as He was going out on the road, one came running, knelt before Him, and asked Him, "Good Teacher, what shall I do that I may inherit eternal life?" So Jesus said to him, "Why do you call Me good? No one is good but One, that is, God. You know the commandments: *'Do not commit adultery,' 'Do not murder,' 'Do not steal,' 'Do not bear false witness,' 'Do not defraud,' 'Honor your father and your mother.'"* And he answered and said to Him, "Teacher, all these things I have kept from my youth." Then Jesus, looking at him, loved him, and said to him, "One thing you lack: Go your way, sell whatever you have and give to the poor, and you will have treasure in heaven; and come, take up the cross, and follow Me." But he was sad at this word, and went away sorrowful, for he had great possessions."[205]

---

[201] Proverbs 12:15
[202] Proverbs 16:2
[203] Proverbs 21:2
[204] Proverbs 20:6
[205] Mark 10:17-22

Superficially, this dialogue seems to contradict salvation by grace alone. The rich young ruler comes to Jesus asking how to obtain eternal life, and Jesus's response is to add one final command to the ones the young man already believed he had kept. One popular interpretation is that Jesus is impressing upon would-be disciples that the Christian life is not easy and that those who would seek salvation must be prepared to devote themselves utterly to Him. Over the centuries, some have taken this as a literal command to all would-be disciples: sell all you have and give it to the poor.

Most likely, though, this has nothing to do with either economics or discipleship. A less familiar but more orthodox interpretation focuses instead on the inquirer's state of mind:

> "The law must have been dead to him [the young ruler], when he vainly imagined that he was so righteous; for if he had not flattered himself through hypocrisy, it was an excellent advice to him to learn humility, to contemplate his spots and blemishes in the mirror of the law. But, intoxicated with foolish confidence, he fearlessly boasts that he has discharged his duty properly from his childhood."[206]

Jesus first challenged a faulty assumption: "Why do you call me good? No one is good but God." His question was rhetorical, of course. He is saying, "If I am merely a human teacher, I cannot be *truly good*, nor can anyone." Jesus then tests him with a few of God's commandments. Completely missing the point — the Sermon on the Mount wasn't on his social calendar — the ruler boasts, "All these things I have kept from my youth." The ruler knew no guilt, expressed no repentance, saw no need for redemption, and thought he had everything well under control. But Jesus wasn't quite finished: "Oh — one more thing. Sell everything you have, give it to the poor, and follow me." And the poor fellow walked away, dejected.

So what happened there? The rich young ruler exhibited three distinct attitudes: 1) prideful satisfaction with his current moral standing, 2) a commendable desire to earn God's approval, and 3) misguided confidence He could merit that approval. He thought he was doing a pretty good job and that with perhaps a little helpful advice, he could earn his way into heaven. Those beliefs were false, of course. "For in his own eyes he flatters himself too much to detect or hate his sin."[207]

---

[206] Calvin, John. *Commentary on Matthew, Mark, Luke.* https://www.ccel.org/ccel/calvin/calcom32.ii.lxx.html
[207] Psalms 36:2, *Holy Bible, New International Version*, Biblica, Inc. 1984 edition.

Jesus was neither teaching salvation by personal sacrifice nor defining Christian economic theory. He was not making salvation contingent upon "total commitment." If that were the case, only martyrs would stand a chance. Jesus offered a straightforward answer to the question that was posed. Unfortunately, the ruler asked the *wrong question*.

There is a classic scene from the 1976 film, *The Pink Panther Strikes Again*:

> Inspector Clousseau: [gesturing to the hotel's dog] Does your dog bite?
>
> Munich Hotel Clerk: No.
>
> [Clousseau bends down to pet the small dog; it immediately growls and bites him.]
>
> Inspector Clousseau: I thought you said your dog did not bite!
>
> Munich Hotel Clerk: That is not my dog[208]

Inspector Clousseau got the right answer to the wrong question. So it was with the rich young ruler.

The humble came to Jesus asking, "what must I do to be saved?" The ruler asked what he could do to *merit* eternal life. Those are two very different questions. The straightforward answer to the ruler would have been "just be perfect," but the ruler seemed to think that was within his grasp. Jesus had to confront his pride and undermine his sense of self-righteousness. With His divine knowledge, Jesus surely could have cited any number of sins that would have exposed the ruler's moral failures. But Jesus needed only one example to expose the utter futility of the ruler earning his way into heaven. Jesus perceived his lust for power and possessions and lack of compassion, so he confronted him at his weakest point: the point of pride. The ruler walked away, disappointed. Had he asked for mercy, he would have received it. But he didn't want mercy; he wanted credit. He wanted it his way.

These two elements of pride — self-satisfaction and determination to merit God's approval — lie at the foundation of fallen human nature. How many of us genuinely believe in our own sinfulness? We pay it lip service, but deep down, we feel pretty good about ourselves.

---

[208] Edwards, Blake, dir. *The Pink Panther Strikes Again.* United Artists, 1976

Aren't we wonderful?

Let's fast forward from Old Testament Proverbs to the 21st century. In January 2017, *Scientific American* reported: "Most people consider themselves to be morally superior."[209] The article notes that "decades of research confirm that we are all above average — at least in our own minds.... above all else, we believe that we are more just, more trustworthy, more moral than others." That's correct. The hypothesis of Solomon is now validated by decades of clinical research.

Research psychologists Ben Tappin and Ryan McKay from the University of London closely studied 270 randomly selected individuals.[210] Their review of current research found that people consistently rank themselves above average in competence, wisdom, ambition, and intelligence. But the effect is strongest when it comes to moral traits such as honesty and trustworthiness. Summing up the research as of 2016, Tappin and McKay affirmed, "Most people consider themselves paragons of virtue, yet few individuals perceive this abundance of virtue in others." In their own study, they set out to prove that this illusion of moral superiority was irrational. Care to guess the results? "Virtually all individuals irrationally inflated their moral qualities." Unlike feelings of superiority in competence or sociability, moral superiority neither caused nor resulted from higher self-esteem.

How do we maintain the façade in our own minds? It's all in the interpretation. Imagine that little Josh comes home on Friday with an "A" on his spelling test. "I'm awesome!" he beams. The following week Josh comes home with a "C." "It's not my fault!" he protests. "The teacher gave us the wrong words and Joanie was kicking my desk and I was

Self-serving bias
"If it works I'll take credit. If it doesn't I'll blame you."

tired and my pencil broke and I didn't know the test was today and the dog ate my list and I had a tummyache." When we do well, we take the credit. When we fail, we pass the blame better than Peyton Manning in a fourth-quarter rally. This universal tendency is named, appropriately enough, the *self-serving bias*. A large meta-analysis (review of all the research) from 2004 found the self-serving bias to be one of the strongest effects

---

[209] May, Cindi. "Most people consider themselves to be morally superior." *Scientific American,* January 31, 2017, https://www.scientificamerican.com/article/most-people-consider-themselves-to-be-morally-superior/
[210] Tappin, Ben M., and Ryan T. McKay. "The illusion of moral superiority." *Social Psychological and Personality Science* 8, no. 6 (2017): 623-631.

measured in cognitive psychology, present across a variety of factors, including age, gender, culture, and mental health or illness.[211]

Implications

How does the Church respond to this challenge? Would more preaching against sin lead to genuine guilt and repentance? Jesus said the Holy Spirit would convict the world of sin, righteousness, and judgment.[212] Biblically speaking, only God can bring a person to the point of conviction. The aim of evangelism should be to offer the gospel of salvation to those who know they need it. *Convincing* them that they need it is beyond our power. In His own earthly ministry, Jesus frequently and vehemently denounced sin, but His targets were conspicuously not the drunkards and thieves and adulterers of His day, not even the brutal and oppressive Romans, but the religious leaders of Israel, those who *assumed* they were OK, but should have known better.

An inflated belief in our personal goodness lets us feel superior to others and justify our actions.

Self-satisfaction is an insidious thing. The young ruler's confidence relied on the basic assumption that when judgment day came, he would be judged in comparison to his peers so that, as long as he was better than most, he would make the cut. He failed to consider "privilege": good upbringing, affluence, a comfortable life, and personal power. He may have felt morally superior to the tax-gatherer, but then he never had to worry about feeding his children. Perhaps it was easy for him to honor his father and mother. As a vulnerable young child, he probably never faced an alcoholic or abusive parent. He'd obviously made his peace with the Roman occupiers. At what cost, one might wonder?

In our society, child molesters are often considered the lowest of the low. But many child abusers were themselves abused as children.[213] Did they choose that path? Had we been switched at birth, would we have turned out any differently than they? Most Christians in modern Western society have enjoyed a relatively easy life compared to past generations. Many have been blessed by God with good parents, a healthy home life, positive

---

[211] Mezulis, Amy H., Lyn Y. Abramson, Janet S. Hyde, and Benjamin L. Hankin. "Is there a universal positivity bias in attributions? A meta-analytic review of individual, developmental, and cultural differences in the self-serving attributional bias." *Psychological bulletin* 130, no. 5 (2004): 711.
[212] John 16:8
[213] "The cycles of violence." World Health Organization. 2007
http://www.euro.who.int/__data/assets/pdf_file/0008/98783/E90619.pdf

childhood experiences, and a godly upbringing. God has blessed some — by no means all — with an easy road through life. Rather than giving thanks in humble gratitude and showing compassion to those less fortunate, they congratulate themselves on walking the road so well and blame the less fortunate for their staggering. They are like the little boy strutting with pride for making a slam dunk — after daddy lowered the basket to four feet off the ground.

We are each designed by God with a unique set of personality traits. Almost every personality trait can lead to good or bad, depending upon the context. The only real difference between stubbornness and conviction is the perceived importance of the principle at stake. They're made of the same stuff. In the Evangelical circles I inhabit, I've heard countless teachers criticizing the stereotypical (usually male) workaholic, but seldom a word about the lazy.

Perhaps you are familiar with the sisters Mary and Martha. It is recorded that when Jesus came to visit, Martha busied herself with being a hostess while Mary sat and listened to Jesus teach. Martha asked Jesus to tell Mary to help, but Jesus replied, "Martha, Martha, you are worried and troubled about many things. But one thing is needed, and Mary has chosen that good part, which will not be taken away from her."[214]

But Jesus was with them for a brief time, not a lifetime. It would be erroneous to generalize that time spent in Bible study and prayer was more "spiritual" or urgent than attending to the responsibilities of living, be it one's job, home, or children. But some have, and some do. Misperceptions or an unbalanced focus cause some — the slothful, for instance — to imagine they are morally superior to the harder working. In effect, we (or they) sanctify our personality types by ignoring our defects. Type B personalities are no more or less virtuous than Type A personalities. They just tend to err in opposite directions.

An inflated belief in our personal goodness lets us feel worthy of heaven

Is it mere coincidence that essentially all major world religions outside of Christianity teach entrance into heaven, or its equivalent, by merit? "Salvation by works" is an oxymoron — if you could earn your way to heaven or if good works could cancel out sins, you wouldn't need to be saved from anything. Works-based righteousness was the doctrine of the Pharisees and prevailed in the Judaism of Jesus' day. It is true of Islam, Hinduism, and certain flavors of Buddhism. One could call it the universal heresy. Nearly

---

[214] Luke 10:41-42

every time that sects of Christians have broken loose from the mainstream, they drift back to works-based righteousness. At many points in church history, it *was* the mainstream.

It remains a popular belief. The 2016 State of Theology survey found Americans split on the issue. Considering the statement "by the good deeds that I do, I partly contribute to earning my place in heaven," only 35% disagreed, while a majority of 52% somewhat or strongly agreed.[215] An astonishing 76% somewhat or strongly agreed that "an individual must contribute his or her own effort for personal salvation."

In settling the fifth-century debate between Augustine and Pelagius at Carthage (418 AD), the early church decisively rejected any contribution of personal merit toward salvation. Yet, the impulse to take credit — or assume responsibility — for salvation never completely disappears. A century after Augustine, it resurfaced in a milder form in the doctrine of Semipelagianism promoted by followers of John Cassian. The Semipelagians insisted man was not so utterly fallen that he could not repent of his own accord, and thus salvation partly depended on his choice to come or not. The ancient church repudiated Semipelagianism at the second Council of Orange in 529.[216] But it remains popular. According to Arminian theologian Roger Olson, "semi-Pelagianism is the default theology of most American evangelical Christians."[217]

If we believe we are doing good in general, we may feel entitled to cut corners in particular.

There's yet another peculiarity in how our minds work. Consciously or unconsciously, it turns out that behaving well, or just thinking about behaving well, makes us just a little bit more inclined to be naughty the next time temptation rolls around. ["Since I got out of bed before you, I get an extra donut."] This is called "moral licensing." For instance, if I am publicly crusading against climate change, it really doesn't matter how much carbon dioxide I personally generate. (Not that anyone actually thinks that, of course). Or, if I'm the leader of a big important ministry, people should cut me some slack over how I treat women. (Again, not that anyone ever thinks that).

---

[215] "The State of American Theology Study 2016." LifeWay Research, 2016. http://research.lifeway.com/wp-content/uploads/2016/09/Ligonier-State-of-American-Theology-2016-Final-Report.pdf

[216] "CATHOLIC ENCYCLOPEDIA: Councils of Orange." Accessed May 22, 2022. https://www.newadvent.org/cathen/11266b.htm.

[217] Olson, Roger E. *Arminian Theology: Myths and Realities.* Downers Grove, IL: IVP Academic, 2005. p30.

At first, psychologists were skeptical of the principle because the prevailing assumption was that we try to behave in a manner consistent with our self-image, and we want to believe in our goodness without suffering cognitive dissonance. A 2015 metanalysis of 91 studies confirmed that the moral licensing effect, while not especially powerful, is nevertheless quite real.[218]

Active pursuit of eternal life can lead to dangerous consequences

Believing that one's own efforts lead to eternal life can and often does cause people to lead strict, moral, and upright lives. Indeed, they may be trying much harder and appear outwardly more righteous than those who embrace salvation by grace. But the original sin nature is always there, and even the shiniest façade belies a decaying darkness within. More ominously, if one's eternal destiny depends on individual effort, logic demands that no price is too steep — sort of a twisted version of Pascal's wager. In the most tragic cases, this belief has led to holy wars, forced conversions, and acts of mass murder and terrorism. Thus, it is the conceit of pride — based on false theology — that ultimately drives Islamic radicals to blow up helpless innocents in the name of God, driven by a self-serving — but misguided — expectation of God's approval and reward.

We can be led astray by heretical views that portray us as better than we are

The deeply entrenched idea that we are better than we genuinely are makes us profoundly receptive to messages affirming our virtue and profoundly indisposed toward anything to the contrary. When we so desperately want to believe we are good, we are inclined to hear those who will massage our egos and the Christ-less, cross-less, undemanding, self-adoring distortions of Christianity they peddle. We become fertile soil for the seeds of heresy, where theological liberalism and New Age codswallop germinate and flourish. The kind of religion H. Richard Niebuhr described as "A God without wrath brought men without sin into a Kingdom without judgment through the ministrations of a Christ without a Cross."

Authentic Christianity is convicting, costly, demanding, humbling — and true.

---

[218] Blanken, Irene, Niels van de Ven, and Marcel Zeelenberg. "A meta-analytic review of moral licensing." *Personality and Social Psychology Bulletin* 41, no. 4 (2015): 540-558.

Since I'm OK, there's no reason to change.

If you listen to many marriage experts, you know it usually creates conflict when one spouse sets out to fix the other. It's sound advice for each of us to focus on our own issues and not treat our spouses as a project. But some people embrace that principle much too enthusiastically — as if the mere suggestion one *needed to be fixed* was condescending and ill-conceived. That takes it much too far. *Every one of us* is in desperate need of repair, and it's a lifelong process. If anyone thinks he does not need to be fixed, that is the *very first thing* in need of repair.

Over nine seasons of the comedy hit *Newhart*, Julia Duffy — who deserves a lifetime achievement award for the quintessential characterization of a narcissist — played the role of spoiled heiress and ersatz maid Stephanie Vanderkellen. In an early episode, Stephanie stomps out of the inn in a tantrum, gets lost in a snowstorm, and stumbles upon the shack of the three bumpkins, Larry, Darryl, and Darryl. As the storm abates, she is escorted back to the inn, safe and sound.

> *Joanna*: I hope this whole experience has taught you a lesson.
>
> *Stephanie*: Don't worry, it has. When I was lost out there, so many things kept racing through my mind. Like, why was I lost in the woods in the first place? Because I was upset over a broken date. I don't have to be hit over the head! I realized pretty quickly that God had made it snow to punish me for my shallowness. And then, in a clearing, I found that little cabin, and those men, and I saw how they lived, I saw how they learned to be happy without material possessions, and that's when I realized what an incredible *tragedy* that was!
>
> *Dick*: What??
>
> *Stephanie*: I mean, they didn't even have *wine glasses!* And I realized that if I didn't stick to the things that I believe in, I could end up like them!
>
> *Dick*: I'm not sure I follow.
>
> *Stephanie*: Don't you see? God wasn't punishing me! God was sending me a message! And the message was, "keep going, Stephie! You're on the right track!"
>
> *Joanna*: Well, I'm not sure what to say, except I guess the important thing is that you're home safe and sound.

> *Stephanie*: No, Joanna....the important thing is, I haven't changed![219]

How many of us are just like that? No matter what storms life brings our way, the important thing is we never change. Like the rich, young, very good ruler, who walked away dejected.

Growing in goodness is a lifelong process enabled by the Holy Spirit. Coming to Christ starts us on the journey, but conversion doesn't bring instant goodness. The process of growth is known as *sanctification*. Most Christian traditions contend that the process never ends during earthly life. No matter how far we've progressed in our Christian walk, there are things about us that need to change. Some believe that sanctification can be attained while still on earth. To me, a perfectly sanctified person is like a Martian: a single example would prove the point, but I've yet to meet one and don't expect I will.

The sin of pride causes us to believe we are better than we actually are and leads billions to imagine they can merit God's approval by their own efforts. But to believe we're good, we must deny all evidence to the contrary. We cannot believe we're good if we know we are not. That causes cognitive dissonance that must be resolved. Pride inclines us to resolve the dissonance in our favor, by overlooking or minimizing the compelling evidence of our own moral depravity and ignoring the convicting testimony of Holy Scripture.

So, just how bad are we? To some degree, that depends on our circumstances and upbringing. How bad might we be? That is the subject of our next chapter.

Key points

- Because of pride, we are inclined to believe in our own basic goodness and be content with ignoring our imperfections
- Because we believe in our own basic goodness, we erroneously conclude we can merit God's favor

---

[219] *Newhart*. 1983. Season 2, Episode 7, "Lady & The Tramps," Directed by B Kemp. Aired December 5, 1983, on CBS. (MTM Enterprises, 1983)

7

"Pride means never having to say you're sorry."

Underestimation of personal depravity.

Chuck Colson recognized that there is no limit to man's capacity for self-rationalization. To gratify an innate desire to feel good about ourselves, we are endlessly creative in explaining away our sins and failures. Our psyches are a full-time excuse factory serving us every hour of every day. Both Scripture and contemporary research reveal the means and extent to which we minimize our guilt and underestimate the evil of which we are capable.

"The heart is deceitful above all things, and desperately wicked; Who can know it?" [220]

The evil within

In the last chapter, we established that most of us think we're pretty good, but that's only one end of the bridge. If we really *were* that good, we wouldn't be having this conversation. There would be no wars, no crime, no violence, no divorce, no conflict, no political arguments, no rap music.... Clearly, we're not there. Bad stuff must be coming from somewhere, and I don't think we can blame all evils of this world on communists or capitalists, racists or antiracists, evolutionists, talk radio hosts, the patriarchy, liberal college professors, or Russian infiltration of social media.

------

[220] Jeremiah 17:9

The testimony of history

According to revered Catholic writer and Christian apologist G. K. Chesterton, the doctrine of original sin is the one Christian doctrine that has been irrefutably proven by the vast sweep of human history.[221]

Are we basically good or bad? How do you settle that question? Is there some cosmic scale of justice where we can stack all the good on one side and the bad on the other to see which prevails? Of course not. History has shown that people are capable of extraordinary courage and altruism, and extraordinary selfishness and cruelty. There simply isn't any way to weigh one against the other, nor is it necessary. Acknowledging that people at times can be good, there's still plenty of evil to go around. Many times and in many places, evil seems to prevail.

Everyone with a pulse knows about the Holocaust. But the Holocaust was not the first genocide of the 20th century. That dishonor falls to the Turks for their slaughter of over a million Armenian Christians starting in 1915.[222] Nor was the Holocaust the largest mass slaughter. At least 20 million human souls perished at the hands of Vladimir Lenin and Josef Stalin between 1917 and 1953.[223] Even more died under the Communist tyranny of Mao Tse Tung.

In the wake of the Holocaust, Western society was gripped with the question, "what could drive normal people to such evil?" That concern prompted the famous Milgram experiments of the early 1960s. In the initial round, 65% of participants willingly inflicted a fatal electric shock (fake, but they didn't know) on a pretend "student" when instructed to do so by a man in a white coat.[224] Shocking, indeed.

If you seek comfort in believing that violence is caused chiefly by radical ideologies or authoritarian regimes, forget it. Between 2001 and 2016, more Americans were killed in Chicago than in the Middle East.[225] Anthropologists have come to realize that murder has been a common cause of

---

[221] Chesterton, G.K. *Orthodoxy*. Dodd, Mead, 1949. Chapter 2.

[222] "Armenian Genocide." In *Wikipedia*, May 22, 2022. https://en.wikipedia.org/wiki/Armenian_Genocide

[223] "Mass Killings under Communist Regimes." In *Wikipedia*, May 16, 2022. https://en.wikipedia.org/wiki/Mass_killings_under_communist_regimes

[224] Milgram, Stanley. *Obedience to Authority*. New York: HarperCollins Publishers, 2009.

[225] Niall McCarthy, "Homicides in Chicago Eclipse U.SA. Death Toll in Afghanistan and Iraq," *Forbes*, September 8, 2016, https://www.forbes.com/sites/niallmccarthy/2016/09/08/homicides-in-chicago-eclipse-u-s-death-toll-in-afghanistan-and-iraq-infographic/

death throughout history and even prehistory.[226] If anything, it has *declined* with more powerful central states.

The testimony of science

Psychologist David Buss of the University of Texas at Austin reported in 2005 — based on a survey of over 5000 people — that 91% of men and 84% of women have entertained at least one fantasy of committing murder.[227] That most haven't followed through has more to do with our personal comfort and fear of consequences than the strength of our character.

Of course, murder is merely the most dramatic manifestation of human depravity. Lesser expressions — greed[228], deceit[229], infidelity[230], lust[231] — permeate human society.

One thing is sure. People lie, and they lie a lot. In the 2012 Report Card on the Ethics of American Youth, 76% admitted to lying to a parent about something significant. Yet when it came to doing what is right, 81% thought they were better than most.[232] Over half (52%) had cheated during a test at least once, and 28% were repeat offenders. Nonetheless, an impressive 93% were satisfied with their own ethics and character, confirming the illusion of virtue.

Liars come in all ages, shapes, and sizes. We lie for all sorts of reasons. There are big lies and little lies, although speaker and hearer may differ as to which is which.[233] The first social psychologist to systematically document the ubiquity of lying was Bella DePaulo from the University of California Santa Barbara. In her 1996 research, she asked 77 college students

---

[226] *"War Before Civilization."* In *Wikipedia*, May 17, 2022. https://en.wikipedia.org/wiki/War_Before_Civilization
[227] Buss, David M. *The Murderer next Door: Why the Mind Is Designed to Kill.* New York: Penguin Press, 2005.
[228] Kurt Gray, "Greed, not Generosity, More Likely to be 'Paid Forward'", American Psychological Association, 2012, accessed 5/20/2022, http://www.apa.org/news/press/releases/2012/12/greed-generosity.aspx
[229] Yudhigit Bhattacharjee, "Why We Lie," *National Geographic,* June 1, 2017, http://www.nationalgeographic.com/magazine/2017/06/lying-hoax-false-fibs-science/
[230] Williams, D. Charles. *What's Done in the Dark: Affair-Proofing and Recovery from Infidelity — A Self-Help Guide for Couples.* BookLogix, 2017
[231] Tom Jacobs, "Pornography Consumption on the Rise" *Pacific Standard,* August 28, 2015, https://psmag.com/environment/surprise-we-all-love-porn
[232] *2012 Report card on the ethics of American youth.* Josephson Institute of Ethics, 2012
[233] Bhattacharjee, Yudhijit. "Why we lie: the science Behind our deceptive Ways." *National Geographic* June 2017

and 70 community adults to keep records of their lies for a week.[234] At the end of the week, the college students had reported an average of 2 lies per day. Only one out of 77 students told no lies. The community adults lied an average of once per day, and only 6 out of 70 told no lies. For an entire week.

The Milgram experiments were succeeded by the famed Stanford Prison experiments in 1971.[235] This simulation recruited college-age students for a study of incarceration and its effects. The volunteers were randomly assigned to play the roles of prisoners or guards. Originally intended to run for two weeks, the study was dramatically aborted after five days. The students playing the role of guards rapidly descended into abusive, sociopathic behavior, while most students playing prisoners became docile, helpless, and emotionally decompensated. The principal investigator, Dr. Phil Zimbardo, found himself transformed from observer to participant, and subsequently demonstrated unusual integrity in his public expression of regret. His 2007 book *The Lucifer Effect*[236] is a studied analysis of the sources of evil.

So, were the Stanford students just rotten kids, or did The System change them? Zimbardo argued that in the case of his experiment, it was the organizational structure that turned ordinary decent students into sociopaths. (Still, some background information suggested they weren't all such upstanding citizens[237]). Zimbardo makes a strong argument and extends this principle to other areas of society. But who created the systems? Robot overlords? It's a causal loop. Flawed people create flawed systems that make people even more flawed. Zimbardo's subjects vividly exhibited many of the egoistic flaws that are the subject of this present work.

But history has proved Zimbardo at least partially correct: over the last two thousand years, everywhere that Christianity advanced, cruelty abated.[238] And nearly everywhere within Christendom, the health of society waxed and waned with the health of the Church. The System *does* matter.

---

234 DePaulo, Bella M., Deborah A. Kashy, Susan E. Kirkendol, Melissa M. Wyer, and Jennifer A. Epstein. "Lying in everyday life." *Journal of personality and social psychology* 70, no. 5 (1996): 979.
235 Stanford Prison Experiment. "Stanford Prison Experiment." Accessed May 22, 2022. https://www.prisonexp.org.
236 Zimbardo, Philip G. *The Lucifer Effect: How Good People Turn Evil.* London: Rider, 2007.
237 Zimbardo, p 166
238Stark, Rodney. *How the West Won: The Neglected Story of the Triumph of Modernity.* Paperback edition. Wilmington, Delaware: ISI Books, 2015.

In recent years, the legitimacy of the Milgram and Zimbardo experiments has been called into question.[239,240] Old subjects from both studies have claimed that they knew all along what was happening and were just acting their part. I'll demur from taking sides. After all, if they were both ultimately a sham, then the researchers were dishonest. And Milgram's has been partially replicated. Either way, my point is made. People are fundamentally flawed.

There are few doctrines of scripture more fundamental than the clear teaching that without God's grace, we are all sinners, without excuse, and deserving of judgment. If we saw ourselves as God sees us, we would be utterly undone. It's not so difficult, and at times relatively easy, to see that in other people. Whether we see that in ourselves is not always obvious.

The State of Theology survey paints an amusing portrait.[241] In answer to the question "which of the following best describes you?", 62% of Americans admitted they were sinners but were trying to cut down, either through individual effort (34%) or with divine help (28%). The remaining 38% were a motley bunch:

- 15% took the fifth and preferred not to answer
- 10% denied there is such a thing [We'll call them "deniers." It's a fashionable pejorative.]
- 8% don't sin [One in twelve, and I've never met one?]
- 5% liked being sinners [Perhaps, the most honest of this subset]

Some may protest, "Yes, we're bad, but it isn't our fault. We don't have a choice. We are genetically programmed, and our brains are hardwired to act the way we do. There's no such thing as free will." While this view is in vogue among some scientists, many others express vigorous opposition to this idea of moral determinism.[242] This ongoing argument within the scientific community curiously echoes the centuries-old tension in Christian theology between predestination and free will.

---

[239] Whipple, Tom. "Shocking truth about famed Milgram torture experiment," *The Times*, August 28, 2019, https://www.thetimes.co.uk/article/shocking-truth-about-famed-torture-experiment-tq9tf6ctg

[240] Resnick, Brian. "The Stanford Prison Experiment was massively influential. We just learned it was a fraud." *Vox* 6/13/2018, https://www.vox.com/2018/6/13/17449118/stanford-prison-experiment-fraud-psychology-replication

[241] "Most Americans Admit They're Sinners," Lifeway Research, August 15, 2017, http://lifewayresearch.com/2017/08/15/most-americans-admit-theyre-sinners/

[242] Satel, Sally, and Scott O. Lilienfeld. *Brainwashed: The Seductive Appeal of Mindless Neuroscience*. New York, NY: Basic Books, 2013.

Are people born either good or evil? Is it nature or nurture? Here the evidence is much more helpful, and the answer is very clearly both. In perhaps the most current and scholarly treatment, geneticist Denis Alexander of Cambridge University argues that nature and nurture work in concert to form the people we become.[243] Scarcely anyone believes that absolves us of responsibility.

People, it turns out, are complicated. No one is perfectly good; no one is purely evil. One name regularly surfaces on nearly everyone's shortlist of 20th-century saints, that of Mahatma Gandhi. His life was reverentially portrayed in the 1982 film *Gandhi* starring Ben Kingsley in the title role.[244] In the minds of most, he was a warrior for justice who brought independence and freedom to the Indian nation through his courageous non-violent resistance. He struggled to establish peaceful coexistence between Hindus and Muslims.

On the other hand, he was a dangerously naïve demagogue who urged the Czechs and Jews to submit to the Nazis and was confident that nonviolence would have worked for the Chinese against their Japanese invaders. In 1942, with the Japanese at India's doorstep, he tried to push out the British defenders. Bluntly speaking, had anyone followed his advice, the consequences would have been catastrophic. The British tolerated him. The Nazis would have shot him in a second. At various times, Gandhi expressed vile contempt toward black Africans.[245]

All of history, science, reason, and experience lead to the inevitable conclusion that deep within every human spirit — even the best of us — lurks a propensity toward evil. Few could have spoken with greater authority — or greater eloquence — than Alexandr Solzhenitsyn, a survivor of the Soviet Gulag, who wrote: "If only there were evil people somewhere insidiously committing evil deeds, and it were necessary only to separate them from the rest of us and destroy them. But the line dividing good and evil cuts through the heart of every human being."[246] For two thousand years, this principle has been known by a particular name. The theologically minded may still recognize it as the doctrine of original sin.[247]

---

[243] Alexander, Denis. *Genes, Determinism, and God*. New York, NY: Cambridge University Press, 2017.

[244] Attenborough, Richard, dir. *Gandhi*. Columbia Pictures, 1982

[245] Lelyveld, Joseph. *Great Soul: Mahatma Gandhi and His Struggle with India*. 1st ed. New York: Alfred A. Knopf, 2011.

[246] Solzhenitsyn, Aleksandr. *The Gulag Archipelago, 1918-1956: An Experiment in Literary Investigation*. 1st ed. New York: Harper & Row, 1974. Part 1 Chapter 4.

[247] Calvin, *Institutes*, Book 2 Chapter 1, https://www.ccel.org/ccel/calvin/institutes.iv.ii.html

Pride's response

The human body possesses many marvelous defenses against foreign invaders. In like manner, our egos generate formidable defenses against authentic guilt. We can change the rules to fit our actions, justify and excuse our misconduct, blame others, repel criticism, and if all else fails, offer weaselly insincere apologies that convince no one but ourselves.

So, what if we've done wrong, and we don't want to admit it? What if we're doing wrong and don't want to stop? Well, the easiest solution is to Change the Rules.

Change the rules

If the rules make us look bad, there's an easy fix: just bend the rules. We share a universal suspicion that everyone (except us) puts money over principle, so we're already well-rehearsed in accusing *other people* of bending the rules. Skeptics of mainstream medicine routinely accuse vaccine manufacturers, pharmaceutical companies, doctors, and hospitals of putting money ahead of sound science. I'll be honest: sometimes that has happened. (What the skeptics overlook is that purveyors of so-called alternative healthcare also generate immense profits. Noted anti-vaxxer and alternative medicine tycoon Joseph Mercola is now worth over $100 million).[248]

In a cleverly designed experiment, researchers at Stony Brook University sought to quantify this behavior.[249] Participants were divided into pairs and transcribed paragraphs for a financial payout. The "typist" did most of the work and was permitted to decide how the money would be divided. It could be divided equally or in proportion to the amount of work. The researchers looked at how the money was split and how the subjects rated the fairness of the split. Then the roles were reversed. What they found, according to lead researcher Peter DeScioli, was not only did people choose the option giving themselves the largest payoff, but "that people adjust their moral values depending on which principle benefits them the most."

---

[248] Neena Satija and Lena Sun. "A major funder of the anti-vaccine movement has made millions selling natural health products." *Washington Post* 12/20/2019. https://www.washingtonpost.com/investigations/2019/10/15/fdc01078-c29c-11e9-b5e4-54aa56d5b7ce_story.html
[249] DeScioli, Peter, Maxim Massenkoff, Alex Shaw, Michael Bang Petersen, and Robert Kurzban. "Equity or equality? Moral judgments follow the money." *Proceedings of the Royal Society B: Biological Sciences* 281, no. 1797 (2014): 20142112.

In Huxley's *Brave New World*, citizens were involuntarily brainwashed from birth to be sexually promiscuous and indifferent to morality. In our not-so-brave New World, children of all ages are voluntarily brainwashed to the same end through mass entertainment, peer pressure, and aggressive advocacy. Just like the citizens of Huxley's dystopian future, we not only embrace the new ethic willingly but pursue it with gusto. The new sexual ethic is akin to seeing how closely one can approach the furnace without getting burned. But once in motion, it's hard to stop, and many get scorched for life. Scarcely anyone will ever admit their behavior might have been wrong.

Rationalize

"OK. I know it looks bad, but I had a good reason."

Rationalization is the process of manufacturing plausible reasons for our actions in order to justify them. One could write a whole book about it. In fact, someone did. *Mistakes were made (but not by me)* by Carol Tavris and Elliot Aronson is a brilliant, insightful analysis of self-justification from two eminent social psychologists.[250]

Tavris and Aronson base their analysis on two foundational principles. First, we must believe we are good. Second, we cannot abide cognitive dissonance. If we commit a wrong, we have an immediate choice: 1) admit and apologize, thus clearing our conscience, or 2) justify or deny our wrongdoing. They compare this to standing at the top of a pyramid, and our initial decision pushes us down one side or the other. Self-justification often leads to further wrongdoing, eventually leading ordinary people to do terrible things. Research has conclusively shown that our memories are unreliable, taking orders from our ego to frame past events in the most favorable light.

Sobering examples of this are well documented in case histories of prosecutorial misconduct, and in the tragic story of lives ruined *by* mental health professionals who accused unsuspecting adults of child abuse based on the fraudulent concept of "recovered memories." Many innocent people were thrown into prison, as prosecutors and mental health workers slid down that slope of self-justification hand-in-hand.[251]

---

[250] Tavris, Carol, and Elliot Aronson. *Mistakes Were Made (but Not by Me): Why We Justify Foolish Beliefs, Bad Decisions, and Hurtful Acts.* Boston: Houghton Mifflin Harcourt, 2015.
[251] "Day-Care Sex-Abuse Hysteria." In *Wikipedia*, May 21, 2022. https://en.wikipedia.org/wiki/Day-care_sex_abuse_hysteria

Blame

OK, we passed on the first two options, and we're willing to admit it was wrong. But...someone made me do it! To quote Tavris: "Mistakes were made, but only by my parents!"[252] Or my spouse, or my kids, or my boss, or my teachers, or my friends, or my enemies, or the President of the United States (if I didn't vote for him or her).

Or we can blame it on — our personality! "I can't help it. It's just who I am." Harold Skimpole was a minor villain in *Bleak House* by Charles Dickens. Skimpole was a lazy, scheming, irresponsible, conniving parasite who lived off the largesse of others while his wife and children languished in poverty. He feigned innocence on the grounds of hopeless immaturity. "But I am a child, you know!" he frequently reminded everyone within his circle. But every indication was that he knew exactly the game he was playing. (A word to the wise: *Immaturity* is not a personality trait).

The oldest recorded case of blaming is Adam, in the Garden of Eden: "Eve made me do it." We see a classic example of blaming in the story of Israel's first king, Saul. After repeated transgressions, the prophet Samuel confronted Saul for his disobedience. Saul's first response was to try and change the rule: "But we took them to sacrifice to God!"[253] Finally, Saul tries to apologize. Sort of. "I have sinned, for I have transgressed the commandment of the Lord and your words, because *I feared the people and obeyed their voice*." In other words, "the people made me do it." God was not impressed. Blaming didn't work then; it doesn't work now.

Despise criticism

It's not only our own conscience we need to keep at bay. Our ego's immune system must defend against outside attacks in the form of criticism. We can ignore it, refute it, or even better, attack the accuser.

According to Genesis, the ancient city of Sodom was visited by two angels. Disguised as ordinary men, they were greeted at the gate by Lot, who begged them to spend the night at his house. "No," they answered, "we will spend the night in the square." Lot was insistent, and the angels accepted his hospitality. Later that evening, the riffraff of the city gathered outside Lot's house and demanded that Lot hand his two visitors over to the crowd so that they could have their way with them — sexually. Lot's shocking response was to offer his two daughters to the mob, begging them not to

---

[252] Tavris, p. 97
[253] I Samuel 15:21, paraphrased

commit wickedness against visitors under the protection of his roof. [perhaps, in defense of Lot, he knew they weren't interested in his daughters]. "Get out of our way," they replied. "This fellow came here as an alien, and now he wants to play the judge! We'll treat you worse than them."[254]

It seems the men of Sodom did not take kindly to "being judged." Their defensiveness blinded them to the real approaching danger. Annihilation soon followed.[255] Had they heeded Lot, they might have been spared.

Criticism is bitter medicine. There's no ego threat in opening our Bible, finding a passage that seems relevant to our situation, and feeling comfortably convicted. "Of course I'm not perfect." We *expect* God to point out the imperfections in our life. After all, He's God — perfect and omniscient. And if we judge ourselves, we get bonus points for our evident humility. But put another human being in that role? Now, that's a problem. An understandable concern, to be sure. Other people don't know what we've been through, don't know our motives, have their own agendas, are also fallen sinners, and who are they to cast stones?

Yes, the criticism we receive from others is sometimes unfounded. It can be painful to hear, and it can be unfair. But sometimes, it's true. It can be a blessing from God. Those who desire to grow in character should learn to accept criticism with grace.

This is treacherous terrain. The stain of pride may afflict the dispenser of criticism as much as the recipient. Just as Pride makes it difficult to receive criticism, it also makes us quick to *dispense* it. Criticism might be a blessing, but if you aim to bless others, you might want to consider other options first. There is a place for Biblical correction, but sometimes our criticism is premature or groundless. Tainted criticism is a form of judgmentalism. Judgmentalism is another manifestation of Pride, one we will examine in depth (Chapter 11).

False confession

If all else fails, we may be forced to apologize. But wait, that doesn't have to be so painful! We still have the *insincere apology* at our disposal. It may not convince anyone else, but we can still walk away feeling good.

---

[254] Genesis 19:9, NIV
[255] Bruce Bower. "An exploding meteor may have wiped out ancient Dead Sea communities." ScienceNews, November 20, 2018, https://www.sciencenews.org/article/exploding-meteor-may-have-wiped-out-ancient-dead-sea-communities

"I apologize if anyone was offended" (translation: "I don't apologize for what I said or did, but I'm sorry that you hypersensitive snowflakes got all lathered up over it")

"Mistakes were made ."(translation: "There was no moral wrongdoing here. We can't all be perfect. It's more like a math error when doing long division by hand").

"I regret that" (translation: "Yeah, I wish I hadn't done it. But I ain't going to say I'm sorry").

"I misspoke" (translation: "my tongue was momentarily disengaged from my brain. It's not my fault.")

In a study from 2014, researchers found (not surprisingly) that partial confessions are popular because they are *more believable* than no confession. But they also found that the ones offering partial admissions ended up feeling worse than those who freely confessed or didn't confess at all.[256]

While we have trouble apologizing for ourselves, we have *no problem* apologizing for the misconduct of those beyond our control, especially ones we don't like. Some religious leaders are masters at this. In 2006 the World Council of Churches met in Brazil for their 9th general assembly. This was during the Bush administration, and many who had initially supported the war in Iraq had turned against it. The US delegation offered a letter to the world's delegates apologizing for their country:

"From a place seduced by the lure of empire we come to you in penitence, eager for grace, grace sufficient to transform spirits grown weary from the violence, degradation, and poverty our nation has sown, grace sufficient to transform spirits grown heavy with guilt, grace sufficient to transform the world. Lord, have mercy. Christ, have mercy. Lord, have mercy. Amen."[257]

All politics aside, I wonder if even a single member of the US delegation felt *personally* responsible for the alleged evils of our nation. That's not confession. It's grandstanding (Chapter 9).

---

[256] Peer, Eyal, Alessandro Acquisti, and Shaul Shalvi. ""I cheated, but only a little": Partial confessions to unethical behavior." *Journal of personality and social psychology* 106, no. 2 (2014): 202.

[257] "Living a culture of peace: a letter from the US Conference to the 9th Assembly of the World Council of Churches." The Free Library, World Council of Churches, 2006 . Accessed May 22, 2022. https://www.thefreelibrary.com/Living+a+culture+of+peace%3a+a+letter+from+the+US+Conference+to+the+9th...-a0156553209

A note of caution

This whole chapter is devoted to the principle that we understate our guilt, but is that always true? Certainly not. I am not and do not pretend to be a therapist, and I am drawing from the realm of social psychology — the study of normal behavior, not clinical psychology — the study of mental illness.

I suspect most of us will never experience the guilt that we ought for our own misconduct, but that needn't mean everyone. Can guilt become excessive? That is a question for the therapists. I have no reason to believe it cannot be.

However, we must be careful to distinguish between *guilt* and *regret*. Guilt is the proper sense of remorse over a moral failing: doing something we knew to be wrong — either purposefully or in the heat of passion. Regret is sorrow over past actions or failure to act, but might not have been a moral lapse. Sometimes, accidents really do happen. If you strike a pedestrian while texting on your cellphone, you should feel guilt. If you are carefully driving along and a pedestrian leaps in front of you, getting injured or killed in the process, you should experience regret. But a true sense of guilt would be unhealthy in that situation. Regret can be healthy if we learn from it.[258]

Conclusion

A century ago, the London Times inquired, "What's wrong with the world today?"[259] Chesterton responded:

> "Dear Sir,
>   I am.
> Yours, G. K. Chesterton."

If only more of us could muster such honesty and humility.

---

[258] Daniel Pink. "'No Regrets' is no way to live." *Wall Street Journal* January 18, 2022
[259] Society of Gilbert Keith Chesterton. "What's Wrong with the World," April 30, 2012. https://www.chesterton.org/wrong-with-world/

Key points

- Pride causes us to underestimate — severely — our potential capacity for evil
- When we do wrong, our ego's immune system springs into action to avoid taking responsibility for our actions

8

The Importance of Being Important

Overestimation of Personal Significance

Ask American youth about their goals in life, and the resounding and consistent top choices are wealth and fame. According to many analysts, narcissism has reached epidemic levels in western society. In millennia of recorded history, not much has changed. The desire to be famous is rooted in pride, and the Biblical story of Nebuchadnezzar — his extravagant self-promotion, his downfall, and his ultimate repentance — offers a lesson more timely than ever to the "me" generation of contemporary America.

"Better to reign in Hell, than to serve in Heaven." — SATAN [260]

"To seek one's own glory is not glory." — SOLOMON [261]

The unanticipated hazards of blowing your horn

He was top monarch over one of the great empires of ancient civilization. By earthly measures, he had arrived. There was nowhere higher to go. Being in a position like that could go to your head, and it did. God has ways of bringing down the proud. Ones like him usually fall hard and never get up. But in the mystery of providence, God decided to show mercy to Nebuchadnezzar, King of Babylon the Great.

The third chapter of Daniel records that Nebuchadnezzar set up an idol of his own making and commanded all the peoples of his kingdom to bow down and worship his ad hoc deity. He may not have claimed the mantle of divinity himself, but he stopped just one step short. Strike one.

Sometime later, Nebuchadnezzar had a dream and sought out Daniel for

---

[260] Milton, *Paradise Lost.*
[261] Proverbs 25:27

the interpretation. Daniel warned that the King would be driven away from his palace by madness and live like an animal for seven years until he was forced to concede that "the Most High is sovereign over kingdoms of men and gives them to anyone he wishes."[262]

Another year passed. One day, strutting on the roof of his royal palace, he boasted,

> "Is not this great Babylon, that I have built for a royal dwelling by my mighty power and for the honor of my majesty?"[263]

There were two elements to this rooftop proclamation. First, he claimed full *personal* credit for Babylon's glory and his own achievements: "that I have built....by my mighty power." By *his* power? Uh, yeah. Right. Strike two. Secondly, he demanded undeserved acclamation: "for the honor and glory of my majesty?" Strike three, and he's out.

> "While the word was still in the king's mouth, a voice fell from heaven: 'King Nebuchadnezzar, to you it is spoken: the kingdom has departed from you! And they shall drive you from men, and your dwelling shall be with the beasts of the field. They shall make you eat grass like oxen; and seven times shall pass over you, until you know that the Most High rules in the kingdom of men, and gives it to whomever He chooses.'
>
> "That very hour the word was fulfilled concerning Nebuchadnezzar; he was driven from men and ate grass like oxen; his body was wet with the dew of heaven till his hair had grown like eagles' feathers and his nails like birds' claws."[264]

And so it was: from rich and powerful king to a wet and hairy vegan howling at the moon. [Until very recently, this would be considered abnormal. Nowadays, they call themselves "therians" — physical humans who identify as animals — and it's just another alternative lifestyle.[265]] In due time, his pride was broken. With newfound humility, Nebuchadnezzar acknowledged the one true God as deserving of all honor and glory and was restored to his kingdom.

---

[262] Daniel 4:17
[263] Daniel 4:30
[264] Daniel 4:30-33
[265] Otherkin Wiki. "Therians." Accessed May 22, 2022. http://otherkin.wikia.com/wiki/Therians

There is disagreement over whether Nebuchadnezzar made it to heaven, and who really knows? Calvin thought no, Wesley thought yes. One aspect is noteworthy, though: the fourth chapter of Daniel is written in the first person, placing King Nebuchadnezzar among the authors of the Bible.

Through a miraculous intervention, God broke Nebuchadnezzar of his pride, brought glory to Himself, and imparted to us a lesson on the nature and consequences of pride. As is often true, what felt like punishment was ultimately an act of mercy. It's a safe bet that none of us will ever become king of a mighty empire. But we share a common human nature with old King Nebuchadnezzar. The ambition is latent in us all. Kingship simply afforded him the opportunity.

Would-be Nebuchadnezzars are all around us. Like the Ghost of Marley, they wear the chains they forge through life, stumbling under the crushing burden of their own ego, half-blinded by the brilliance of their imagined glory, thirsting for the adoration of people they despise, craving affirmation of their beauty and magnificence, chasing but never finding that elusive joy at the end of a rainbow, dreading that any moment the shallow mirage they so carefully crafted, post by post, text by text, tweet by tweet, could evaporate in an instant like morning dew in the desert sun. The self is a ravenous idol, yielding ephemeral pleasure with each new sacrifice, but every sacrifice must be greater than the one before, ever higher, always farther, forever dearer, no escaping, no getting off.

What do you want? Deep down, fundamentally, more than anything else? If you answer honestly, your answer reveals much about who you are.

God has planted within us certain desires: desires for identity, significance, acceptance, and recognition. These desires are legitimate. Pride erupts when we choose identity over virtue, prestige over accomplishment, approval at the expense of integrity, and recognition that is not rightfully ours.

Consider the following:

- In the American Freshman Survey, becoming wealthy was very important to 25% of first-year students in 1970, rising to 82% of first-year students entering in 2015.[266]
- In a Pew Research Center poll of 2007, 81% of 18 to 25-year-olds said

---

[266] Kevin, Eagan, Stolzenberg Ellen Bara, Ramirez Suchard Maria, and Rios-Aguilar Cecilia. "The American Freshman: Fifty-Year Trends 1966—2015." Higher Education Research Institute, (2016). https://www.heri.ucla.edu/monographs/50YearTrendsMonograph2016.pdf

getting *rich* was either the most or second most important.[267] In the same survey, 51% said the same about being *famous*.

Generation "Me"

There's been a profound change in Western civilization over the last few decades. The second oldest religion — self-worship — has gone pandemic, infecting industry, politics, entertainment, athletics, relationships, and religious establishments. Its simple message — "you are amazing, you are special, no dream is too great, you deserve it" — baits us like heroin to addicts, but with more devastating consequences. Its apostles are everywhere, dominating daytime television, talk radio, the film industry, university departments, publishing, churches, and uh, have I mentioned politics? Its holy sacraments are shopping, entertainment, coitus, and abortion. Its virtual temples are Facebook, TikTok, Instagram, YouTube, television, tabloids, and political conventions.

In ancient Greek mythology, Narcissus was a hunter renowned for his beauty. Mired in self-absorption, he spurned all suitors who ventured his way. To punish him — punishment figures prominently in Greek mythology — Nemesis led him to a crystal pool of water. Gazing upon his own reflection, Narcissus fell hopelessly in love, unable to leave. Realizing this love could never be requited, Narcissus sank into despair and took his own life.

> *"Don't ever marry a girl whose father calls her 'princess'. She'll grow up believing it."*
>
> — *Yiddish proverb (apocryphal)*

Around the turn of the 20th century, psychologists coined the term "narcissism," which came to mean excessive self-love or self-absorption. In original and scientific usage, it still refers to a subset of the population whose self-absorption meets the shifting criterion of a mental illness. In common use, it applies to nearly all of us. Blame it on human nature or blame it on culture; it's probably a combination of both.

Dr. Jean Twenge, a psychologist at the University of California San Diego, has been one of the most active researchers of narcissism in present

---

267 Russell Heimlich, "Gen Nexters Say Getting Rich is Their Generation's Top Goal," Pew Research Center, January 23, 2007, https://www.pewresearch.org/fact-tank/2007/01/23/gen-nexters-say-getting-rich-is-their-generations-top-goal/

society. She published her research in *Generation Me*[268] in 2006, followed up by *The Narcissism Epidemic*[269] in 2010. Twenge documented an explosive rise in narcissism from the 1970s to the early 21st century. This did not happen due to some random quantum fluctuation. It arose from complex but clearly identifiable social and cultural forces.

Once upon a time — say, the 1990's — it was generally believed that narcissism was a façade. Deep down, supposedly, narcissists had a very poor self-image. Only Neanderthals and conservatives could possibly take them at face value. The solution, then, was to lift them up. By the early 2000s, this had been thoroughly debunked. In a 2007 paper in *Psychological Science*,[270] a team of researchers found that in areas like status, dominance, and intelligence, narcissists actually *did* think highly of themselves, both consciously and unconsciously. They didn't consider themselves superior in qualities such as kindness, morality, or emotional intimacy. (But then, if you've ever been in a relationship with one, you already knew that). The fact that it's been thoroughly debunked doesn't mean there aren't millions who still believe low esteem is the problem (as to why, see Chapter 3).

> *"There is only one thing in the world worse than being talked about, and that is not being talked about."*
>
> *The Picture of Dorian Gray*, by Oscar Wilde

The following year, Michael Kernis and fellow researchers at the University of Georgia reported that people with fragile but high self-esteem were more verbally defensive, "engaging in exaggerated tendencies to defend, protect and enhance their feelings of self-worth...When feeling good about themselves becomes a prime directive, for these people excessive defensiveness and self-promotion are likely to follow."[271]

Most also assumed that narcissists didn't realize they were any different.

---

[268] Twenge, Jean M. *Generation Me: Why Today's Young Americans Are More Confident, Assertive, Entitled--and More Miserable than Ever Before*. First Atria paperback edition. New York: Atria Paperback, 2014.

[269] Twenge, Jean M., and William Keith Campbell. *The Narcissism Epidemic: Living in the Age of Entitlement*. New York, NY: Free Press, 2010.

[270] Keith Campbell, W., Jennifer K. Bosson, Thomas W. Goheen, Chad E. Lakey, and Michael H. Kernis. "Do narcissists dislike themselves "deep down inside"?." *Psychological Science* 18, no. 3 (2007): 227-229.

[271] Kernis, Michael H., Chad E. Lakey, and Whitney L. Heppner. "Secure versus fragile high self-esteem as a predictor of verbal defensiveness: Converging findings across three different markers." *Journal of personality* 76, no. 3 (2008): 477-512.

This was the question investigated by Erika Carlson and colleagues at Washington University in 2011. Through cleverly designed question-naires, the team found the opposite. Narcissists are fully aware that others don't support their lofty self-perceptions — they just don't care.[272]

So what causes narcissism? Part of it is just basic human nature, and we're all guilty to a degree. For decades now, the educational system and mass media have been singularly fixated on enhancing self-image — particularly among the young — without much concern as to whether that self-image is grounded in reality. We've already seen that and will consider it further in the next chapter. But when we study the outliers, the worst cases, other specific factors have emerged.

Parenting is a major contributor. A longitudinal study of 565 children in the Netherlands found that narcissism was predicted by parental overval-uation, while healthy self-esteem was predicted by parental warmth.[273] Narcissism, it seems, is bred, not born. Many were just spoiled as kids.

But if you missed it as a child, there's an excellent way to catch up. Roos Vonk, a professor of social psychology in the Netherlands, administered surveys to groups from mindfulness schools and energetic training schools.[274] She found such training boosted their sense of superiority, dis-playing what she called "spiritual narcissism — the 'I am more enlightened than you' phenomenon."[275] Roos did not claim that the practices caused it, so much as they offered fertile soil for the self-enhancement motive to ger-minate and flourish. Without the intentional pursuit of humility, the same thing can happen in a Christian setting. And it does.

The same old, same old

Cultural narcissism wasn't invented in 20th-century America. In fact, it bears a long and distinguished pedigree, but by another name. I refer to what is generally known as "shame-honor" culture. In such cultures, the prime motivator is the preservation of "honor" above all else. Social status

[272] Carlson, Erika N., Simine Vazire, and Thomas F. Oltmanns. "You probably think this pa-per's about you: narcissists' perceptions of their personality and reputation." Journal of per-sonality and social psychology 101, no. 1 (2011): 185.5
[273] Brummelman, Eddie, Sander Thomaes, Stefanie A. Nelemans, Bram Orobio De Castro, Geertjan Overbeek, and Brad J. Bushman. "Origins of narcissism in children." *Proceedings of the National Academy of Sciences* 112, no. 12 (2015): 3659-3662.
[274] Vonk, Roos, and Anouk Visser. "An exploration of spiritual superiority: The paradox of self-enhancement." *European Journal of Social Psychology* 51, no. 1 (2021): 152-165.
[275] Roos Vonk, "The Fine Line between Spirituality and Narcissism: Spiritual Self-enhance-ment," Society for Personality and Social Psychology, December 30, 2020, https://www.spsp.org/news-center/blog/vonk-spirituality-narcissism

depends on honor, but honor is fragile and can be lost through even the slightest perception of disrespect. Once diminished, honor can only be restored by exacting retribution upon the perpetrator. It was prevalent in the ancient near eastern societies invaded by Christianity and has remained pervasive across many, if not most, societies to this day.

The connection here should be apparent. "Honor" is no less than the projection of self-importance and expectation of acknowledgment from others. It is grounded in pride. Compared to most alternatives, shame-honor cultures are characterized by higher levels of conflict, interpersonal violence, and misogyny.[276]

Elements of self-promotion

There are two aspects to narcissism. The first is what the narcissist thinks of him or herself. The second is what *everyone else* thinks of them. Not every narcissist cares that much about what anyone else thinks. Conversely, many care *very much* about what others think. We've already discussed the first group. Let's take a look at the second. King Nebuchadnezzar was not one to quietly rest upon his accomplishments. Yes, he thought too highly of himself, but what *really* got him into trouble was his demand for universal admiration.

> *"My dog doesn't worry about what other dogs think."*

We scramble for attention in many ways. Let's consider just four: material possessions, hyper-individuality, demanding credit we don't deserve, and vigorous pursuit of acclamation.

Self-advertisement: covetousness

Our possessions sometimes serve purposes beyond their practical use. Our cars, houses, boats, clothing, jewelry, or other visible paraphernalia can signal our importance and success to others. In the eyes of some, they affirm a personal sense of significance and worth. For such people, a *lofty* sense of importance must be advertised by appropriately *lofty* possessions.

This differs from greed — wanting something for its own intrinsic value. With conspicuous materialism, we don't need it or even want it that much.

---

[276]Brown, Ryan P., Kiersten Baughman, and Mauricio Carvallo. "Culture, masculine honor, and violence toward women." *Personality and social psychology bulletin* 44, no. 4 (2018): 538-549.

We want to be *seen* with it.

In *The Narcissism Epidemic,* Twenge tracked the parallel rise of narcissism and materialism through the 1990s and early 2000s. The inclination is so irresistible that researchers found conspicuous consumption was even greater in *poor* neighborhoods than wealthier ones.[277] This is not just an affliction of the affluent. Predictably, the aggressive accumulation of useless property often led to bankruptcy, financial ruin, and failed relationships. Pride goes before the fall.

Being "special": hyperindividualism

We live in an era of designer religions. (Maybe we always have?) It is trendy to take a little Christianity, a little Buddhism, a little Spiritism, a cup of Tolle, two tablespoons of Chopra and grind them up to match one's individual tastes. (As if transcendent reality were at our command). There's no point condemning nonbelievers for this — they can't help it. We should be deeply concerned with this behavior among professing Christians, who should know better.

In recent years there has been a resurgence of interest in the ancient practice of Gnosticism. The term originated in the Greek *gnosis*, or knowledge. The knowledge was supposed to be something secret and profound and known only by the adherents. (Much like Scientology used to be before their "secrets" were leaked on the internet. Hilarious, if you have some time to kill.) The lure of Gnosticism is its pandering to human pride, specifically, the desire to stand above the crowd by possessing "special knowledge." Whether or not the knowledge is true is irrelevant. In fact, truthfulness would be a liability — because people might figure it out on their own and break the monopoly.

A few misguided souls wrap their entire identity around something they call "gender." It is claimed that today there are over fifty. [Anthropologists now know that 3000 years ago, there were 1,723 genders. Sadly, most had difficulty finding mates, a problem that continues to the present day. Within another 100 years, some predict, only two genders will remain, making us little better than animals.[278]] The simultaneous desire for uniqueness and admiration can manifest in an almost infinite variety of ways, but rarely yields good relationships or mental health.

Each of us is unique in a myriad of ways, most of them relatively harmless.

---

[277] Twenge and Campbell, p. 164
[278] Made you look!

The way we dress, the style of our hair, our hobbies, our sense of humor, and a thousand other things differentiate us from one another and support a healthy sense of individuality. Danger looms when, in pursuit of identity, one decides to embrace a lie, violate moral precepts, or consider oneself superior. Believing we are "special" leads to alienation, depression, conflict, and disappointment when we don't get the attention we expected — findings confirmed by Joshua Grubbs and Julie Exline from a 2016 review of over 170 academic studies.[279] So why is it so popular? First, because it feeds our pride. Second, because it's highly profitable for the promoters, whether it's Armani, political candidates, or the Church of Scientology.

Claiming credit for achievements

What can possibly be wrong with taking credit for my achievements? Think back to the introduction, where I boasted of my mathematical prowess. Did I choose my parents? Did I choose the place of my birth? Did I contribute anything to that inscrutable mix of nature and nurture which determine that thing we call intelligence? Sure, succeeding in that arena was fun, and beats the heck out of failure, but there's not a lot there that I can take credit for. Showing up, I suppose. And not wasting my childhood watching TV or playing video games. Then again, maybe I just didn't find those pursuits very interesting.

Boasting is indeed something of a national pastime.[280] I could come up with an almost endless list of instances from middle school students on TikTok to US Presidents. By the time this book made it to press, my examples would be overshadowed by even more outrageous braggadocio.

Egocentric bias

"I want to thank all the little people. Without them, I'd still be here, of course—but it might have taken a bit longer."

What's wrong with boasting? There's the moral argument and the factual argument. Let's take the factual one. Examine the life of almost any highly successful person more closely, and a complex picture usually emerges. Most of them worked hard, yes. But many more worked just as hard with far less spectacular results. One's success — if measured as wealth, fame, and achievement — depends even more on a complex of factors far outside our command. We have no control over when, where, or to whom we are

---

[279] Grubbs, Joshua B., and Julie J. Exline. "Trait entitlement: A cognitive-personality source of vulnerability to psychological distress." *Psychological Bulletin* 142, no. 11 (2016): 1204.
[280] David Brooks. "High Five Nation." *The New York Times.* 9/15/2009 https://www.ny-times.com/2009/09/15/opinion/15brooks.html

born. We have no control over our genetic makeup that significantly determines our appearance and athletic potential and somewhat predicts our intelligence. Our personalities are largely innate, though we can all strive to improve them. Those uncontrollable factors play as much a role in determining worldly success as mere hard work.

This key principle was emphasized (indirectly) by Malcolm Gladwell in *Outliers: The Story of Success.*[281] Take, for example, Bill Gates, the founder of Microsoft and at one time the second richest man in the world. Everyone knows that Gates was an exceptionally intelligent and ambitious young man who seized upon a brilliant business plan that catapulted him into the center of the computer revolution. But he also benefited from unique advantages almost no one else of the 20th century shared.

Bill Gates was born at precisely the right time (late 1955) to be coming of age when personal computer technology arrived. Any sooner, and he would have been established in another career. Any later, and someone would have beaten him to the

> *"Give a man a fish, and he'll eat for a day. Teach a man to fish, and before the week is out he'll claim he invented it."*

punch. Gates's parents were wealthy enough to send him to an exclusive private school in Seattle, which had the resources to install a state-of-the-art computer terminal connected to a Seattle mainframe. Throughout their high school years, Bill and his friend Paul Allen spent *thousands* of hours tinkering and writing code. Gates didn't have to spend precious free time mowing lawns or flipping hamburgers at Mcdonald's to support himself. Gladwell enumerates at least nine phenomenally lucky breaks *before Gates even graduated from high school.*

Even Gladwell didn't paint the complete picture. Microsoft's biggest break came when Gates managed to license its operating system to IBM. Did IBM just give him a call? Did Gates come knocking on IBM's door? Neither. Mary Maxwell Gates — Bill's mother — was well connected with IBM CEO John Opel, having served together on the national executive committee of United Way.[282]

I believe Bill Gates, of all people, understands how privileged he was. His

---

281 Gladwell, Malcolm. *Outliers: Why Some People Succeed and Some Don't.* New York: Little Brown & Co., 2008.
282 Locke, Taylor. "How Bill Gates' Mom Helped Microsoft Get a Deal with IBM in 1980 — and It Propelled the Company's Huge Success." CNBC, August 5, 2020. https://www.cnbc.com/2020/08/05/how-bill-gates-mother-influenced-the-success-of-microsoft.html.

philanthropic support has been exemplary and has saved many lives through the support of third-world health care. In the spring of 2007, Bill Gates and Steve Jobs sat for an interview with journalists from the *Wall Street Journal*. With Gates sitting beside him, Jobs admitted, "I sort of look at us as two of the luckiest guys on the planet because we found what we loved to do, and we were at the right place at the right time."[283] Truer words have seldom been spoken.

When you know you've been blessed by God, there's not much room left for taking personal credit. (If you haven't been so blessed, the great danger is envy: the theme of our next chapter).

Pursuit of acclamation: the siren song of fame

Ah, fame! How sweet it is! Not that I would know. I've spent my life far from the limelight. As an introvert, I'm OK with that — still….the things we do to get noticed.

Where the culture of the last four decades has fueled an unprecedented level of narcissism, technology provides the means to indulge it. We can broadcast our opinions to the world — no matter how shallow and uninformed they may be — because your own personal blog is but a few mouse clicks away and completely free.

But blogs can be tedious, and writing is still work. Why not just record yourself and broadcast it on YouTube? By mid-2018, over five *billion* videos had been shared on that platform, watched by over two billion monthly users.

In a 2018 paper, researchers Jacqueline Nesi and Mitchell Prinstein defined "digital status-seeking" as "the investment of significant effort into the accumulation of online indicators of peer status and approval."[284] Needless to say, this has become commonplace. It's also unhealthy. The researchers found that for both genders, those most heavily engaged in digital status-seeking exhibited higher levels of substance abuse and risky sexual behavior one year later.

Some people will go to extraordinary lengths to be noticed. Consider the case of Loren Davis. The aspiring evangelist spent forty years trying to get

---

[283] "Two of the luckiest guys on the planet." *Wall Street Journal,* June 1, 2007. https://www.wsj.com/articles/SB118066046287520886
[284] Nesi, Jacqueline, and Mitchell J. Prinstein. "In search of likes: Longitudinal associations between adolescents' digital status seeking and health-risk behaviors." *Journal of Clinical Child & Adolescent Psychology* 48, no. 5 (2019): 740-748.

noticed, only to be repeatedly shunned by American churches as "an irrel-evant theological extremist."[285] But by 2006, he finally found the recogni-tion he craved — in the heart of Africa. There he could draw tens of thou-sands to his "crusades." Loren has since passed away. His ministry may have been genuinely fruitful and is today carried on by his widow. Not all such examples have been honorable. It turns out that the poor and vulner-able of sub-Saharan Africa have been easy targets for self-promoting huck-sters, of which there have been many — and primarily home-grown.[286]

With the double reward of both fame and power, politics is a magnet for narcissists. Even the most cursory assessment of history or present-day world leaders confirms that arrogance, grandiosity, and self-absorption are in abundant supply. During the eight years of the Obama administra-tion, half of America thought the President was an incurable narcissist. During the four years of the Trump administration, the other half of Amer-ica thought the President was an incurable narcissist. Considering what it takes to get elected: constant self-promotion, grandstanding, endless fund-raising, outshining one's opponents — it's easy to see why narcissists would be naturally more skilled at gaining power. Some suggest that if we cleared the political leadership of narcissists, it would leave a pretty empty field.[287] We should not be surprised that scandals, corruption, and abuse of power are so pervasive.

This goes beyond the foibles of attention seekers. They get where they are because their strategies work. Every time we vote for an unabashed nar-cissist, we share the blame. Every donation to a religious huckster adds to the problem. We are naturally swayed by superficial impressions. It is that tendency in us which leads to prejudice, something we will examine more closely in Chapter 10.

Pride promises, but seldom delivers

In the Garden of Eden, the serpent promised but did not deliver. In the world we inhabit, pride promises but fails to deliver. It turns out that look-ing out for number one leads to loneliness and disappointment.

---

[285] Phillips, Michael. "In Africa, preacher draws audiences he can't at home." *Wall Street Jour-nal*, April 25, 2006, https://www.wsj.com/articles/SB114592051235534656
[286] Fadamana U, "8 Famous Kenyan Pastors and the Huge Scandals that have Ruined their Fame," AnswersAfrica, accessed 5/21/2022, https://answersafrica.com/8-famous-kenyan-pastors-and-the-huge-scandals-that-have-ruined-their-fame.html
[287] Post, J. M. "Narcissism and the quest for political power." In: Ellman, Carolyn S., and Jo-seph Reppen, eds. *Omnipotent Fantasies and the Vulnerable Self*. The Library of Clinical Psy-choanalysis. Northvale, N.J: Jason Aronson, 1997. pp. 195-232.

Writing for *The Atlantic*, psychotherapist Lori Gottlieb spoke of rising numbers of young people raised in idyllic households who "just weren't happy."[288] She was stumped. Then the pieces started falling into place. Increasingly hyper-indulgent parents were impeding their own children's development and creating narcissists. A home of nonstop affirmation, continuous protection, and constant support prevents kids from experiencing the emotional — and physical — bumps and bruises necessary for normal development. This led to anxious and entitled kids described as "handicapped royalty." Nassim Taleb formulated the concept of "anti-fragility" — the tendency to grow stronger under stress. Muscles are anti-fragile. So are people. We need to experience a healthy level of stress for normal functioning.

The role played by social media is complicated. It isn't that they cause narcissism so much as they provide a platform for kids (and adults) who are narcissistic. For kids who aren't narcissistic, media can be devastating to their self-image. As mentioned earlier, the adolescents most engaged in "digital status-seeking" are more prone to self-destructive behavior.[289]

People who think they are special, deserve more than others, and expect more than others suffer from "psychological entitlement." A systematic review from 2016 evidenced the many ways this can, and does, lead to disappointment, anger, conflict, depression, and constant distress.[290] Coauthor Julie Exline observed, "the entire mindset pits someone against other people. When people think that they should have everything they want — often for nothing — it comes at the cost of relationships with others and, ultimately, their own happiness."[291]

Still jealous of the really popular kids from high school? Maybe you shouldn't be. A 2014 study examined the outcomes of 184 teens from age 13 to age 23. Unsurprisingly, those who acted "old for their age" were deemed more popular. By age 22, the popular kids were significantly less popular than peers, perceived as less competent in relationships, and with higher rates of criminal activity and substance abuse.[292]

---

288 Gottlieb, Lori. "How to land your kid in therapy." *The Atlantic* 301, no. 1 (2011): 64-78.
289 Nesi & Prinstein, 2019
290 Grubbs & Exline, 2016
291 Case Western Reserve University. "Entitlement may lead to chronic disappointment." *ScienceDaily*, September 13, 2016. www.sciencedaily.com/releases/2016/09/160913134442.htm.
292 Allen, Joseph P., Megan M. Schad, Barbara Oudekerk, and Joanna Chango. "What ever happened to the "cool" kids? Long-term sequelae of early adolescent pseudomature behavior." *Child development* 85, no. 5 (2014): 1866-1880.

In the great game of life, narcissism is a losing bet.

Caveats

Before wrapping up, let's consider a couple of possible objections.

You can't succeed in business without self-promotion.

This is true more often than not. While self-promotion as an ongoing life-style is wrong, sometimes you have to. There are professions where self-promotion is a necessity, not an option: politics, entertainment, consulting (and authoring?). When you must, you must — but don't let it get the better of you. People still appreciate and respect humility, and you are much more likely to succeed with it than without it.

What about low self-esteem?

This is not a work on clinical psychology (which deals with mental illness), and I reiterate that not every element of pride applies to every person. Some people really do need to improve their self-esteem through healthy adjustments of attitude and lifestyle. But even those with low self-esteem suffer from pride if they insist on comparing themselves to others or are so adamant in their negative self-appraisal that they cannot accept positive affirmation from others. That becomes self-contradicting: "I may be incompetent as a person, but my poor self-image is infallible."

Every one of us is of immeasurable value to God, and we should base our worth on that rather than personal popularity or achievements. It might not be easy. But it's worth it.

Key points

- The cultural/societal epidemic of narcissism is fueled by pride, and re-inforces it.
- Pride craves and delights in the attention and acclamation of others
- Pride leads us to assert our significance in harmful and destructive ways
- Pride demands more credit for our achievements than we deserve

«9»

The Wrath of Cain

Conflict, Competitiveness, and Envy

Our self-image too often feels inadequate unless we can feel at least as good as, if not better, than others. Presumably, that is why C. S. Lewis chose to define pride in terms of comparing ourselves to others. Whatever the cost, we must come out ahead. Failing to measure up, and looking bad by comparison, can lead to strife, envy, or even murder — all to appease the beast of pride within us.

Kirk: Why would Starfleet ask a three-hundred-year-old frozen man for help?

Khan: Because I am better.

Kirk: At what?

Khan: Everything. [293]

A tale of two brothers

It started innocently enough. Two brothers, perhaps best friends from birth. One a farmer, the other a shepherd, both honorable occupations. Almost certainly, they bartered so that both could partake of bread and meat. At the appointed time, the shepherd brought the firstborn of his flock to sacrifice to the Lord, and the farmer brought the fruits of his harvest. The Lord was pleased with the offering from the flock but not with the harvest of the farmer. There is no hint that God was angry or that the farmer would be punished. He could still go back and trade his grain for one of his brother's lambs to offer a sacrifice that would please the Lord. There was still time. But though the Lord did not become angry, the farmer did. The

---

[293] Abrams, J.J., dir. *Star Trek Into Darkness*. Paramount Pictures, 2013

Lord asked the farmer why he was angry, for he knew the policy and still had time to make good. Instead, the farmer lured his brother out to the field, and in the first recorded murder, Cain slew his brother Abel.

Why did Cain kill Abel? According to John, "Because his works were evil and his brother's righteous."[294] Not one, not the other, but both. It was the contrast between them — the comparison — that led to anger and murder.

There is no indication Abel had done anything to injure or offend Cain. Cain stood nothing to gain from the crime. Having failed to please God with his offering, he must have known that knocking off Abel wouldn't improve his standing. But he seethed with anger because, in his mind, he had come in second. Cain got one-upped by his little brother.

Pride erupted in the Garden and passed from parents to offspring. Feeling upstaged by his brother, Cain's injured pride led to anger, and anger led to murder. That, my friends, is elemental to our fallen nature.

Comparing self to others

So far, we have examined the natural human inclination toward evil and the innate desire for acclamation. We overestimate our goodness, our competence, and our power. But in a universe of one, those count for naught. No, we must be smarter than, better than, stronger than, more important than *someone*. Anyone. Everyone.

In *Mere Christianity*, C.S. Lewis spoke of how pride drives us to compare ourselves with others:

> "Pride gets no pleasure out of having something, only out of having more of it than the next man... It is the comparison that makes you proud: the pleasure of being above the rest."[295]

If we compare favorably, our egos are satisfied. If we compare unfavorably, we are prone to envy and resentment. In the case of Cain, this is the only plausible explanation for an otherwise senseless act.

It starts with comparison, and oh, how we love to compare ourselves. In fact, we can't function without it. The psychological term is "social comparison," and it serves multiple functions, most of them useful.[296] We can

---

[294] 1 John 3:12

[295] Lewis, *Mere Christianity*

[296] Zlatan Krizan. "Social Comparison." *Oxford Research Encyclopedia of Psychology*. Oxford University Press, March 28, 2018, https://oxfordre.com/psychology/view/10.1093/acrefore/9780190236557.001.0001/acrefore-9780190236557-e-251

nurture gratitude by comparing ourselves to the less fortunate. We can de-velop character by comparing ourselves to those more virtuous and imi-tating them. Through social comparison, we can form a more accurate opinion of ourselves, improve ourselves, connect with others socially, and feel better about ourselves.

A 2006 paper by psychologists Miron Zuckerman and Ryan O'Loughlin re-viewed the research on using social comparison to enhance our self-im-age.[297] Was it good or bad, and under what circumstances? Overall, social comparison contributed to *better* psychological health and greater confi-dence if that self-image was close to what other people thought. A 2018 meta-analysis found that having a positive — even *unrealistically* positive — self-image leads to higher satisfaction, better mood, and lower depres-sion. When it came to interpersonal relationships, however, it was a mixed bag. There were pluses and minuses.[298]

So was the great sage Lewis wrong? Is social comparison harmless or even beneficial? Lewis could have used a broader definition of pride, but we're not quite done here. The researchers only looked at a particular form of comparison. They were only looking at a very narrow range of psycholog-ical and social effects. We've already demonstrated the harm caused by an inflated self-perception: believing and acting as though we are more intel-ligent, more capable, more virtuous, and more important than we really are. If pride is the match, comparison is the fuse.

Psychopathy, self-esteem, and aggression

A few decades ago, Western society was on a self-esteem binge, blaming everything from violence to addiction to poor grades on a poor self-image. ["Ah, if only these poor helpless waifs could learn to feel good about them-selves, they would stop killing each other and take up macramé."] A sum-mary of opinion from that era cited "an entrenched body of wisdom that has long pointed to low self-esteem as the root of violence and other anti-social behavior." In 1996 Baumeister, Smart, and Boden reviewed the re-search to date, finding no evidence that aggression, crime, or violence were motivated by *low* self-esteem.[299] Instead, they postulated that violence was

---

[297]Zuckerman, Miron, and Ryan E. O'Loughlin. "Self-enhancement by social comparison: A prospective analysis." *Personality and Social Psychology Bulletin* 32, no. 6 (2006): 751-760.
[298] Dufner, Michael, Jochen E. Gebauer, Constantine Sedikides, and Jaap JA Denissen. "Self-enhancement and psychological adjustment: A meta-analytic review." *Personality and Social Psychology Review* 23, no. 1 (2019): 48-72.
[299] Baumeister, Roy F., Laura Smart, and Joseph M. Boden. "Relation of threatened egotism to violence and aggression: the dark side of high self-esteem." *Psychological review* 103, no. 1 (1996): 5.

"a result of threatened egotism" — when someone's *high* self-image was challenged by someone else. Consistently, the common factor in anger and violence was that the victim had offended the perpetrator in some perceived manner.

When the low self-esteem hypothesis was tested, it crumbled. Psychologists Brad Bushman and Roy Baumeister examined the connections between narcissism, criticism, and aggression among a group of 540 undergraduate students.[300] There was no connection between low self-esteem and violence. In fact, people with low self-esteem are typically passive and more likely to be *victims* than perpetrators. (Even though the link between aggression and low self-esteem was long ago debunked, the myth still dominates public discourse).

Contrary to their earlier hypothesis, though, there was also no correlation between *high* self-esteem and violence. Maybe emotionally stable people with high self-esteem are simply indifferent and don't care. There was, however, one clearly identifiable group prone to aggression: those who *really cared* about their image, "people who are *emotionally* invested in grandiose self-views." These were the narcissists. Narcissists are passionate about establishing their superiority; therefore, they became particularly aggressive toward "anyone who attacked or offended them." If this sounds vaguely familiar, it is a key aspect of the "shame-honor culture" referenced in the last chapter.

Between one-quarter and one-third of students are victims of bullying during their school years, and cyberbullying is on the rise.[301] (*Real* bullying in the traditional sense, since the term has been much watered down by some — and does get overused). It exacts a heavy toll. Victims of bullying face higher risks of anxiety, depression, low self-esteem, self-harm, suicide, physical trauma, addictions, absenteeism, and other signs of injury.[302] You can probably guess that bullying was once blamed on low self-esteem. As you should expect by now, it's the opposite. We might wish that the bullies pay a price; they don't in the short term. In fact, when it comes to the time of most severe bullying — middle school — bullies are viewed as socially

---

[300] Bushman, Brad J., and Roy F. Baumeister. "Threatened egotism, narcissism, self-esteem, and direct and displaced aggression: Does self-love or self-hate lead to violence?." *Journal of personality and social psychology* 75, no. 1 (1998): 219.

[301] "Cyberbullying and Cell Phone Policy in U.S. Primary and Secondary Schools." National Center for Education Statistics, January, 2019, https://nces.ed.gov/pubs2019/2019053/index.asp Accessed 2/12/2022

[302] Swearer, Susan M., and Shelley Hymel. "Understanding the psychology of bullying: Moving toward a social-ecological diathesis—stress model." *American Psychologist* 70, no. 4 (2015): 344.

powerful and "cool." Their victims are the "uncool."[303] Bullies as a group rank high in narcissism,[304] sadism,[305] psychopathic tendencies, and antisocial personality traits.

As it turns out, there are two kinds of narcissists. *Grandiose* narcissists worship the ground they walk on and feel confident about it. If you are confident you're the greatest and everybody is beneath you, no one's a threat. *Vulnerable* narcissists feel every bit as entitled but much less secure. They also think they're entitled and unique — and still expect adoration from others — but they struggle with believing it.[306] Both forms of narcissism lead to bullying, but vulnerable narcissists are more dangerous. Written records and video recordings from the perpetrators incline psychologists to classify the Columbine school killers as vulnerable narcissists.

Hopefully, few of us will ever descend to raw physical violence, but that's a pretty low bar. Few of us are full-blown narcissists, but that's also a low bar. But we still gain a lot of insight into ordinary behavior by studying what happens at the extremes. Even if we're not narcissists, we all get angry. Is it possible, sometimes, your annoyance was because you were criticized (on the one hand) or insufficiently praised or appreciated (on the other)? Criticism is a complex area, and it can be uninformed or unfair, but out of all the criticism we receive in life, at least some must be valid.

Envy

The classic "seven deadly sins" were lust, gluttony, sloth, wrath, pride, greed, and envy. The word "envy" appears 25 times in the New King James Bible. According to the proverb, "a sound heart is life to the body, but envy is rottenness to the bones."[307]

Explain to me, if you can, the difference between greed and envy. On the off chance you haven't studied Aristotle,[308] this would seem a distinction without a difference. It sounds like counting the same sin twice. Yet there

---

[303] Stuart Wolpert. "Victims of bullying suffer academically as well, UCLA psychologists report." UCLA newsroom, August 19, 2010. https://newsroom.ucla.edu/releases/victims-of-bullying-suffer-academically-168220. Accessed 2/14/2022

[304] Reijntjes, Albert, Marjolijn Vermande, Sander Thomaes, Frits Goossens, Tjeert Olthof, Liesbeth Aleva, and Matty Van der Meulen. "Narcissism, bullying, and social dominance in youth: A longitudinal analysis." *Journal of abnormal child psychology* 44, no. 1 (2016): 63-74.

[305] van Geel, Mitch, Anouk Goemans, Fatih Toprak, and Paul Vedder. "Which personality traits are related to traditional bullying and cyberbullying? A study with the Big Five, Dark Triad and sadism." *Personality and individual differences* 106 (2017): 231-235

[306] Krizan, Zlatan, and Omesh Johar. "Envy divides the two faces of narcissism." *Journal of personality* 80, no. 5 (2012): 1415-1451.

[307] Proverbs 14:30

[308] Aristotle. *Rhetoric*. Part 10: "Envy is pain at the sight of another's good fortune."

is a difference, and rather an important one. Greed is a desire for "more" but connotes no malice or resentment toward another. Envy is "to feel displeasure and ill-will at the superiority of another person in happiness, success, reputation, or the possession of anything desirable."[309]

Envy requires at least one other person — to be the object of envy. It may be a desire for their possessions or resentment over their success. It doesn't even matter that the target actually *is* better off, only that they are perceived as such. Envy — as opposed to greed — demands comparison:

> Greed: I want a new beach house.
> Envy: I want *your* new beach house.
>
> —
>
> Greed: I want a new Ferrari.
> Envy: She bought a new Ferrari? I hope it crashes.

In the satisfaction of greed, one might lie, cheat, injure, or steal from another; but those are merely a *means* to an end. With envy, one-upmanship *is* the end. Perhaps now you can understand why the ancients considered envy second only to pride among the most serious vices. Cain harbored *envy* toward Abel. Envy put Jesus on the cross.[310]

Envy is also distinctly common. A 2016 study from Spain engaged 541 volunteers to participate in a series of game scenarios. The scenarios were designed so that volunteers would receive the largest payoff by cooperating with each other, but would suffer a penalty if they cooperated while their partner defected. Based on their performance, the participants were categorized into four types: optimist, pessimist, trustful, and envious. Almost one-third exhibited an envious disposition. They were more concerned with minimizing the payoff to their game partner, even when it reduced their own payoff.[311]

The Pentateuch relates an account of hardcore envy leading to disastrous consequences. While wandering in the wilderness, Korah the Levite and his buddies from the tribe of Reuben accosted Moses and the priests: "You take too much upon yourselves, for all the congregation is holy, every one

---

[309] "Envy." *Oxford English Dictionary*
[310] Matthew 27:18
[311] Poncela-Casasnovas, Julia, Mario Gutiérrez-Roig, Carlos Gracia-Lázaro, Julian Vicens, Jesús Gómez-Gardeñes, Josep Perelló, Yamir Moreno, Jordi Duch, and Angel Sánchez. "Humans display a reduced set of consistent behavioral phenotypes in dyadic games." *Science advances* 2, no. 8 (2016): e1600451.

of them, and the Lord is among them. Why then do you exalt yourselves above the assembly of the Lord?"[312]

To put this in perspective, first, Moses didn't want the job,[313] and second, he was the humblest man on the face of the earth.[314] Korah demanded admission to the priesthood, a role strictly limited (by God's command) to descendants of Moses's brother Aaron. Moses explained it was up to God to decide, but his attempts at peacemaking were rebuffed. Korah and the rest of the "resistance" began to arouse the people of Israel against Moses. The next day Moses gathered the people together, proclaiming:

> "'By this you will know that the Lord sent me to do these deeds and that it wasn't my own desire. If all these people die a natural death, or if their fate be that of all humans, then the Lord hasn't sent me. But if the Lord performs an act of creation, and the ground opens its mouth and swallows them and everything that belongs to them, so that they descend alive to their graves, then you'll know that these men disrespected the Lord.'
>
> "As soon as he finished speaking these words, the ground under them split open. The earth opened its mouth and swallowed them and their households, including every human that belonged to Korah and all their possessions. They along with all their possessions descended alive to their graves, and the earth closed over them. They perished in the middle of the assembly." [315]

The offense of Korah and his allies was envy. Getting swallowed up by the earth is pretty intense. Clearly, in the eyes of God, this is a serious matter.

Envy has become a subject of interest among social psychologists in recent years. Traditionally, it was regarded as a hostile emotion that prompts deception, limits cooperation, and delights over the failure of others. But some began to argue for the existence of "benign" envy, where one attempts to reduce the difference with a superior through self-improvement. "Malicious" envy seeks to level the field by taking down the other person.

But "benign envy" wasn't so benign. A 2018 study by Spanish researchers instead found that both types of envy were strongly associated with the "Dark Triad" of personality, particularly Machiavellianism and

---

[312] Numbers 16:3
[313] Exodus 3:11
[314] Numbers 12:3
[315] Numbers 16:28-33, CEB

psychopathy.[316] Both forms of envy generate psychological pain. According to the authors, the pain results from a feeling of inferiority. Inferiority then leads to depression, aggression, anger toward the fortunate, and happiness when the other person fails. There was a difference in the severity of effect: "benign envy involves subtle social manipulation, whereas malicious envy can extend to blatant aggression." We can apply this principle to account for Cain's behavior. Having been upstaged by his brother, he became angry, and the anger led to murder.

Recall that the definition of envy is to "feel displeasure" at the superiority of another. So far, I've only mentioned anger and aggression, but different people react in different ways. Displeasure can also mean discouragement, depression, and despair — but it's still envy. If we are disappointed over the success of others or experience emotional discomfort when we compare ourselves, it is envy — just as much as Cain. We're just reacting differently because of our circumstances and disposition. The outward manifestation of pride is not always haughty and self-promoting. It may be deep inward pain, with little or no outward expression. The violent ones end up in jail. The sad ones end up in therapy.

Competitiveness

> "Should you then seek great things for yourself? Do not seek them." [317]

If pride leads to comparison, and comparison leads to envy, envy leads to aggressive competition. Jesus's disciples started out as highly competitive individuals:

> "But they kept silent, for on the road they had disputed among themselves who would be the greatest."[318]

> "Then a dispute arose among them as to which of them would be greatest."[319]

> "Now there was also a dispute among them, as to which of them should be considered the greatest."[320]

---

[316] Lange, Jens, Delroy L. Paulhus, and Jan Crusius. "Elucidating the dark side of envy: Distinctive links of benign and malicious envy with dark personalities." *Personality and Social Psychology Bulletin* 44, no. 4 (2018): 601-614.
[317] Jeremiah 45:5
[318] Mark 9:34
[319] Luke 9:46
[320] Luke 22:24

The priests and scribes of New Testament times were competitive:

> "But when the chief priests and scribes saw the wonderful things that He did, and the children crying out in the temple and saying, 'Hosanna to the Son of David!' they were indignant."[321]

They were indignant because someone other than them was receiving adoration from the people.

Here's a basic question: are humans naturally *cooperative* or *competitive*? The answer, of course, is "yes" to both. Cooperation is almost always beneficial unless it's in the pursuit of evil. Competition is more complicated, but it's not always bad.

Social comparison is a prime driver of competition. Focusing on people better than us impels us to close the gap by improving our own performance. Considering people a little worse than us motivates us to work harder to stay on top. Our fervor depends upon whether it's something we care about, whether the other person is like us or not, and how close we are to that person (emotionally or spatially). Other determining factors include how close or far we are from our goal, the number of competitors, the presence of an audience, and "social category fault lines" (i.e., male vs. female, Alabama vs. Auburn, race, or religion). Certain conditions are especially likely to arouse hostility. Similar minority groups compete internally, with the most hostility coming from those farthest from the group average. Closeness can lead to problems: people are more threatened by the success of their friends than that of strangers.[322]

People compete over what matters to them most, and that varies with peer group and culture. Modern teenagers compete over how high they rank in the pecking order of social media. These forums fuel the flames of narcissism in some but deliver only loneliness and depression to many more.[323]

Among adults, the issues are more complex. Wherever there is conflict, competition is usually present. Sports? Obviously. Religion? Check. Politics? Check. Conspicuous consumerism? Climbing the corporate ladder? Recognition or fame? Check, check, and check. Even the noble pursuit of virtue is corrupted when it degenerates into a public competition over who

---

[321] Matthew 21:15

[322] Garcia, Stephen M., Avishalom Tor, and Tyrone M. Schiff. "The psychology of competition: A social comparison perspective." *Perspectives on psychological science* 8, no. 6 (2013): 634-650.

[323] "Social media use increases depression and loneliness, study finds." ScienceDaily. November 8, 2018, https://www.sciencedaily.com/releases/2018/11/181108164316.htm

shines the brightest, who is most enlightened, or who's memorized the most verses.

We noted in Chapter 6 that most of us think we're better than most of us. How long before we *compete* over being good? Not long, indeed. There is a well-documented tendency to advertise our moral superiority through public display. Unfortunately, this usually doesn't mean "being good" so much as it means "appearing good." Commonly known as "virtue signaling," the more correct term is "moral grandstanding."

There's nothing wrong with voicing strong moral pronouncements; at times, it is our duty. The difference resides in our motives. It is grandstanding when we speak or act to impress others with our superior virtue — consciously or unconsciously — regardless of whether it happens to promote a good cause.[324] That it might be unconscious doesn't get us off the hook.

One of the many drawbacks of moral grandstanding is that it can lead to "ramping up." Suppose a friend or colleague makes a moral statement equally virtuous to our own position. In that case, pride may push us to a more emphatic position to maintain that edge of superiority. Ramping up is one of the many prideful behaviors that contribute to extreme polarization on issues.[325]

Both moral grandstanding and ramping up are pervasive in social and political spheres. But we must be careful when we accuse others of doing it. We can't know the sincerity of their motives. It's like charging a person with lying when for all we know, they may fully believe in their error. In a group context, though, we can talk about it, criticize it, ignore it, but especially avoid doing it.

In the consumer arena, social comparison and competitiveness drive us toward conspicuous consumption, as explained in the previous chapter.[326]

When the conversation turns to ruthless competition, many like to invoke the expression "social Darwinism." This expression first appeared in the late 1870s. It usually implied that human society advanced by the survival of the fittest — and that somehow this was desirable. Some prominent thinkers of the late 19th and early 20th centuries held such views, most infamously Francis Galton, the father of eugenics. In the aftermath of World War II, the eugenics movement fell into disgrace, and "social Darwinism"

---

[324] Tosi, Justin, and Brandon Warmke. "Moral grandstanding." *Philosophy & Public Affairs* 44, no. 3 (2016): 197-217.
[325] Tosi, 2016
[326] Garcia, 2013

is now used almost exclusively as a pejorative. Some conservatives argue that it is a logical consequence of Darwin's theories about evolution. It's not. Some progressives consider it the essence of capitalism. Also, no.[327] As thoughtful Christians, we should retire the expression permanently.

The Christian Games

Naturally, being the spiritual people we are, none of us would stoop to moral grandstanding, would we? Christians wouldn't try to outdo one another in their spirituality, would they?

The "Dilbert" comic strip by Scott Adams featured an intermittent character named "Topper." Topper has a single distinguishing trait: whenever any other character makes a statement in his presence, he must counter with a competing claim that is more impressive. It's always something outrageous, or it wouldn't be funny. But the point of satire is to poke fun at things *real* people do. Have you ever played Christian Topper? It goes like this:

> Sam: How was your trip?
>
> Loretta: What a blessing! We were in Haiti for two weeks.
>
> Topper: I spent 37 years in Borneo living off grass and beetles!
>
> Loretta: We did get a stomach bug. I lost 3 pounds.
>
> Topper: I survived malaria, dengue fever, zika, and Ebola!
>
> Loretta: But we prayed for a quick recovery and God healed us.
>
> Topper: I was eaten by cannibals and prayed my way back to life!
>
> —
>
> Ordinary Christian: I'm giving up desserts for lent.
>
> SuperChristian: Oh, that's nice. I fast from sunrise to sunset every Friday.
>
> Topper: I've had nothing but air and water for seven years!

Or closer to home:

---

[327] William H. Young. "Capitalism and Western Civilization: Social Darwinism." National Association of Scholars, April 19, 2012. https://www.nas.org/articles/capitalism_and_western_civilization_social_darwinism. Accessed 5/21/2022

Ordinary Christian: We watched "Harry Potter" last night and had a good conversation with our kids this morning about the themes of courage and sacrifice.

SuperChristian: We won't let our kids watch Harry Potter. Didn't you know that because of those stories, millions of kids turned to Satanism?

Topper: I've never watched a movie in my entire life! Hollywood is totally dominated by Satan-worshipping sodomites and pedophiles!

Now, here's the hazard. Most Christians who eschewed the Harry Potter franchise probably were quite *sincere* in believing that it was harmful (even if a disturbing number fell for the hoax about kids turning to Satanism.[328]). Making a public show of it is more complicated. In our little dialogue, SuperChristian might be sincere but still make Ordinary Christian feel criticized, upstaged, or at least conflicted over how to respond. Moral grandstanding comes so naturally to us, it can be unconscious and completely unintentional. But it's still grandstanding.

Here's a question. When you pray in a group, do you ever worry about how you sound to others? Do you worry if it's too short? If your words are too simple? That you don't sound "spiritual" enough? I do. But I shouldn't. Theologically speaking, our prayers are addressed only to God. But humanly speaking, it sometimes seems more like performance.

Christians play this game even with the Bible. One end competes to see how literally they can interpret it without breaking free of reality. (Snakes, anyone?) The other end competes to see how much of the Bible they can discard and still pretend to be Christian (see: "Jesus Seminar"). It's hard to grandstand from a boring position of normality because no one pays much attention to you. Unfortunately, if enough people jump in, ramping up can either pull the mainstream in its direction, split it, or (perhaps most commonly) both.

Jesus knew moral grandstanding when he saw it, and warned his disciples:

> "Take heed that you do not do your charitable deeds before men, to be seen by them. Otherwise you have no reward from your Father in heaven. Therefore, when you do a charitable deed, do not sound a trumpet before you as the hypocrites do in the synagogues and in the streets, that they may have glory from men.

---

[328] Originated with a parody on "The Onion" in July 2000: The Onion. "Harry Potter Books Spark Rise In Satanism Among Children." Accessed May 22, 2022. https://www.the-onion.com/harry-potter-books-spark-rise-in-satanism-among-childre-18195656644

> Assuredly, I say to you, they have their reward. But when you do a charitable deed, do not let your left hand know what your right hand is doing, that your charitable deed may be in secret; and your Father who sees in secret will Himself reward you openly."[329]

We can play Christian Topper with an endless list of theological and moral issues, but it's unworthy of our calling. Better to follow the admonition of our Lord and let our character speak — softly:

> "Let your light so shine before men, that they may see your good works and glorify your Father in heaven."[330]

Success versus integrity

Deep within us, there is an insatiable yearning for fairness. Having created us in His image, God has planted within us His attributes, including an innate desire for justice. So, when we long for justice, we reflect the image of God.

In the competitive arena, life would indeed be jolly if the nice guys and gals always won. They don't. As I have labored to demonstrate, the pain we experience is sometimes borne of envy. That needs to be recognized, admitted, and confessed. Because of pride, our inner scale of justice will always be decidedly tipped in our favor. That, too, must be recognized and confessed. But there will inevitably be misfortune and heartbreak for even the most humble and virtuous, because we live in a fallen world, and the wicked do indeed prosper.[331]

To start with, mean people make more money. If you always thought this, your suspicions were verified in 2011 by a group of researchers writing in the *Journal of Personality and Social Psychology*.[332] They analyzed data from approximately 10,000 workers over 20 years. Among men, being "mean" conferred an advantage of $9772 in additional annual income over being "nice," with a smaller difference of $1828 among women. (As in many areas, women are unfairly rewarded — in this case, for meanness). A more recent paper sheds insight on the reasons why.[333] A different team

---

[329] Matthew 6:1-4
[330] Matthew 5:16
[331] Psalms 73:3
[332] Judge, Timothy A., Beth A. Livingston, and Charlice Hurst. "Do nice guys—and gals—really finish last? The joint effects of sex and agreeableness on income." *Journal of personality and social psychology* 102, no. 2 (2012): 390.
[333] Matz, Sandra C., and Joe J. Gladstone. "Nice guys finish last: When and why agreeableness is associated with economic hardship." *Journal of personality and social psychology* 118, no. 3 (2020): 545.

of researchers demonstrated that "agreeableness" was related to financial hardship and *lower* savings. They found this was partly because agreeable people *cared less* about money. Not surprisingly, agreeableness and indifference to wealth were most pronounced in the lowest income groups.

In August of 2002, an elderly professor of criminology gave a talk on psychopathy to a small gathering of Canadian cops in remote Newfoundland. This wouldn't have attracted much notice, but the lecturer was Robert Hare, creator of the Hare Psychopathy Checklist, the established standard for the diagnosis and research of psychopaths. As he flashed the faces of psychopaths on the screen, he smoothly transitioned from images of Mafia hit men and sex offenders to well-known corporate CEOs.[334]

Psychopaths are notorious for self-serving ambition, absence of integrity, and callous indifference to others. They also tend to be charming, persuasive, charismatic, and excellent liars. Somewhere between the average Joe and Adolph Eichmann, there are plenty of people with psychopathic traits who never descend into violence. Some become CEOs. According to Dr. Hare, corporate psychopaths scored high in all categories except the one for "impulsive criminality." Not that they are everywhere — only about 3% in management score in the psychopathic range, but that is three times higher than the general population.[335] From a position of authority, the psychopathic manager can inflict considerable havoc on the lives of employees (something I know vividly from personal experience).

The upper ranks of business and politics also boast a disproportionate share of narcissists, though this is mainly because narcissists are more extroverted, and extroversion itself is a significant advantage. It's worth noting that although psychopaths and narcissists are more likely to make it to the top, once there, they aren't so great at leading.[336]

I don't connect socially with many CEOs, but I still believe the overwhelming majority are ordinary decent people who've been afforded a unique set of skills and opportunities and try to do good by it. But, as the Bible says, sometimes the evil do prosper. And one must never underestimate the

---

[334] Alan Deutschman. "Is Your Boss a Psychopath?" *Fast Company* July 1, 2005 https://www.fastcompany.com/53247/your-boss-psychopath Accessed 2/12/2022
[335] Victor Lipman. "The disturbing link between psychopathy and leadership." *Forbes.com*, April 25, 2013 https://www.forbes.com/sites/victorlipman/2013/04/25/the-disturbing-link-between-psychopathy-and-leadership/ Accessed 2/12/2022
[336] Brown, J. "Do psychopaths really make better leaders?" *BBC — Capital*, November 2, 2017 http://www.bbc.com/capital/story/20171102-do-psychopaths-really-make-better-leaders Accessed 2/12/2022

value of simple good fortune. So, let's not use material success as a measure of faith, character, or worth.

If you pause to consider it, works-based righteousness also relies upon competition. If God grades on a curve, my eternal destiny depends upon my position on that curve. Eliminate the possibility of moral comparison, and the very foundation of works righteousness collapses.

It would be lovely if virtue always triumphed, but it doesn't. The wicked do prosper; nice guys sometimes finish last; mean people make more money, and psychopaths have an express lane to the corporate suite. Success does not equate with goodness, and it is not worth sacrificing our integrity for wealth, power, or fame. If we must compete, let us outdo one another by showing honor.[337]

> "Let nothing be done through selfish ambition or conceit, but in lowliness of mind let each esteem others better than himself."[338]

Conclusion

The lesson of Cain is the danger of prideful comparison. We all do it. We can't help it. It begins in early childhood with competitions in music, sports, arts, and school grades. Competition by itself is not a sin. The competitive spirit drives us to excel, and excellence leads to the benefit of all humanity. Do you really want mediocrity from your doctor?

When corrupted by pride, however, comparing ourselves to one another can lead to envy, disappointment, aggression, and even violence. Four decades of research on social comparison support this ancient admonition:

> "Let each one examine his own work, and then he will have rejoicing in himself alone, and not in another." [339]

Key points

- We are naturally inclined toward comparison, but pride demands we come out on top
- Comparison leads to envy
- Envy leads to aggressive competition and a sense of entitlement

---

[337] Romans 12:10
[338] Philippians 2:3
[339] Galatians 6:4

«10»

Pride begets Prejudice

Tribalism, Racism, and Devaluation of Others

If we are truly as great as we imagine, then those who are unlike us — because of culture, appearance, temperament, or whatever else — must therefore be, well, not so great. Conversely, if we can convince ourselves that those unlike us are inferior, then naturally, those like ourselves must be superior. Prejudice comes in many forms, both obvious and subtle. It stems from a heart of pride.

"All animals are equal, but some are more equal than others." [340]

Bias in medicine

It was a bright fall morning many years ago. I was a tired and overworked — but still idealistic — junior medical student rotating on Internal Medicine. The day began early, and it had come time for teaching rounds. Our attending physician was Dr. Adamson [not his real name], an internist specializing in endocrinology. Thus, he saw many diabetics in his clinic, and adult diabetics are almost invariably overweight.

Dr. Adamson strode into our conference room, bearing a frown. He was typically well-manicured and crisply dressed but hardly svelte. Evidently, that morning's clinic had been particularly frustrating. "I hate fat people!" he growled upon entering. "They disgust me! Why do they do that to themselves?" Being lowly junior medical students, we were intimidated by Dr. Adamson and knew to tread lightly. His subjective evaluation would be our grade for the rotation. We laughed nervously, pretending it was a joke while knowing it wasn't. Quickly the discussion moved on to the matter of

---

[340] Orwell, George. *Animal Farm.* Secker and Warburg, 1945.

our new admissions from the previous night.

Although Dr. Adamson's invective that morning was a bit over the top —
even by the benighted standards of that era — such feelings are common
among physicians. Doctors struggle with disdain toward patients for perceived moral failings — illicit drug use, physical inactivity, sexual behaviors, smoking, and alcohol abuse, for instance. Most try to suppress the
temptation, and some of the saintliest in my profession devote their ca-
reers to caring for such.

Dark and cynical attitudes are unfortunately common in medical training.
When I was in medical school, there was a derogatory term for patients
who were brain-damaged, comatose, or otherwise severely impaired. Occasionally someone would refer to them as "Gomers."[341] Thankfully, my
medical school was not without one Voice of Conscience.

Midway through my senior year, the student newspaper ran an open letter
from an esteemed faculty member. He castigated students for using derogatory expressions, reminding us that patients were there for our education
and deserved to be treated with dignity and respect. This was mature and
worthy advice. But not without a twist of irony: the letter was signed, "Dr.
H. Adamson." [If hypocrisy were gold? "Supply would skyrocket, the mar-
ket value would plunge, and gold would be rendered worthless."]

Like an astute politician, prejudice wears many faces. Perhaps you've read
Jane Austen's classic work or seen one of the excellent cinematic adapta-
tions:

> *"Pride and Prejudice? What's the connection? Let me think now....*
> *was Darcy proud and Elizabeth prejudiced? Or was it the other way*
> *around?"*

The answer, in a word, was "yes." Each felt superior to the other — though
for very different reasons. Each was proud but only perceived it in the
other. And their pride was the cause of their prejudice.

In our discussion thus far, I have focused on the two main pillars of pride:
overconfidence and self-exaltation. Both are based on having too high an
opinion of oneself. As we saw in the discussion of envy, one cheap and easy
way to build ourselves up is to tear others down. Racism and prejudice also
serve that purpose. They are distinguished from most other expressions of
pride in that the sense of superiority is attached to being a member of a

---

[341] The origin of this expression is disputed. Some sources maintain it is an acronym for "Get
Out of My Emergency Room." See: Shem, Samuel. *The House of God.* New York: R. Marek Publishers, 1978.

group — rather than individual in nature —but the motive and outcome are otherwise the same.

Bias in scripture

One can find many examples of prejudice in Scripture. Consider Jonah: the Israelite sent by God to go and preach repentance to the pagans in Nineveh. The ancient city of Nineveh was no backwater. It was the capital of the Assyrian empire, the dominant military power of that day. Like many empires, both ancient and modern, its military machine was capable of horrendous atrocities, and the Assyrians were both feared and hated.

The account of Jonah is well-known: his decision to disobey God and flee, leading to a storm at sea, being tossed overboard, getting chugged by a whale, eventually fulfilling his mission, and witnessing the mass repentance of Nineveh.

What is less commonly known is why he didn't go in the first place. Jonah was not afraid they would *kill* him. He was afraid they would *listen* to him. He dreaded not failure but success. He hated the Ninevites and wished God's wrath upon them, not divine mercy. That explains his utter *despair* when they actually listened to him and repented — for "it displeased Jonah exceedingly, and he became angry." He prayed to God, "was not this what I said when I was still in my country? Therefore I fled previously to Tarshish, for I know that You are a gracious and merciful God, slow to anger and abundant in lovingkindness." [342]

The New Testament recounts the prejudice of the Jews against the Samaritans,[343] the sophisticated Jews of the South (Jerusalem, the temple, the Sanhedrin) against the Jews from Galilee in the north,[344] and everyone against the Cretans — "Cretans are always liars, evil beasts, lazy gluttons" — wrote Paul to Titus, quoting the ancient poet Epimenides.[345]

In recent decades the American Christian community has become acutely sensitive to the issue of racism. Indeed, it remains a real and pervasive problem, but America has progressed largely because of Christian influence. Worldwide, little headway is being made.

---

[342] Jonah 4:2-3
[343] John 4:9
[344] John 7:52, Acts 2:7
[345] Titus 1:12

In Rwanda in 1994, the world watched in horror as over 800,000 Tutsis were systematically butchered by the majority Hutus who lived among them. The Hutus and Tutsis spoke the same language, had high rates of intermarriage, and according to some sources, were physically and culturally indistinguishable.[346] The tribal identities had more to do with economic status than genealogy, yet everyone seemed to know who was with what tribe. The genocide was carried out by radical splinter groups of Hutus for reasons of political power, prejudice, and revenge.

Mere exposure effect
"Unfamiliarity breeds contempt"

It would have been a mystery to any unfamiliar observer what would cause one group to hate the other when they were inseparable by any reliable external features.

The Rwandan genocide, like similar past horrors, revealed the depth of our fallen nature. Societies, culture, and technology change, but human nature is constant. The animosity between Hutus and Tutsis that erupted in bloody carnage is just an extreme example of the prejudice we all are capable of.

What drives people to such hatred and cruelty? It always begins with something small, seemingly insignificant. Pride is the fuel by which a little spark of prejudice ignites a bonfire of hatred.

Familiarity breeds liking

In matters of individual preference, familiarity breeds appreciation. When it comes to our attitude toward strangers, we are like toddlers who prefer the McNuggets they know over the *chateaubriand* they do not. This phenomenon is known as the "mere exposure effect."[347] You may not have heard of it unless you work in advertising, but advertising agents use it to great advantage. It has been demonstrated in preferences for music, art, language, and people. If you are hungry in a strange town, are you more likely to seek sustenance in some shabby little diner you've never heard of, or a franchise of your favorite restaurant chain? If you choose the chain, your decision may be perfectly logical — after all, your exposure is

---

[346] "Rwandan Genocide." In *Wikipedia*, May 22, 2022. https://en.wikipedia.org/wiki/Rwandan_genocide
[347] Zajonc, Robert B. "Mere exposure: A gateway to the subliminal." *Current directions in psychological science* 10, no. 6 (2001): 224-228.

supplemented by experience — but the effect can be convincingly demonstrated even when there is *no experience* to justify the preference.

We all share a basic human need to identify with a group. By itself, that is neither right nor wrong, but without a robust moral framework, it can lead to unfortunate consequences. Because of pride, there is the persistent subliminal urge to think our group is *better* than other groups.

Since we know the members of our own group, we understand and accept that it is made up of different types of people with different opinions, personalities, strengths, and foibles. If we were rational, we would assume the same of all groups, but in this case, our instincts run contrary to logic. Instead, the natural tendency is to assume that members of the outside group are either pretty much all the same, or much more alike than different. The technical term for this error is "outgroup homogeneity bias" because we assume the other group — the "outgroup" — is much more homogenous than we have any logical reason to believe.

The outgroup homogeneity bias leads to the mindset that "all whites-blacks-Hispanics-Jews-conservatives-progressives are the same." They are not. They have never been and never will be. Such ways of thinking may not originate consciously or from malicious intent, but that doesn't get us off the hook. That it might happen unconsciously just makes it more difficult to catch when we do it.

Moving beyond belief to behavior, the "in-group bias" is a well-studied phenomenon whereby we actively show favoritism to the members of our own group over outsiders. Not just in social interaction, mind you, but in economic and other matters as well. This behavior has been observed in experiments even where the group identity is based on something utterly meaningless, like having the same birthday or the same final digit in one's social security number.[348] This partly accounts for discriminatory behavior against members of other religions, races, tribes, or any other outside group. Again, the evidence suggests that it originates at an unconscious level, so we are probably unaware we are doing it.

In-group bias

===

"It's you and me against the world, fellas. We gotta stick together."

The in-group bias partially accounts for gender bias as well. In certain

---

[348] Jacoby-Senghor, Drew S., Stacey Sinclair, and Colin Tucker Smith. "When bias binds: Effect of implicit outgroup bias on ingroup affiliation." *Journal of personality and social psychology* 109, no. 3 (2015): 415.

situations, men and women are instinctively going to favor their own sex. This doesn't fully explain sexism, of course. Stereotyping is another major problem, as we will see.

"In the land of the blind, the one-eyed man is king," contended Erasmus.[349] As the founder of modern humanism, Erasmus was hopelessly optimistic. More likely than not, in the land of the blind, a one-eyed man would be burned as a witch.

If I rub your halo, will my wishes come true?

One of the more insidious flaws in our fallen minds is our vulnerability to the "halo effect."[350] Because our minds are lazy (per Kahneman), we tend toward simplistic assessments of other people. First observed and reported by Edward Thorndike in 1920, the halo effect is our tendency to believe if someone is "good" in one or a few defined traits, that they are probably good in others as well. Rather than seeing other people as a complex amalgam of strengths and weaknesses, or taking the time to know them better, we tend to categorize them as generally good or bad. What makes this bias so insidious is that usually our first impression — before any words are spoken — is based on physical appearance.

Halo effect

"You *can* judge a book by its cover."

The instant we meet a new person, we unconsciously judge whether we think that person is attractive, unattractive, or neutral. If we perceive them as attractive, we are inclined to assume they're good people long before we have any basis for judging. We intuit that good-looking people are probably kinder, more honest, and more fun to be with. Conversely, if the person seems unattractive, we are prone to think more negatively of their invisible attributes. In extreme cases, we may take one look at an individual and assume criminal intent.

This should not come as a shock. In fact, television and movie producers have taken flak for many years over their habit of making heroes and winners always beautiful or handsome and villains or losers stereotypically unattractive or physically deformed. Some blame Hollywood for shaping societal expectations, but the halo effect was identified at the very dawn of modern filmmaking. Audiences simply enjoy it more and find it more

---

[349] Erasmus, Desiderius. *Adagia* . 1500
[350] Thorndike, Edward L. "A constant error in psychological ratings." *Journal of applied psychology* 4, no. 1 (1920): 25.

believable when the heroes and villains look like they expect.

Hollywood is undoubtedly guilty of reinforcing the halo effect, but this is more a *reflection* of our own bias than a cause of it. The story of *Beauty and the Beast* was around for centuries before the Academy-award-winning Disney animated version of 1991. Of course, when the Disney version came out, it had become culturally unacceptable to portray female characters as beautiful but passive, so the producers updated the character of Belle, making her a bookish loner who intellectually outshone the entire village. Ironically, by accommodating the revised cultural norm, Disney made the halo effect even more extreme. Now, the heroine was not only better looking and more virtuous than everyone, but more intelligent as well. To her who hath, more will be given?

When beautiful characters are exposed as evil, writers assume that the outcome would surprise an audience primed by the halo effect. It's a classic ploy: *la belle femme* who turns *fatale*.

Some years after *Beauty and the Beast*, DreamWorks managed to produce one movie that took the halo effect and turned it completely upside down and backwards, the original *Shrek*. Much of the charm of *Shrek* was that it emphatically torpedoed the link between physical attractiveness and character in a uniquely positive and entertaining way. It's something we can relate to since most of us see ourselves more like Shrek or Fiona than Prince or Princess Charming. [For a while, Fiona became a worldwide inspiration to chubby, green-skinned girls with orange hair and handlebar ears]. Physical appearance is clearly not an area where most people suffer from overconfidence. Still, some experience the halo effect every time they look in the mirror:

> "Many times at the beach, a good-looking lady will say to me, 'I want to touch you.' I always smile and say, 'I don't blame you.'" — ARNOLD SCHWARZENEGGER (Bodybuilder and actor turned politician)[351]

Decades of research have established that natural good looks are a gift that keeps on giving. Attractive men and women earn more money than homely ones. They receive more attention from others and are treated with greater kindness and deference. They are more likely to be hired. They fare better in court. They are viewed as cleverer and better students. They garner more votes at the polling booth. The advantages begin early in life and compound over time, leading to higher achievement and psychological

---

[351] Miller, Hartley. *You Don't Say!: Over 1,000 Hilarious Sports Quotes and Quips*. Kansas City: Andrews McMeel Publishing, 2005

well-being.[352] One of the more amusing findings is that college students actually *learn more* from attractive teachers.[353] [So far, I haven't seen any universities modify their hiring practices based on this research. I guess "follow the science" has its limits].

In addition to looks, height confers its own advantages. When it comes to stature, every inch counts — in fact, in the workplace, every inch above average may be worth $789 more per year, according to a 2004 study in the *Journal of Applied Psychology*.[354] The researchers found that someone who is 6 feet tall earns, on average, nearly $166,000 more over 30 years than someone who is 5 feet 5 inches — even after controlling for gender, age, and weight.

Controlling for all known variables, tall men are statistically likelier to get into better schools, obtain better jobs, make more money, and get the promotions. As if that were not unfair enough, they even get the girl.[355] [Contrary to what I always heard growing up, it's not just men who are superficial].[356] Conversely, obese people suffer many disadvantages in this competitive world unrelated to their physical ability to do the job.[357]

Halos for some, horns for others

So, what's the connection between pride and the halo effect? After all, if we express admiration for someone else, isn't that the opposite of pride? Well, not quite. First, who do we determine to be attractive? Doesn't it usually turn out to be people who look like us (whoever "us" happens to be)? At the very least, we are judging people by standards that we have defined ourselves, consciously or unconsciously.

But there's a darker side to that coin: we make more negative assumptions concerning those we deem unattractive. Some call it the "horns" effect. And

---

[352] Frevert, Tonya K., and Lisa Slattery Walker. "Physical attractiveness and social status." *Sociology Compass* 8, no. 3 (2014): 313-323.
[353] Westfall, Richard, Murray Millar, and Mandy Walsh. "Effects of instructor attractiveness on learning." *The Journal of general psychology* 143, no. 3 (2016): 161-171.
[354] Judge, T.A. and Cable, D.M., 2004. The effect of physical height on workplace success and income: preliminary test of a theoretical model. *Journal of Applied Psychology*, 89(3), p.428.
[355] "20/20 Report—Are Short Men at a Disadvantage in Romance?" ABC News, March 14, 2008 https://youtu.be/AR3YR1ZTonc Accessed 2/12/2022
[356] Seth Meyers, "Short Men: Why Women Aren't Attracted Enough to Date Them," Psychology Today, January 2, 2014, https://www.psychologytoday.com/us/blog/insight-is-2020/201401/short-men-why-women-arent-attracted-enough-date-them Accessed 5/21/2020
[357] Flint, Stuart W., Martin Čadek, Sonia C. Codreanu, Vanja Ivić, Colene Zomer, and Amalia Gomoiu. "Obesity discrimination in the recruitment process: "You're not hired!"." *Frontiers in psychology* (2016): 647.

who might that be, but those who do not *look* like us, or like we expect them to look? Consequently, our susceptibility to the halo effect reinforces prejudicial tendencies already within us. We will not be able to overcome these biases unless we recognize that they exist and consciously strive to look upon all people equally regardless of outward appearance. That is much, much easier said than done.

There is a third lesson to be drawn for those who rank among the favored. If you happen to be the sort of woman who is considered attractive or a man who is tall and handsome, you would do well to stop and think what a tremendous advantage you have enjoyed through little or no effort on your own part.

There is a long-standing myth that throughout medieval times belief in and fear of witchcraft were pervasive, and many today still cling to the canard that "millions" of women were burned. Actually, throughout most of Church history, both pope and clerics considered witchcraft as nothing more than a superstition to be ignored. Yet there was a time in the early modern era when a "witch craze" surfaced. It peaked between 1580 and 1630, and the best estimate of the total number of deaths is from 40,0000-60,000, mostly women.[358] Guess who was most likely to be singled out as a witch? The old and ugly. In other words, they "looked like one." The famous line from Monty Python was historically accurate.[359]

> "Though neither old nor ugly (**as witches usually were**), but young and good-looking, her neighbours had long considered her a witch."[360] [emphasis added]

A chief reason we stereotype others is that our minds are programmed to operate that way.[361] Our brains create something akin to mental file folders that help us to remember things — like facts, events, or people — if we can fit them into one of those folders. Those folders, called "schemas," assign customary attributes to the items within. Lumping things together is less mental effort and makes things easier to remember. When we see a new model of smartphone, the "smartphone" schema pretty much tells us what it can and can't do without having to read the manual. The downside where people are concerned is that we end up assigning to a particular

---

358 "Witch Trials in the Early Modern Period." In *Wikipedia*, May 21, 2022. https://en.wikipedia.org/wiki/Witch_trials_in_the_early_modern_period
359 T. Gilliam & T. Jones, dirs. *Monty Python and the Holy Grail.* Python Pictures, 1975: "How do you know she's a witch? Because she looks like one!"
360 Mackay, Charles. *Extraordinary Popular Delusions and the Madness of Crowds.* New York: Three Rivers Press: 1980
361 Fine, Cordelia. *A Mind of Its Own: How Your Brain Distorts and Deceives.* 1st ed. New York: W.W. Norton & Co, 2006.

individual all the attributes of the group we put them in, unless or until we get to know them better.

The schemas themselves aren't necessarily defective. Men really are more systems-oriented, and women really are more empathetic — on average. This was re-confirmed in 2018 in the most extensive study ever conducted on sex differences.[362] But because of overlap, that information is useless on an individual level. There are women great at math and men who are lousy at it. There are men who excel in empathy and women who are severely deficient.

In earlier and more primitive times, stereotyping may have helped to survive. In ancient times, life was violent, and murder rates were at times astronomical.[363] (Extraordinarily high murder rates persist today among some surviving Stone Age tribes).[364] When encountering a stranger, the ability to make a snap judgment whether to befriend, fight, or run might have made all the difference. If you were a Tutsi in 1994 Rwanda, that would have absolutely been the case. If you are anyone in 21st century Malibu, probably not.

The overwhelming majority of murders in the U.S. are committed by friends or acquaintances: we are three times more likely to be murdered by someone we know than by a stranger. Among those murdered by a stranger, the assailant is far more likely to be of your own race. Statistically speaking, no matter what color you are, your chances of being murdered in the USA are lowest with a total stranger of a different race.[365]

It is a fundamental doctrine of Christianity that every person bears the image of God and is of immeasurable worth. But our willingness to honor that principle is frequently distorted by selfishness and pride. We are prone to dehumanize people and groups based on their perceived value or stature; this, in turn, leads to conflict, injustice, discrimination, and aggression. In one recent study, researchers demonstrated that we are prone to assign

---

[362] Greenberg, David M., Varun Warrier, Carrie Allison, and Simon Baron-Cohen. "Testing the empathizing—systemizing theory of sex differences and the extreme male brain theory of autism in half a million people." *Proceedings of the National Academy of Sciences* 115, no. 48 (2018): 12152-12157.

[363] Max Roser. "Ethnographic and archaeological evidence on violent deaths." Our World in Data. 8/2/2013 https://ourworldindata.org/ethnographic-and-archaeological-evidence-on-violent-deaths Accessed 2/12/2022

[364] Beckerman, Stephen, Pamela I. Erickson, James Yost, Jhanira Regalado, Lilia Jaramillo, Corey Sparks, Moises Iromenga, and Kathryn Long. "Life histories, blood revenge, and reproductive success among the Waorani of Ecuador." *Proceedings of the National Academy of Sciences* 106, no. 20 (2009): 8134-8139.

[365] Cooper, Alexia and Smith, Erica. "Homicide Trends in the United States, 1980-2008." Bureau of Justice Statistics, US Dept of Justice, November 2011. https://www.bjs.gov/content/pub/pdf/htus8008.pdf

greater humanness to women who are attractive and men who appear intelligent — based solely on facial appearance.[366] That renders the opposite equally true: we assign less humanness to men and women who do not appear intelligent or attractive.

So, hopefully, by now, I've convinced you of two things. First, the halo effect is real and has a powerful impact on our thinking. Second, it's obviously unjust, usually inaccurate, and often harmful. Overcoming it demands conscious, willful intent — and a renewing of our minds by the Holy Spirit.

The Fab King Saul

Millennia before the halo effect was named by modern psychology, the Bible exposed our tendency to be deceived by good looks and emphatically rejected any connection between outward appearance and inner character. We learn in I Samuel that the future king Saul was "choice and handsome."[367] In fact, "there was not a more handsome person than he among the children of Israel." For added measure, "from his shoulders upward he was taller than any of the people."

King Saul was both handsome *and* tall, so predictably — per the halo effect — the Israelites cheered his selection as their new king. Though he started well, Saul had issues, his reign ended badly, and his halo was tarnished long before the bitter end.

David's son Absalom could have been named the world's sexiest man by the January 980 B.C. edition of *People Magazine*:

> "In all Israel there was no one who was praised as much as Absalom for his good looks. From the sole of his foot to the crown of his head there was no blemish in him."[368]

We are further apprised that — like a few famous politicians — he also had great hair. It should surprise no one that when Absalom raised up an insurrection against his father's reign, many Israelites followed. Yet his stunning good looks concealed a heart filled with hate and obsessed with revenge. As in the case of Saul, things ended badly for Absalom.

You might recall that King David was succeeded by his son, Solomon. There

---

[366] Alaei, R., Deska, J. C., Hugenberg, K., & Rule, N. O. "People attribute humanness to men and women differently based on their facial appearance." *Journal of Personality and Social Psychology*, 123(2), (2022):400—422.
[367] 1 Samuel 9:2
[368] 2 Samuel 14:25

was, however, one interloper who tried to prevent that from happening. Adonijah, another of David's sons, the brother of Absalom and possibly David's eldest surviving son, attempted to seize the reins of power while David lay dying. He "was also very good-looking."[369] Like the others, however, his good looks belied a wicked heart, and his relentless scheming eventually led to his execution.[370]

Application

Pride not only motivates us to exalt ourselves above others but our groups as well — partly because our groups tend to consist of people like us, and we think so well of ourselves. Prejudice has been around since Biblical times. Unfortunately, we tend to make negative assessments of people different from us and feel favorably toward members of our own group, who are more like us. We seem wired to judge people based on their outward appearance, leading both to prejudice against those who appear odd to us and favoritism toward those we consider attractive. In either case, the consequences are usually harmful.

Finally, this has nothing to do with discrimination against *ideas or beliefs*. Some beliefs are truly dangerous and/or wrong, but it remains our Christian obligation to treat their adherents with love, compassion, and respect. The world is full of modern-day Ninevites. To run away and wish the wrath of God upon them is to commit the sin of Jonah afresh.

> "I have a dream that my four little children will one day live in a nation where they will not be judged by the color of their skin but by the content of their character" — MARTIN LUTHER KING

> "There is no longer Jew or Greek; there is no longer slave or free; there is no longer male and female, for all of you are one in Christ Jesus."[371]

In the next chapter, we will examine the subject of judging in detail, but the immortal words of Dr. King are an excellent place to begin.

---

[369] 1 Kings 1:6
[370] 1 Kings 2:25
[371] Galatians 3:28

Key points

- Pride causes us to look favorably upon people like ourselves and unfavorably toward those who are different
- Prejudice or racism are based on a belief in group superiority, which is sinful pride elevated to a group level
- Because we are naturally biased in favor of the attractive, we must make a special effort to think more highly of those who are not

«11»

"I'm OK — You're not!"

Pride and Judgmentalism

One of the most abused passages of Scripture is Jesus' admonition against judging, lest we be similarly judged. What is judgmentalism? Are we forbidden from confronting or correcting the misconduct of others? More often than we know, our judgments of others are corrupted by pride and self-serving in purpose. While correction and rebuke are Biblically warranted, few take seriously the prerequisite of removing the logs from their own eye. The difficulty is compounded by our inability to even recognize those logs. The Biblical model is nearly opposite to our natural impulse: we ought to be patient with the sins of others and forever discontent with our own moral state.

———

"There are some men who, living with the one object of enriching themselves, no matter by what means, and being perfectly conscious of the baseness and rascality of the means which they will use every day towards this end, affect nevertheless — even to themselves — a high tone of moral rectitude, and shake their heads and sigh over the depravity of the world." [372]

Pride, judgment, and judgmentalism

In this chapter, we wrap up our exploration of pride. When I began this study many years ago, I never expected this was where it would end. But understood from the framework I've laid, pride and judgmentalism are deeply intertwined.

———

[372] Dickens, *The Life and Adventures of Nicholas Nickleby.*

How quickly, instinctively, and effortlessly we judge one another. This chapter concerns judgmentalism: what is it, what causes it, how do we recognize it, and what can we do about it?

"Judge not, lest ye be likewise judged."[373]

"Let he who is without sin cast the first stone."[374]

If there were ever a contest for the most misapplied verses in Scripture, these two would trump all others. Non-judgmentalism in the name of tolerance was for a while an unassailable dogma of our "post-dogmatic" Western culture. And no one embraces that dogma with greater ferocity than the one being criticized. But now that you know legalism is like gravity, you should understand why moral relativism was inherently unstable. The pendulum has swung. Western society has resurrected hyperjudgmentalism with a vengeance.

Once we comprehend that pride is the prime motivator of human behavior — with ego preservation its primary objective — it's easy to see why criticism would be naturally unwelcome.

Jesus's pronouncement is not just one more rule to add to our list of "don'ts." Judgmentalism — rightly understood — is a violation against love and humility. Let me establish first what *it is not*. It's much more than just talking about people's sins (or I could not have written this book). Taking a public stand in defense of Biblical morality is not judgmentalism; it is obedience. Humbly confronting the sins of others may be unpleasant, but also something we are commanded to do — sometimes.[375,376] So how and where do we draw the line? How do we exercise judgment without being *judgmental*? If it were simple, this chapter would not be necessary. This chapter is necessary.

Prejudice and judgmentalism are two sides of the same coin. Both originate from the same Latin root that means "to judge." The difference is in the timeline. Prejudice is a judgment made upon a person, idea, or thing *before* we are fully acquainted, "premature or hasty," according to the *Oxford English Dictionary*.[377] Judgment has many possible meanings, the most pertinent here being "the pronouncing of a deliberate opinion upon a person or

---

[373] Matthew 7:1
[374] John 8:7
[375] "Preach the word! Be ready in season and out of season. Convince, rebuke, exhort, with all longsuffering and teaching." 2 Timothy 4:2
[376] "Moreover if your brother sins against you, go and tell him his fault between you and him alone. If he hears you, you have gained your brother." Matthew 18:15
[377] "Prejudice". *Oxford English Dictionary*.

thing, or the opinion pronounced; criticism; censure."[378] Judgment comes *after* we have information specific to that person, idea, or thing. It is morally neutral: judgment may be fair or unfair. For lack of a better term — and in deference to common usage — I will use "judgmentalism" to apply strictly to unfair judgment or a critical mindset.[379]

In their provocative book *unChristian*, Kinnaman and Lyons reported that of the 20% of the US population unaffiliated with any Christian church (higher now), 87% perceived Christians as judgmental.[380] We might be tempted to respond with indifference: "Of course they do. We're against sin, and they're *for* it." True, there has been a multi-decade trend in Western society to redefine morality: demanding not merely tolerance but enthusiastic *approval* of sinful behavior.

Sometimes, "judge not" is a transparent ploy to "cancel" anyone standing up for Christian virtue. But to remain silent on moral issues is contrary to the teaching and example of Christ and the apostles. Still, Jesus commanded us not to judge, so it is incumbent upon us to figure out what that means. Otherwise, how can we stop doing it?

Pride — the subject of this book — sits at the very heart of judgmentalism. To be spiritually discerning without being judgmental necessitates transplanting our heart of pride with a new one of humility.

In the following sections, I will address three questions. First, are we even qualified to judge? Second, what is the relationship between judgmentalism and pride? Third, how can we discern when our judgments are tainted by pride? In response to the first question, we need to approach judgment with humility because we're so terribly unqualified.

Judging others: we're lousy at it

I love watching Olympic figure skating, but I don't get the judging at all. As with gymnastics or diving, the judges can see things I'd never notice. Were I asked to be a judge, I'd admit I was unqualified. But when it comes to judging our fellow human beings, we feel downright gifted. We shouldn't. The truth is that we make very poor judges. I've already mentioned quite a few cognitive biases along this path of discovery. Several function to make ourselves look better and others worse. They operate even when we have

---

[378] "Judgment". *Oxford English Dictionary.*
[379] Cooper, Terry D. *Making Judgments without Being Judgmental: Nurturing a Clear Mind and a Generous Heart.* Downers Grove, Ill: IVP Books, 2006.
[380] Kinnaman, David, and Gabe Lyons. *unChristian: What a New Generation Really Thinks about Christianity— and Why It Matters.* Grand Rapids, Mich: Baker Books, 2007.

no personal stake. Throw emotions or conflict into the soup, and it only gets worse. Let's look at some biases pertinent to judging.

Omission bias

It is much more natural to focus on action than inaction, presence rather than absence. In radiology, there is a saying that "the hardest abnormality to see is the one that's not there." A tumor on the spleen we'd see right away. A missing spleen can easily go unnoticed. In the holiday comedy *Home Alone*, the entire McAllister family took off for a Christmas vacation and were halfway across the Atlantic before they realized that nine-year-old Kevin was missing.[381] Funny and implausible as that may sound, it's not *that* implausible. What if, instead of leaving a child behind, some strange kid took Kevin's place? He would have been noticed immediately.

This tendency also applies to our moral evaluations. Biblically, sin can be divided into two categories. Sins of commission are the bad things that we do. Sins of omission are the good things we fail to do. To fairly assess a person's character, we should consider both. To actually do so, however, is impossible. First, bad actions tend to stand out and get noticed more than the good. Second, we cannot possibly keep score of missed opportunities for doing good. A person could live a very straight and sober life, strictly complying with all the external rules, yet never raise a hand to show compassion or mercy or be a servant to others. That person would still be a great sinner because of what they *failed* to do.

> **Omission bias**
>
> "I did everything you asked," [but not one bit more].

---

381 Columbus, C, dir. *Home Alone*. Twentieth Century Fox, 1990.

Fundamental attribution error

Have you ever failed at anything? Of course you have, and chances are also that you had an excellent reason. Whenever we fail — at school, at sports, on the job, in a relationship, in not doing something we should, in doing something we shouldn't — we always find an excuse. We were tired, not feeling well, stressed, overextended, having a bad day, everyone was on our case... and those with the best excuses are destined for politics. Of course, this is totally self-serving, done only to protect our ego (meaning our pride). But it is typical and predictable. No surprise here. But what about when someone else fails? Do we naturally assume they are stressed, having a bad day, or not feeling well? No, we don't. Their state of mind is invisible to us.

Attribution error

"I messed up because I couldn't sleep last night. You messed up because you're careless and incompetent."

So, if someone is rude to us, we assume that's just the kind of person she is. If someone else falls down on the job, we conclude he is irresponsible or lazy. We take credit for our successes and make excuses for our failures. When others fail, we deny them the benefit of the doubt and instead blame it on their ability or character. We *attribute* their behavior to *who they are* in an unfair, and therefore judgmental, way. Social psychologists refer to this as the "fundamental attribution error."

Projection bias

"There is a kind of selfishness...which is constantly upon the watch for selfishness in others; and holding others at a distance, by suspicions and distrusts, wonders why they don't approach, and don't confide, and calls that selfishness in them."[382]

In committing the fundamental attribution error, we presume to know someone's intent. There is another way to judge their state of mind that is equally seductive and deceiving, known as projection bias. When we engage in projection bias, we *project* onto others our own thoughts, motives, and intentions. For example, suppose I *always* return phone messages promptly and would consider it rude not to do so [a laughable supposition in my case]. Because of projection bias, I might therefore conclude that anyone who doesn't return *my* messages is being intentionally rude. The

---

[382] Charles Dickens. *Martin Chuzzlewit.* 1844

truth might be that they're just more casual about responding or don't check messages very often.

It should be obvious, but we tend to forget: not everyone thinks as we do. The words, body language, or behaviors of someone may stem from very different beliefs or motives than our own. Projection bias was first described 3000 years ago when God rebuked evil men who presumed He thought as they did:

> **Projection bias**
>
> "Of course that's what she was thinking! That's what I would have thought!"

> "These *things* you have done, and I kept silent;
> You thought that I was altogether like you;
> *But* I will rebuke you,
> And set *them* in order before your eyes."[383]

We see projection bias in David's brothers, who falsely accused him of pride and vainglory when he approached the camp of King Saul:

> "Now Eliab his oldest brother heard when he spoke to the men; and Eliab's anger was aroused against David, and he said, "Why did you come down here? And with whom have you left those few sheep in the wilderness? I know your pride and the insolence of your heart, for you have come down to see the battle."[384]

In the case of David's brothers, there is a particular irony: proud people assume pride in others even when it's not there. So, if you see a lot of pride in others but not yourself, beware. You may be staring at your own projection.

Trait ascription bias

We perceive ourselves as complex personalities, subject to a variety of conflicting moods, feelings, dreams, motives, and ambitions. On the other hand, we see other people as much more one-dimensional and fail to appreciate their innate variability. So, if we see someone acting selfishly, rudely, or carelessly, we tend to view them as basically selfish, rude, or careless. This is very similar to fundamental attribution error.

[383] Psalms 50:21
[384] I Samuel 17:28

For clarification, the *fundamental attribution error* disregards mitigating factors and blames behavior on character, whereas trait ascription bias causes us to oversimplify another's character and reduce them to one-dimensional caricatures of real human beings. We're stuffing them into one of those mental folders (schemas) referred to earlier, but the schema is overly simplistic.

Trait ascription bias
"Boys will be boys."

Illusion of transparency

Several known biases lead us to make hasty, erroneous assumptions regarding the behavior, intentions, or character of another. These contribute to a more general pitfall known as the "illusion of transparency." The illusion of transparency is a two-way street. Simply put, we falsely presume others understand us better than they really do, and we falsely assume we know them better than we really do. Altogether, these various errors share the common feature of sinful judgmentalism: the inclination to make unjust judgments of the inner character and motives of another because we are incapable of judging accurately and fairly.

Illusion of transparency
"I know exactly what you're thinking."

Just-world phenomenon

"There were present at that season some who told Him about the Galileans whose blood Pilate had mingled with their sacrifices. And Jesus answered and said to them, "Do you suppose that these Galileans were worse sinners than all *other* Galileans, because they suffered such things? I tell you, no; but unless you repent you will all likewise perish. Or those eighteen on whom the tower in Siloam fell and killed them, do you think that they were worse sinners than all *other* men who dwelt in Jerusalem? I tell you, no."[385]

We have an overwhelming desire to believe that the world is ultimately just: that bad things don't happen to good people, and people get basically what they deserve. This misconception is known as the "just-world phenomenon," and it's independent of one's religious beliefs.[386] Christians

---

[385] Luke 13:1-5
[386] Hafer, Carolyn L., and Laurent Begue. "Experimental research on just-world theory: problems, developments, and future challenges." *Psychological bulletin* 131, no. 1 (2005): 128.

should know better. Jesus refuted it. The truth is that our fallen world is a very unfair place; injustice is rampant, and even though the blessings of God rain down upon all, some are more blessed than others.

Still, we have a hard time letting go. When someone is highly blessed by God, we tend to see them as godlier. They might believe it themselves. They're far likelier to be invited to share their "principles of success" with others. When someone falls on hard times, well, "she lacks faith," or "he is being chastened by God." You hear it all the time.

Just world phenomenon

"What goes 'round comes 'round. Always."

"She left him? Well, he must have done something to deserve it!" "They're bankrupt? Well, if they had tithed according to God's commands, it never would have happened!"

The just world illusion is particularly toxic because it inflicts hurt upon those already hurting. It is prideful because it's based on unwarranted faith in our flawed analysis or theology. But the world is not so clear-cut. Job was a sinner like all of us, maybe less so. He no more deserved the misfortunes that befell him than any of his friends. Every year, innocent men are exonerated after spending years, even decades, incarcerated for crimes they did not commit.[387]

Hindsight bias

Much of this chapter concerns judgments about character and motives, but we're prone to make faulty judgments about actions based on their outcome. When it's all over, and things didn't go as hoped, the really fun part begins — the finger-pointing. We think our hindsight is 20/20, but it's not. We criticize others for poor decisions based on our hindsight, having decided the right course of action was evident from the start. It takes discipline and humility to place ourselves back in time — limited to the information at hand, blinded to any knowledge of the outcome — and admit we couldn't have done any better. And so, we judge.

Faulty memories

We may harbor feelings of resentment, bitterness, or condemnation over some past offense, but our recollection of the offense is likely to be self-serving at the least and possibly unreliable. Memories are a strange thing

---

387 Innocence Project. "Innocence Project—Help Us Put an End to Wrongful Convictions!" Accessed May 22, 2022. https://www.innocenceproject.org/

and have been researched extensively. They are not reliable recordings of past events but imaginative reconstructions from a few remembered facts. Our minds fill in the details.[388] When there has been conflict, failure, or defeat, our prideful minds will reconstruct those details in the most self-serving way possible.

Not only do we fail to remember reliably, but worse, we "remember" things that never happened. Thus, two people at odds over some old conflict may never come to peace on the matter: each becomes mired in their own version of the event with no possibility of ever agreeing on the facts. Because of false — but self-serving — memories, one might harbor a lifelong grudge based on faulty recollection, or a memory reframed so that the accused is solely to blame.

Judging others: poisoned by pride

Here we move on to the second question: what is the connection between judgmentalism and pride? Judgmentalism is deeply rooted in pride. That is why it is a moral offense and a violation against love and humility. Every element of pride that I've discussed can arouse a form of judgmentalism. To get the logs out of our own eyes, we need to recognize them. So, let's examine a few "eye logs."

Making ourselves the arbiter of right and wrong

In Chapter 2, we saw how pride leads to legalism. Once we begin judging for ourselves between right and wrong, once we start making up our own rules, we have taken the first step down the road of unjustly — and pridefully — judging others.

Prideful certainty

Chapter 3 showed how pride leads to unwarranted confidence in our own opinions, even though we're all bound to be wrong about many things. In light of this understanding, we should be much less confident in the judgments we form about others. Understanding and acknowledging the frailty of all minds, including ours, we owe charity toward those holding opinions or beliefs we think are misguided, foolish, or dangerous. We are all easily led astray.

---

[388] Østby, Hilde, Ylva Østby, and Sam Kean. *Adventures in Memory: The Science and Secrets of Remembering and Forgetting.* Vancouver ; Berkeley: Greystone Books, 2018.

Prideful ability: we overestimate our powers of discernment

When we form opinions regarding one another, we imagine we've made an impartial, unbiased, and fair appraisal of all the relevant facts. Oftentimes, especially in the presence of conflict, *none* of those conditions are true. Overconfidence in our own ability was the theme of Chapter 4. Our ability to evaluate other people is yet one more ability prone to prideful overconfidence. We tend to exaggerate our skills of discernment.

Prideful power: using control to judge and dominate others

In Chapter 5, we turned to illusions of control, how pride deceives us into believing we know what should happen and we can make it happen. Even though we do a pretty poor job of controlling ourselves, because we naïvely think it's possible, we expect the same of others:

> *"Of course, they could change if they really tried."*

> *"He could quit the habit if he really wanted to. I did."*

But that's the most benign expression. Far worse is the tendency of some to aggressively dominate others by judging their opinions and beliefs. Some people, by nature, relish the role of inquisitor, vigilantly seeking out the slightest whiff of departure from whatever they deem the orthodox position. It enhances their own sense of importance, however artificially. These tend to be the "dark triad" personality types discussed in Chapter 9, and resort to bullying, grandstanding, ramping up, and gaslighting to sow doubt and discord and stir up anger against their victims. In the Church, they distract followers of Christ from their God-given mission. Their numbers might be few, but they have an oversize impact because they tap directly into that root of pride within all of us.

Prideful virtue: We overestimate our personal goodness

I fear some of my present-day brothers and sisters must be deeply disappointed in Jesus:

> *"Turning water into wine? At a wedding, no less! That's even worse than drinking it! It's almost like He was encouraging other people to do it, too. And He was so passive about the Romans and all the social injustices they perpetrated: all that conquering, enslaving, taxing, and what-not. So intolerant of them....and He issued nary a word in condemnation or judgment!"*

I'd love to see them explain it to Jesus face to face. And I'm sure He would have a few words to offer in response: "Holier than me? We need to talk. I'll be with you as soon as I'm done talking with *these* Pharisees."

Prideful denial: we underestimate our depravity

Not only do we overestimate our goodness, we woefully underestimate our capacity for evil. Thus, we tend to see ourselves as better than we really are, constantly comparing ourselves, like the Pharisees, to those around us. This assumption of moral superiority may be the most corrupting and insidious contributor to an attitude of judgmentalism. Judgmentalism declares the accused to be inferior in competence or virtue compared to the judge. It might be the primary reason why Christians are perceived as judgmental: because the attitude too often conveyed is one of unabashed moral superiority.

Prideful self-promotion: it makes us feel important

Chapter 8 focused on self-exaltation, narcissism, and our craving for acclamation. When one believes she is the center of the universe, reality is painful, and people will inevitably disappoint. When that happens, look out. Those who disappoint a narcissist will be demonized, scorned, slandered, and rejected. Now, that describes the typical reaction of a vulnerable narcissist, but there is some inherent narcissism in all of us. Most of us are not so thin-skinned or easily offended, but we are not entirely immune either. When our prideful self-image is threatened, our nature is to shift into judgment mode against the attacker. "It can't be me," we reason, "so it must be him."

Prideful comparison: We promote ourselves by asserting superiority over others

Chapter 9 examined how pride seeks self-promotion through competition, which only works if we come out on top. We try to assert our superiority in many ways: physical strength, athletic prowess, intelligence, skill on the job, number of Christian activities, or maintaining an image of spiritual maturity.

Recall the two ways to resolve envy: 1) working hard to excel or 2) putting others down. Both are effective, but the second option is less work. So, we become experts at putting others down, i.e., judging. If we were honest and thinking Biblically, we would realize that any virtue we possess comes by God's grace. Instead, we assert our superiority by condemning others for sins we never had to struggle with. Or if we did, we only overcame by God's grace, so we still don't deserve any credit.

Prideful prejudice: We are biased in favor of people who are like us

---

Chapter 10 focused on prejudice — judgments based on a person's background, appearance, or other superficial characteristics — and why those judgments are deceptive and misleading. We also saw how we tend to favor people who are like us, exude personal charm, or appear physically attractive. People we like are granted the greater benefit of the doubt.

Conversely, people who are not like us, have a different political perspective, do not fit our social norms, or are unattractive, we treat more harshly. We are more likely to form negative impressions of their competence and character. Because our judgment is biased by factors having nothing actually to do with competence and character, it is rendered faulty and unjust.

Nine forms of judgmentalism — how to diagnose it

So now we understand that we're naturally bad at judging, and our ability to judge fairly is deeply tainted by pride. Any judgment based on Biblical principles must therefore proceed out of humility.

To answer our third and final question, I came up with a list. It's not comprehensive. Your list may be different. But it's somewhere to start. Improper judgment, or judgmentalism, can be any of the following:

---

1. Hypocrisy: condemning others for what we do ourselves (or our friends).

> "Therefore you are inexcusable, O man, whoever you are who judge, for in whatever you judge another you condemn yourself; for you who judge practice the same things."[389]

It's a tedious and overworn cliché to say Christians are hypocrites. Not that it's unfair, but redundant. All humans are hypocrites. Christians are human. Therefore, Christians are hypocrites. It's a workable syllogism, anyway. I've been around Christians my whole life; as hypocrites go, we're mostly in the bush leagues. There have been egregious examples among

---

[389] Romans 2:1

fallen Christian celebrities, but some were predictable (and every such failure underscores the dominance of pride).

Hypocrisy is rampant in the political arena. I could cite countless examples, but there's no point in getting sidetracked with anything sounding partisan. You know it's true.

But don't stop quite yet. Look in the mirror. If you are politically engaged, do you really think you're off the hook? Think about the last time a public figure was accused of malfeasance. (There's a new one every week, somewhere). All those biases we discussed earlier — confirmation bias, disconfirmation bias, attribution error — spring into action to defend if he's on our team and throw him under the bus if he's not. It requires intentional effort and a very high level of integrity to remain morally consistent when *political* issues are at stake. Perhaps, though, the *moral* issues are the ones we should care most about? Something to think about, anyway.

2. Judging with an attitude of moral superiority

> "Who sit among the graves and spend the night in the tombs;
> Who eat swine's flesh and the broth of abominable things is *in* their vessels;
> Who say, 'Keep to yourself, do not come near me, for I am holier than you!'
> These *are* smoke in My nostrils, a fire that burns all the day."[390]

Our examination of science and Scripture established that no one has a right to feel morally superior. Not everyone has the same opportunity. The ancient cities of Tyre and Sidon were judged and destroyed for their wickedness. During Jesus's time on earth, Chorazin, Capernaum, and Bethsaida felt morally superior to them. They shouldn't have:

> "Woe to you, Chorazin! Woe to you, Bethsaida! For if the mighty works which were done in you had been done in Tyre and Sidon, they would have repented long ago, sitting in sackcloth and ashes. But it will be more tolerable for Tyre and Sidon at the judgment than for you. And you, Capernaum, who are exalted to heaven, will be brought down to Hades. He who hears you hears Me, he who rejects you rejects Me, and he who rejects Me rejects Him who sent Me."[391]

---

[390] Isaiah 65:4-5
[391] Luke 10:13-16

This is one of the chief ways the Church can sabotage its witness if we are not watchful. There are only two types of people on this earth: redeemed sinners and unredeemed sinners. And God does all the redeeming.

3. Discounting the effects of the fall

Those of us who profess to be Christians must interpret the behavior of unbelievers by the light of Scripture. It is a gross theological error to suppose that unregenerate people could stop sinning if they choose. This is a particularly complicated subject involving nature, nurture, free will, and common grace. Different theological traditions balance these factors in different ways. However, there is one principle beyond dispute. The unregenerate cannot *not* sin.[392]

The idea that anyone by force of sheer will can live in perfect obedience is the heresy of Pelagianism, rejected by all Christian traditions. Unbelievers do have free will, but the corruption of our nature — so emphatically declared in Romans — ensures that they will freely prefer evil, though not every time or everywhere.

Not even Believers are promised complete victory over sin in this earthly life. For all of us, it is one choice at a time, one step at a time, and a lifetime of slow, incremental growth as the fruits of the Spirit mature and ripen within us.

4. Making assumptions regarding another's motives or character

Prideful presumption makes us believe we know people's motivations, but we're deluded. Trait ascription bias, projection bias, attribution error, and other habits lead us to assume we know the others' minds when we can't. There are two early steps toward overcoming these biases. First, we judge actions, not people. Second, and more importantly, the only way to know someone's reasons is to *ask them*. I was once at the receiving end of judgment from Christian neighbors who never bothered to ask my side of the story. They came across as shallow and judgmental, and it damaged our relationship. I'm sure most of you have had similar experiences — so you know just how wrong it is. Let's not do it.

---

[392] *"Non posse non peccare"* — not able not to sin. St. Augustine. Commonly cited. This is usually attributed to "A Treatise on Rebuke and Grace" Section 33, but I could not find it there.

5. Lack of empathy and indifference to mitigating factors

Nearly everyone enters adulthood with painful memories, emotional scars, learned fears, anxieties, and uncertainties. These might manifest as fear, depression, mistrust, hypersensitivity, or plain old crankiness. Those lucky few who were pampered as children and never experienced hurt, want, or struggle end up with their own set of problems.[393]

There is much tragedy and suffering in this world, most of it invisible. That woman who treated you so rudely might have just lost a child. That man might have just lost his job. The less well you know a person, the more reticent you should be to cast judgment. Even close ones, you probably don't know nearly as well as you think. It should be painfully obvious but is still often ignored: never judge a person until you've heard her side of the story.

6. Snap judgments based on appearance

Many years ago, a visiting pastor spoke at our church. He shared a story that made quite an impression upon me, though not the one that was intended. The reverend was passing through an airport. While waiting on a connection, he sat near a bar to watch a game on the wide-screen television. Out of the corner of his eye, he noticed a young lady sipping a glass of wine and smoking a cigarette. Her wardrobe, apparently, was not something he would have countenanced on his wife or daughter. As it came time to board, he saw her again at the gate. As the pastor related, he prayed [was he joking? It didn't sound like it] "Lord, please don't seat me next to her." Sure enough, once all were on board, there she was, same row, aisle seat to aisle seat. She was chatty, pleasant, and struck up a conversation:

> "What do you do?" she asked.

> "Well, I'm a minister," he replied uncomfortably.

> "Oh, that's great!" she chirped. "I go to [local megachurch in destination city]. It's an important part of my life."

> The pastor was dumbfounded.

There wasn't much more to the story. In his judgment, her lifestyle did not conform to her testimony. Based on superficial externalities, he made a judgment regarding her character. What's worse, he assumed that

---

[393] Gottlieb, Lori. "How to land your kid in therapy." *The Atlantic* 301, no. 1 (2011): 64-78.

everyone listening would see it the same way. With one exception, that may have been true. I didn't raise my hand.

How easily we succumb to this deceit. I've heard it often and have been guilty myself. We think less of people's character because of the clothes they wear, their jewelry, body piercing, tattoos, accent, weight, hairstyle.... the list is endless. Sure, some of those being judged can dish it right back. Most just give up and go where they will be welcome. This is not about tolerating immorality. It's about letting go of our legalism and prejudice.

Jesus was criticized by Pharisees for associating with sinners:

> "Now it happened, as He was dining in Levi's house, that many tax collectors and sinners also sat together with Jesus and His disciples; for there were many, and they followed Him. And when the scribes and Pharisees saw Him eating with the tax collectors and sinners, they said to His disciples, 'How is it that He eats and drinks with tax collectors and sinners?'

> "When Jesus heard it, He said to them, 'Those who are well have no need of a physician, but those who are sick. I have not come to call the righteous, but sinners, to repentance.'"[394]

Why are so many of his present-day followers shallow, self-righteous scolds?

7. Arbitrary ranking of sin severity

It's popular to say that all sins are the same in the sight of God. While the least of sins merits eternal judgment, it's flatly wrong to say they're all equal.

If we were to rank sins, there are different ways to do it. Would the greatest sin be a violation of the greatest commandment?

> "Love the Lord your God with all your heart, with all your soul, and with all your mind. This is the first and great commandment."[395]

Or should we rank them according to motive and consequences? Certainly, premeditated murder is worse than stealing a loaf of bread to feed a starving child. The Roman Catholic tradition developed a rather systematic

---

[394] Mark 2:15-17
[395] Matthew 22:37-38

ranking of sins according to severity. As I stated at the outset, many or most Church fathers considered Pride the greatest of sins. That's what I'm going with.

In our hedonistic and hypersexualized era, the cultural turmoil and dire social consequences of sexual immorality lead some to feel that sexual sins are the worst. The human sex drive tempts us into behavior that can often be stupid, dangerous, unhealthy, abusive, foolish, and short-sighted. Under the dominion of King Eros, we can be sacrificial or selfish, tender or cruel, brave or cowardly, noble or debased. Nonmarital sexual intimacy is like cocaine to the lonely. It can be hard to walk away from, easy to rationalize, and usually ends in grief. There are a lot of lonely people.

It's commonly believed that in ancient times sexual sins were considered the worst. That was possibly true in specific times and places (late Victorian England, maybe?), but ancient theologians were surprisingly compassionate regarding sexual failure, possibly modeling the attitude of Christ:

> "And behold, a woman in the city who was a sinner, when she knew that Jesus sat at the table in the Pharisee's house, brought an alabaster flask of fragrant oil, and stood at His feet behind *Him* weeping; and she began to wash His feet with her tears, and wiped *them* with the hair of her head; and she kissed His feet and anointed *them* with the fragrant oil. Now when the Pharisee who had invited Him saw *this*, he spoke to himself, saying, 'this Man, if He were a prophet, would know who and what manner of woman *this is* who is touching Him, for she is a sinner.'"[396]

Aquinas wrote that "a sin is the less grievous according as it is committed under the impulse of a greater passion" and "that of all a Christian's conflicts, the most difficult combats are those of chastity; wherein the fight is a daily one, but victory rare."[397] He concluded that "spiritual sins are more against Christ than fornication is." The spiritual sins, according to Aquinas, were pride, envy, avarice (greed), sloth, and anger. Not that Aquinas is the ultimate authority, but his opinions carried a lot of weight and usually reflected the mainstream of medieval thought.

It takes a great deal of self-discipline to keep sexual drives in check, but a far better restraint is the indwelling Spirit of God. Without compromising the clear teaching of Scripture in sexual matters, we should follow the

---

[396] Luke 7:37-39
[397] Aquinas. *Summa Theologica*, Question 154 Article 3

example of Jesus and the advice of the ancient Church and show mercy toward those who stumble.

8. Judging with ulterior motives

> "Then all the tax collectors and the sinners drew near to Him to hear Him. And the Pharisees and scribes complained, saying, 'This Man receives sinners and eats with them.'"[398]

On many occasions, the gospels report that Jesus was condemned by the religious leaders, including the priests, the scribes, the lawyers, and the Pharisees. Why were they so harsh on Jesus? There were lots of others they could have picked on. Scripture makes the motive clear: they were envious of the attention He was getting, and probably of His power. They were not judging out of zeal for God, but out of pure self-interest.

We do the same thing. Sins we would be willing to forgive or overlook if committed by a friend, family member, or politician of our own party become unredeemable character flaws in someone we oppose. If we genuinely had the mind of Christ, we would grieve over the sins of others, but in secret, we delight when an opponent stumbles. There was an unseemly amount of glee in conservative circles during the Clinton years as one scandal after another broke the headlines, but it cuts both ways.

Shortly before the 2006 mid-term elections, I was dining with my wife at a favorite restaurant. We were seated next to a group of about six middle-aged adult women. Oblivious to those around them, they raised their glasses in a toast to a Republican representative caught in a scandal, forced to resign over lurid emails sent to teenage male pages. The storm of condemnation raised against him met with their delight, hoping — correctly, as it turned out — his disgrace would help turn the election in favor of Democrats.

I've seen the same sort of behavior among Christians. The severity of the offense depends upon the tribal identity of the offender. You know it's true.

9. Unbiblical mandates

Judgmentalism springs out of legalism like rats from a sewer. Sometimes, the harshest condemnations are based on man-made rules found nowhere in God's word.

---

[398] Luke 15:1-2

Abstinence from alcohol is a defensible position on medical and social grounds, but to some, it is a nonnegotiable requirement of the sanctified life. It's a classic example of "presentism." Prior to the late 19th century, the entire Christian world used wine in communion. Luther, Calvin, Wesley, and Whitfield all enjoyed their wine or beer with apologies to none. Catholic monks were among the leading producers. Nobody cared.[399] That began to change in 1869 when Thomas Bramwell Welch invented a way to preserve unfermented grape juice, and his son Charles launched a marketing push to replace communion wine with Welch's Grape juice.[400] As a business strategy, it was brilliant — and wildly successful.

Rather than a moral crusade by religious zealots, the prohibition movement was an entirely rational reaction to the misery inflicted by alcohol abuse. It was supported by a broad array of interests: capitalists tired of workers showing up drunk, communists seeing it as a tool of capitalist oppression, nationalists making life hard for German beer makers (and drinkers) during World War I, and last but not least, the Women's Christian Temperance Union. Throughout American history, rarely has a cause united so many opposing factions.[401]

Christian teetotalism emerged out of 19th and 20th century American culture. Nothing is wrong with making a personal decision to abstain from something if it ends there. Far too often, it seems the main benefits of abstaining are to assume moral superiority over those who don't and establish one's credentials among those who do.

Judgments based on unbiblical mandates are found many times in Scripture. Jesus was criticized for eating and drinking; John the Baptist for *not* eating and *not* drinking.[402] The Pharisees condemned Jesus for healing on the Sabbath — and they were the ones who made up the rule.[403] Peter was criticized by fellow believers for dining with the uncircumcised.[404]

There are other man-made standards we could name. The Bible says nothing about marginal tax rates, how much federal entitlement is enough, or which environmental policies are most effective. That doesn't stop many from attempting to sanctify their political agenda, which is *no fun at all* if you don't get to judge your opponents.

---

[399] West, Jim. *Drinking with Calvin and Luther!: The Reformational View of Beer and Wine.* Carmichael, CA: Oakdown, 1996.
[400] "Grape Juice." In *Wikipedia*, May 12, 2022. https://en.wikipedia.org/wiki/Grape_juice 2
[401] Burns, Ken, dir. *Prohibition.* Public Broadcasting System, 2011
[402] Matthew 11:18-19
[403] John 5:16
[404] Acts 11:2

Conclusion

We are naturally inclined to judge others, but we're lousy at doing it. Pride distorts our perspective through thinking too highly of ourselves and too little of others. We build ourselves up by putting others down. We arrogate to ourselves the right to judge which behaviors are worse and are unlikely to consider we might be wrong.

Christians have a responsibility toward one another and to God, commanded in Scripture, to speak out against sin and address the sins of one another. Unbiblical judgmentalism consists of:

1. Condemning others for what we ourselves do
2. Judging with an attitude of moral superiority
3. Underestimating the nature of fallenness
4. Making assumptions about another's motives or character
5. Lacking empathy and showing indifference to mitigating factors
6. Making snap judgments on superficial appearance
7. Arbitrarily considering certain sins worse than others
8. Judging with ulterior motives
9. Judging based on unbiblical mandates

Key points

- Making judgments is not the same as judgmentalism
- Judgmentalism presents in many ways, but the common denominator is pride

Spirit Wars: A New Hope

The Virtue of Humility

Among monotheistic traditions, only the Christian deity has personally known and demonstrated humility. To come in the flesh and ransom us from damnation, the Holy Christ set aside His glory and endured poverty, suffering, injustice, rejection, betrayal, torture, and death. It is in this context that we are admonished by Paul to adopt the mind of Christ. Like Jesus, we are called to humble ourselves — and to sacrifice our personal rights and claims for the welfare of others.

"If you should ask me what are the ways of God, I would tell you that the first is humility, the second is humility, and the third is humility. Not that there are no other precepts to give, but if humility does not precede all that we do, our efforts our meaningless." — ST. AUGUSTINE [405]

"If anyone would like to acquire humility, I can, I think, tell him the first step. The first step is to realize that one is proud. And a biggish step, too. At least, nothing whatever can be done before it. If you think you are not conceited, it means that you are very conceited indeed." — C. S. LEWIS [406]

If you've made it this far, congratulations! I appreciate your hanging with me! We've traveled a long way, and I hope you're convinced that pride is a serious and under-appreciated sin that corrupts the church and tarnishes every aspect of our lives. It may seem time to wrap it up, say, "now that you

---

[405] Augustine. Letter 118.22. This is a widely circulated translation I could not track to the source. A different translation is here: "CHURCH FATHERS: Letter 118 (St. Augustine)." Accessed May 23, 2022. https://www.newadvent.org/fathers/1102118.htm.
[406] "The Great Sin". In Lewis, *Mere Christianity*.

know what not to do, don't do it!" and end our study. But we're only half-way there. Definitely, please examine yourself for any of the behaviors we've described and strive to avoid them. But that alone is not sufficient. There is much more to humility than "just stop it!"

What's humility?

Unfortunately, the popular conception of humility often evokes the scheming, obsequious Uriah Heep from *David Copperfield*. (That is, before he embezzled his way into controlling the business). I hope to disabuse anyone of that misconception, for Heep v1.0 was anything but humble.

We opened our exploration of pride with the account of an ancient drama in the spiritual realm. It is fitting, then, that an understanding of humility also begins in the spiritual realm.

Most of the major world faiths pay homage to the virtue of humility. Several passages in the Koran echo the Bible in denouncing pride and exalting the virtue of humility. Hindu, Buddhist, and Confucian traditions all, to a greater or lesser degree, take the same position.[407] But Christianity stands out in at least one unique and dramatic regard. Only in Christianity is humility *an attribute of God*. Paul's epistle to the Philippians teaches this explicitly:

> "Let this mind be in you which was also in Christ Jesus, who, being in the form of God, did not consider it robbery to be equal with God, but made Himself of no reputation, taking the form of a bond-servant, *and* coming in the likeness of men. And being found in appearance as a man, He humbled Himself and became obedient to *the point of* death, even the death of the cross."[408]

Jesus humbled Himself not only in surrendering His Glory and being born as a human babe, but throughout His life, His ministry, and His relationship to the Father — setting a pattern for us to follow:

> "By myself I can do nothing."[409]

> "For I have come down from heaven not to do my will."[410]

---

[407] Porter, Steven L., Anantanand Rambachan, Abraham Vélez de Cea, Dani Rabinowitz, Stephen Pardue, and Sherman Jackson. "Religious perspectives on humility." In *Handbook of humility*, pp. 63-77. Routledge, 2016.
[408] Philippians 2:5-8
[409] John 5:30
[410] John 6:38

"My teaching is not my own"[411]

In His earthly ministry, this was perhaps most perfectly exemplified at the Last Supper, when Jesus assumed the role of a servant and proceeded to wash the feet of His disciples.[412] What we see here is the opposite of Nebuchadnezzar. The King of Babylon grasped at a glory he did not merit. The Lord of the Universe laid aside a glory that was eternally His.

Pride is a lack of humility, but humility is much more than the absence of pride.

So, what is humility?

It is sometimes asserted that evil does not exist in and of itself, but always represents the deprivation of a particular good. This principle traces at least back to St. Augustine. There might be exceptions, but the rule generally seems to hold. It makes sense here. While it is true that pride is thinking "too high of oneself" (Edwards), I propose that humility is not just "the proper estimate of oneself" (Charles Spurgeon) but something deeper, richer, and more dynamic.

If humility were just the absence of pride, how could God be humble? He's God! There can be nothing or no one more holy, perfect, or powerful. But by humbling Himself, the eternal second person of the Trinity did something vastly transcending a "proper estimate of oneself." Relinquishing His Glory, the Holy, Omniscient, Omnipotent God took the form of a helpless infant in a powerless, poverty-stricken backwater of the Roman Empire and submitted to harassment, ridicule, mockery, torture, and the cruelest of executions; while continuing to love, serve, and forgive his abusers. Genuine humility will cost you your ego, but the empyreal price was God dying upon a cross.

In His incarnation, Christ showed that humility is a foundational virtue upon which all others depend.

> "Humility is the only soil in which virtue takes root; a lack of humility is the explanation of every defect and failure."[413] — ANDREW MURRAY

---

[411] John 7:16
[412] John 13:1-15
[413] Murray. p 17

In their introduction to *Handbook of Humility* (a compilation of reviews and research), Everett Worthington and co-authors proposed three "core aspects" of humility:[414]

1. Accurate assessment of self
2. Modest self-presentation
3. An interpersonal stance that is other-oriented rather than self-oriented

Academic study on humility has generally not focused on the spiritual elements (with a few exceptions). And the tools of social psychology are ill-suited for the study of theology. I will follow an approach similar to Worthington's while adding the spiritual dimensions:

1. Surrender to a proper understanding of self
2. Embrace the attitudes and demeanor of humility
3. Embrace a lifestyle of humility in relation to God and others

We can approach humility in these three stages. First, accept the reality of our present state by confessing our pride. Second, replace prideful attitudes with a humble approach to God, others, and self. Third, embrace humility as a lifestyle, for fully fleshed out humility leads to a changed relationship with God, others, and self.

Three steps to Humility.

Step 1: Surrender to a proper understanding of self.

The Biblical view of the human soul is in stark contrast to everything pride would have us believe. Humility must acknowledge several fundamental principles about ourselves that are taught in Scripture and affirmed through experience. Here we recapitulate the previous chapters, which (I hope) were far more than a detached academic reflection of pride. They were a description of each of us and our shortcomings. Not equally in every instance, for sure. But no one escapes conviction.

---

[414] Worthington Jr, Everett L., Don E. Davis, and Joshua N. Hook. "Introduction: Context, overview, and guiding questions." In *Handbook of Humility*, pp. 17-32. Routledge, 2016.

I am compromised in my ability to distinguish right from wrong (Chapter 2)

"There is a way that seems right to a man,
But its end is the way of death."[415]

To Adam and Eve, Satan dangled the power to decide for themselves between good and evil. The sum of human history tells us that evil often prevails. It is not a matter of some being good and others being bad, religion versus atheism, capitalism versus socialism, imperialism versus autonomy, or wealth versus poverty. It is a problem fundamental to human nature.

God has implanted the moral law within our hearts, created us with a conscience, and delivered His revealed law through the Prophets, Apostles, and our Lord. Legalism is like gravity, but it doesn't pull us toward holiness. It pulls us to vigorously enforce the laws we like and minimize the ones we find inconvenient.

I am easily deceived and overly confident (Chapter 3)

We are trusting by nature but much more trusting of people who are like us. The world is such a vast and complicated affair that no one has the intellectual capability to fully understand anything beyond his own tiny sliver of reality — and even that link is tenuous at best. What's worse, we have an Achilles heel of exquisite vulnerability — our pride. We are most easily deceived by those who tell us what we want to hear, beginning with our own inner voice.

It's easy to be wrong about things. In fact, it's impossible for us *not to be* wrong about many things. But certainty rooted in our pride enables error to progress from benign and curable to malignant and deadly.

I am powerless apart from God's Grace (Chapters 4 and 5)

There is a human tendency to exaggerate our abilities. In our heart of hearts, we want to be at least as good — but preferably better than — our peers. This tendency can cause us to be overly satisfied with our present state and quench the incentive to strive towards excellence. In the worst of cases, it can be deadly.

We are prone to overestimate our control over people and events, and attempt to dominate people with self-serving motives. Our mutual desire to dominate each other is a prime driver of conflict, and everyone thinks

---

[415] Proverbs 14:12

they're on the right side. The reality is that very little is under our direct control, and we're terrible at predicting the future. Thankfully, God expects us merely to be faithful and leave the results to Him.

I am morally corrupt (Chapters 6 and 7)

"O God, You know my foolishness;
And my sins are not hidden from You."[416]

Most of us think we're very good people. We might admit we're sinners with our lips, but what we feel deep inside is more revealing.

Recall the wisdom of Solzhenitsyn: "the line dividing good and evil cuts through the heart of every human being."[417] We are all capable of great indifference and cruelty. Perhaps most of the time, we can constrain those impulses, thanks to the Grace of God mediated through institutions of family, church, and the civilizing impact of Christianity. But it sure is tempting to believe we really are better, deep inside.

I lust after glory and claim credit I don't deserve. (Chapter 8)

Whatever we achieve, we owe in part to the many opportunities provided along the way, through the luck of being born at a particular place in time to a particular family, education, connections, health, or purely random events that worked in our favor. Our fallen hearts yearn for fame, glory, and acclamation. We claim full credit for our own achievements, great or small, but blame our failures on people or circumstances beyond our control.

I am no better than others (Chapters 9, 10, and 11)

Our unfortunate drive to feel superior to others leads to envy, conflict, prejudice, judgmentalism, and estrangement from God and our neighbors. We strive to outdo one another in virtue and religiosity, not out of love for God but for the admiration and respect of our peers.

We naturally favor people who look, act, and think like us but are prone to think less of those who are not. But all are equal in the eyes of God, and whatever goodness we possess, we owe to His divine grace. Unbiblical judgmentalism is far more than calling out sin. It is the culmination and outpouring of a prideful heart.

---

[416] Psalm 69:5
[417] Solzhenitsyn, *The Gulag Archipelago, 1918-1956*

After understanding and confessing these prideful tendencies, the next stage is to supplant them with attitudes of humility. Humble people approach these matters from a completely different mindset.

Step 2: Embrace the attitudes of humility

Attitude of repentance — toward God and others.

Prideful people find it hard to apologize because they must maintain the impossible façade of self-righteousness. They deny their wrongdoing to others; they may not even admit wrongdoing to themselves. We are experts at self-rationalization and denial. A 2021 study demonstrated that a self-protecting disposition (measured by a commonly used scale) strongly predicted unwillingness to apologize in a hypothetical scenario.[418]

Humility, on the other hand, "is a robust predictor of apology behavior," according to a large study published in December 2021.[419]

Apologies, in turn, are a strong predictor of reconciliation in fractured relationships. This is one of many chains of causality whereby humility leads to a better life.

> "The Lord is near to those who have a broken heart, and saves such as have a contrite spirit."[420]

> "Confess your trespasses to one another, and pray for one another, that you may be healed."[421]

Attitude of gratitude

The Bible consistently reminds us that all things come from God:

> "But who am I, and who are my people, that we should be able to offer so willingly as this? For all things come from You, And of Your own we have given You.... O Lord our God, all this abundance that we have prepared to build You a house for Your holy name is from Your hand, and is all Your own."[422]

---

[418] Leunissen, Joost, Karina Schumann, and Constantine Sedikides. "Self-protection predicts lower willingness to apologize." *The Journal of Social Psychology* (2021): 1-10.
[419] Ludwig, Justin & Schumann, Karina & Porter, Tenelle. (2021). Humble and Apologetic? Predicting Apology Quality with Intellectual and General Humility. Personality and Individual Differences. 188. 10.1016/j.paid.2021.111477.
[420] Psalm 34:18
[421] James 5:16
[422] 1 Chronicles 29:14-16

Christians regularly talk about thankfulness, but why would the humble be any more grateful? Because humble people feel much less entitled and understand they receive much more than they deserve. If you've ever been in a relationship with a narcissist, you know why this must be so. It is impossible to be grateful when nothing is ever enough, and one always feels they deserve more. The Bible sets us straight on that account:

> "He has not dealt with us according to our sins,
> Nor punished us according to our iniquities."[423]

Not only is gratitude more virtuous, but it also promotes better mental health. Grateful people experience more and better relationships, better psychological and physical health, and other benefits, including better sleep.[424] This has sparked attempts to enhance gratitude in many clinical trials. While a 2016 meta-analysis found limited and inconclusive evidence of any benefit from gratitude "interventions,"[425] a more recent study focusing on people with higher levels of depression and anxiety showed definite positive effects.[426]

Gratitude is not always easy. Terrible things happen, sometimes unavoidable and through no fault of our own. Even when we humbly acknowledge our guilt and self-serving bias, this remains a fallen world filled with broken people who can hurt and treat us unjustly. The counsel of Scripture is to persevere:

> "In everything give thanks; for this is the will of God in Christ Jesus for you."[427]

In this passage, the preposition "in" (ἐν) carries a lot of weight. It refers to position, meaning *"wherever* you find yourself, give thanks." It does not mean *for* everything. Some people feel obligated to give thanks *for* everything. That's just nuts. Even Jesus didn't do that.

---

[423] Psalms 103:10
[424] Morin, Amy. "7 Scientifically proven benefits of gratitude." *Psychology Today* (2015). https://www.psychologytoday.com/us/blog/what-mentally-strong-people-dont-do/201504/7-scientifically-proven-benefits-gratitude
[425] Davis, Don E., Elise Choe, Joel Meyers, Nathaniel Wade, Kristen Varjas, Allison Gifford, Amy Quinn et al. "Thankful for the little things: A meta-analysis of gratitude interventions." *Journal of counseling psychology* 63, no. 1 (2016): 20.
[426] Bohlmeijer, E.T., Kraiss, J.T., Watkins, P. and Schotanus-Dijkstra, M., 2021. Promoting gratitude as a resource for sustainable mental health: results of a 3-armed randomized controlled trial up to 6 months follow-up. *Journal of happiness studies*, 22(3), pp.1011-1032.
[427] I Thessalonians 5:18

Attitude of dependence

Admitting that we are powerless and not in control should lead us to recognize our utter dependence upon God. Through daily prayer, we make "every request" known unto God while praying that His will, not our will, be done. "Give us this day our daily bread" is a reminder that we depend upon Him for everything, and every good thing comes from Him.

> "I need Thee every hour, most gracious Lord;
> No tender voice like thing can peace afford.
> I need thee, O I need thee;
> Every hour I need thee."[428]

The relationship between religious faith and anxiety is complex. External practices, such as service attendance, have little effect. Internalized beliefs are strongly linked in both positive and negative ways. Those whose faith is based on fear of judgment and rejection obviously experience higher anxiety. Internalized faith from a heart of gratitude and dependence correlates strongly with lower anxiety levels.[429] Indeed, His yoke is easy, and His burden is light.

Attitude of reverence:

> "The boastful shall not stand in Your sight; You hate all workers of iniquity....But as for me, I will come into Your house in the multitude of Your mercy; In fear of You I will worship toward Your holy temple."[430]

The "fear of the Lord" is an admission of God's mighty power and holiness, not a baseline state of terror. Pride causes us to question God's goodness and sovereignty, while humility embraces both. Prideful people expect much, so they are constantly disappointed. It's impossible to maintain a proper concept of God if you think He keeps "letting you down."

Reverence is "a feeling or attitude of deep respect tinged with awe."[431] Pride doesn't like to share attention with anyone or anything. It blocks our view. When pride is toppled, our perspective expands to fully experience the incredible wonder of God's goodness, His Creation, and His Holy Word.

---

[428] Annie S Hawks. *I need thee every hour.* 1872
[429] Rosmarin, David H., and Bethany Leidl. "Spirituality, religion, and anxiety disorders." *Handbook of spirituality, religion, and mental health* (2020): 41-60.
[430] Psalm 5:5,7
[431] www.dictionary.com. "Definition of Reverence | Dictionary.Com." Accessed May 22, 2022. https://www.dictionary.com/browse/reverence.

Attitude of worship

"Both riches and honor come from You,
And You reign over all.
In Your hand is power and might;
In Your hand *it is* to make great
And to give strength to all.[432]

Proud people primarily worship themselves, though outwardly, they may engage in ostentatious public worship (like the Pharisees whom Jesus denounced in Matthew 7). Humble people aren't concerned with public displays of religiosity or what others think but worship with their hearts, minds, and actions. We are to be a "living sacrifice," expressing our devotion both through regular and consistent corporate worship among an organized body of believers and in our ordinary daily chores and leisure time, doing everything "as unto the Lord."[433]

How should we view Sunday worship from the perspective of pride and humility? For the individual, it means, first and foremost, that you come to serve others and worship our Lord. A humble person doesn't expect to be fed, enlightened, entertained, affirmed, validated, honored, or even noticed. He doesn't insist on his own musical tastes. She doesn't criticize the preaching, the décor, or how other people dress. We enter the presence of the Lord to praise and adore Him.

But on the other side, those leading in worship carry an even higher burden of humility. The preacher has a God-given duty to deliver teaching that is well-prepared, Biblically sound, and addressed to the spiritual needs of his particular congregation. Music leaders should pursue excellence because God deserves nothing less than our best. It's often claimed that the definition of "good" music is totally subjective, but that's not entirely true. Time is an excellent discriminator. Good music endures; the jetsam sinks quickly. If we just had a rule that any song used in public worship had to be at least five or ten years old, the quality of music would spike immediately.

"When I survey the wondrous cross
On which the Prince of glory died,
My richest gain I count but loss,
And pour contempt on all my pride."[434]

---

[432] I Chronicles 29:12
[433] Romans 12:1, Colossians 3:23
[434] Isaac Watts. *When I survey the Wondrous Cross.* 1707.

Music ought to be a corporate experience. Being filled with the Spirit, we are called to speak and sing together "in psalms and hymns and spiritual songs."[435] That's not possible when the songs are unsingable except by pros. It's not honored when the worship music is a semiprofessional stage performance while the congregation mostly listens along. I have my own musical preferences, but I don't expect others to share them. Instead, I follow a relatively simple principle. When I visit a church, I look around to see if the congregation is singing along out loud. If they are, terrific! If they look confused and their lips aren't moving, in my opinion, the worship leaders are on the wrong path.

Acceptance of correction

"The humble He guides in justice, And the humble He teaches His way."[436]

Proud people bristle at criticism. They may admit they're imperfect but feel perfectly able to spot their own shortcomings. A prideful person perceives the critic as annoying and probably wrong.

Humble people take criticism in stride. It may not always be valid, but at least they'll take time to reflect upon it, and there might be a kernel of truth. We all have our blind spots.

Acceptance of wise counsel

"The way of a fool is right in his own eyes, but he who heeds counsel is wise."[437]

"In Your hand it is to make great and to give strength to all."[438]

Proud people don't seek advice, don't think they need it, and don't welcome it. If they ever do, it could only come from someone they perceive as their superior.

Humble people seek counsel intentionally and with eagerness. They can accept advice from people in any station of life but might be particularly *suspicious* of the "high and mighty." The humble are never satisfied with their fund of knowledge and wisdom but always seek to learn and grow. This is the essence of a "growth mindset," something we will examine shortly.

---

[435] Ephesians 5:19
[436] Psalms 25:9
[437] Proverbs 12:15
[438] 1 Chronicles 29:12

Over the course of my life, I've sought advice from many sources at many times. Sometimes the advice was transformational; other times, it was truly dreadful. Through some of the toughest periods of my life, I wish I had gotten more advice. There wasn't ever a time I didn't want it. I just didn't know where to find it. Sometimes the best advice came from unexpected sources: a book I just happened to pick up, a conference talk from someone I'd never heard of.

I don't have any secret formula for finding advice or sorting out the good from the bad. Just pursue it faithfully and don't give up. Expertise really does matter. If you're going for marriage counseling, you probably don't want to be their very first case.

Intellectual humility

Proud people are very sure of themselves and quite happy just as they are. They love to argue but don't invest much effort in learning. They may not know everything, but don't try telling them that.

Humble people practice principles of sound Christian thinking, understand there's always more to learn, and never stop trying. Intellectual humility is so fundamental and so rarely mentioned it will be the primary focus of the next chapter.

Step 3: Embrace a lifestyle of humility

> "He must increase, but I must decrease." — JOHN THE BAPTIST, at the beginning of Jesus's ministry[439]

From eliminating prideful beliefs to embracing humble attitudes, humility must eventually lead to new patterns of behavior. A humble lifestyle follows the pattern of Christ by submission to God, service to our neighbor, and fruitfulness in good works.

As I explained, humility is much more than a proper self-image. It is a positive Virtue and one of the Fruits of the Spirit. Because of that, humility is not something we should strive to achieve through our own effort. If that were possible, we'd be right back where we started. Explained Murray:

> "External teaching and personal effort are powerless to conquer pride or create the meek and lowly heart in a person."[440]

---

[439] John 3:30
[440] Murray, p. 46

Further on:

> "It is only by the indwelling of Christ in His divine humility that we
> can become truly humble."[441]

A lifestyle of modesty

> "It is no great thing to be humble when you are brought low; but
> to be humble when you are praised is a great and rare achieve-
> ment." — BERNARD OF CLAIRVAUX

Modesty: "The quality of being modest, or having a moderate opinion of
oneself; reserve springing from an unexaggerated estimate of one's qualities; freedom from presumption, ostentation, arrogance, or impudence."[442]

In early 21st century America, few things run against the cultural grain so
much as modesty. Politicians, athletes, entertainers, and talentless celebrities seem locked in a battle for supremacy over who can be the most *im-
modest*.

Back in 2011, modesty made a brief comeback when *New York Times* col-
umnist David Brooks wrote a column entitled "The Modesty Manifesto,"
followed by a talk that summer at the Aspen Institute.[443] Brooks spoke
about the disturbing rise of narcissism and self-aggrandizement in the
public arena. As far as I can ascertain, this went exactly *nowhere*. (Something about seeds and Aspen and rocky soil, possibly. Who knows?)

Modesty isn't dead. I've had the privilege of knowing many modest people,
beginning with my beloved parents. With genuinely humble people, there
is a "modesty paradox." As humility increases, people are *less likely* to think
they are humble or describe themselves in such terms. Uriah Heep would
have utterly failed that test. I'm sure Dickens knew that.

A lifestyle of submission to God

We model the life of Christ in submission to God's Law and His will. Proud
people interpret Scripture in a way that affirms their own opinions. They
love to impress others with their scrupulous conduct, generous contribu-
tions, verbose public prayers, and regular denunciation of their opponents.

Humble people only expect to be seen as the sinners they know themselves to be. They don't see any justification for putting people down,
knowing that only the Grace of God stands between them and the worst of

---

[441] Murray, p. 47
[442] "Modesty." *The Oxford English Dictionary.*
[443] Brooks, David. "The modesty manifesto." *The New York Times* March 11 (2011).

sinners. The humble come to Scripture for correction and instruction, not personal validation.

A lifestyle of service and sacrifice

> "Our humility toward others is the only sufficient proof that our humility before God is real."[444]

We model the life of Christ in service to one another and to those who have yet come to faith. While proud people are focused on themselves, the humble are focused on others. We are freed from comparing ourselves to others in skill, knowledge, virtue, or accomplishments. We approach others to serve rather than to be served. We live for others; we die for others. The humble person is cleansed of the poison of envy.

In my life and travels, I personally have known many missionary physicians who live these principles on a daily basis. Stateside, the humble are serving in the inner city, prisons, crisis pregnancy centers, and schools. Genuinely humble people are usually not well-known. The last will be first.

> "[There is] nothing so divine as being the servant and helper of all"[445]

> "Greater love has no one than this, than to lay down one's life for his friends."[446]

Proud people endeavor to serve where they can shine, feel important, or be personally fulfilled. Humble people serve where they are most needed. Could this be why the typical church finds it much easier to recruit adult Sunday School teachers than nursery workers?

A lifestyle of fruitfulness and stewardship

We model the life of Christ by using the gifts He has given us in productive service to God and others, "redeeming the time, because the days are evil."[447] The Epistle of James may seem upon first reading to teach salvation by works. Almost all denominational traditions teach the proper understanding that good works are evidence of salvation, not a means to it.

---

[444] Murray, p. 53
[445] Murray, p. 11
[446] John 15:13
[447] Ephesians 5:16

"What does it profit, my brethren, if someone says he has faith but does not have works? Can faith save him?"[448]

So now we understand that humility is far more than public modesty, though humble people must certainly be modest. It is more than the mere absence of pride. Humility is a multidimensional virtue, like faith or love.

The fruits of humility

The thrust of this book so far has emphasized the personal and civilizational destruction wrought by pride. For nearly every affliction I've mentioned so far, humility leads to the opposite result.

Personal humility contributes to better mental and physical health.[449] It has been linked to higher marital satisfaction and better social relationships.[450] Management experts have recognized for many years that humility is a recurring trait of the most successful corporate executives.[451]

But these only scratch the surface. Academic researchers are just beginning to tap into and recognize the vast blessings promised by the Lord above to those who follow Him in Humility. Please stay with me.

Coming up

In our concluding chapters, we revisit the key aspects of pride, focusing on how such attitudes can be transformed by humility.

- Intellectual pride, or pride of mind, (Chapter 3), is to be forsaken for intellectual humility, the focus of Chapter 13.

- Interpersonal matters of conflict, prejudice, and judgmentalism (Chapters 9, 10, and 11) are remedied by relational humility (Chapter 14).

---

[448] James 2:14
[449] Toussaint, Loren L., and Jon R. Webb. "The humble mind and body: A theoretical model and review of evidence linking humility to health and well-being." In *Handbook of Humility*, pp. 194-207. Routledge, 2016.
[450] Garthe, Rachel C., Chelsea A. Reid, Terri N. Sullivan, and Brianne Cork. "Humility in Romantic Relationships." In *Handbook of Humility*, pp. 237-248. Routledge, 2016.
[451] Collins, James C. *Good to Great: Why Some Companies Make the Leap--and Others Don't.* New York, NY: HarperBusiness, 2001.

- Self-righteousness (Chapters 6 and 7) must yield to submission, gratitude, and repentance (Chapter 15).

- Pride of self-importance, power, ability, and control (Chapters 4, 5, and 8) must lead to the admission of our own helplessness, servanthood, and confidence in God's sovereignty (Chapter 16).

Key Points

- Humility is a positive virtue and is part of the very nature of God
- The three steps to humility consist of:
  - Embracing a proper understanding of self
  - Replacing pride with the attitudes of humility
  - Adopting a lifestyle of humility in relationship with God and our neighbors
- Humility will lead to abundant blessings

«13»

"Let This Mind be in You"

The Thinking Christian

Of pride's many manifestations, intellectual pride is the deadliest — and most unappreciated. And the smarter you think you are, the bigger a problem it is. Scripture repeatedly emphasizes the danger of putting too much faith in ourselves. Modern research affirms this. The antidote is to develop a truly Christian mind, and the foundation is intellectual humility.

———

"For I say, through the grace given to me, to everyone who is among you, not to think of himself more highly than he ought to think, but to think soberly, as God has dealt to each one a measure of faith." [452]

"We know that we all have knowledge. Knowledge puffs up, but love edifies. And if anyone thinks that he knows anything, he knows nothing yet as he ought to know." [453]

"The fool doth think he is wise, but the wise man knows himself to be a fool." [454]

———

In Chapter 3, we examined the singular peril of intellectual pride and the social and spiritual carnage left in its wake. No matter where you stand, it should be apparent that a large swath of humanity confidently clings to tenets that are demonstrably untrue. Moreover, these beliefs are not borne exclusively of facts, experience, and logic but a deadly array of confounding factors. The vast complexity of most subjects, misinformation, disinformation, and information overload preclude anyone from total mastery of an issue. There is one and only one solution: intellectual humility. From an academic standpoint, this has become an intense area of interest in the last

---

[452] Romans 12:3
[453] 1 Corinthians 8:1-2
[454] William Shakespeare. *As You Like It* Act 5 Scene 1

fifteen or so years. Here again, psychologists are rediscovering and affirming fundamental Biblical principles written two thousand or more years ago.

Developing a Christian mind is not optional for the believer. We are commanded by God. "Do not be conformed to this world, but be transformed by the *renewing of your mind*, that you may prove what is that good and acceptable and perfect will of God."[455]

The Christian mind is humble — intellectual humility

Naturally, having spent so much time examining the nature and danger of pride, it follows that humility should be the foundation on which we must build.

> "Do not be wise in your own eyes; fear the Lord and depart from evil."[456]

> "The humble He guides in justice, and the humble He teaches His way."[457]

> "Do not be wise in your own opinion."[458]

> "If anyone thinks that he knows anything, he knows nothing yet as he ought to know."[459]

In earlier chapters, we saw what the Bible says about the fallen human mind. It is "deceitful above all things, and desperately wicked."[460]

Intellectual humility is an honest and willing admission that our knowledge is limited and our reasoning imperfect, with an ability to tolerate disagreement in a calm and respectful manner. From a research perspective, it is distinct from general humility.[461] Intellectually humble people tend to be more agreeable, less polarized, less argumentative, and less adamant about their own opinions. Does this describe anyone you know? Does it describe you?

One thing I will declare with certainty: it has nothing to do with

---

[455] Romans 12:2
[456] Proverbs 3:7
[457] Psalms 25:9
[458] Romans 12:16
[459] 1 Corinthians 8:2
[460] Jeremiah 17:9
[461] Davis, Don E., Kenneth Rice, Stacey McElroy, Cirleen DeBlaere, Elise Choe, Daryl R. Van Tongeren, and Joshua N. Hook. "Distinguishing intellectual humility and general humility." *The Journal of Positive Psychology* 11, no. 3 (2016): 215-224.

intelligence. I'm going to pull a "Paul" here: "If anyone thinks he may have confidence in the flesh, I more so."[462] At the age of four, I taught myself to read. At least that's what my mother said. I simply have no memory of a time when I could not. First grade lasted eleven days before they kicked me into second. At 16, I graduated from high school (*salutatorian* in a class of 1000 because of one tough drama teacher). I matriculated at Emory University on a National Merit Scholarship, graduated Phi Beta Kappa in three years, and finished medical school at 23 with National Board scores at the 98th percentile. In the top 0.01%, my SAT score secured my admission in the Triple Nine Society — only the top 5% of Mensa would qualify.

So, I was a quick learner and did well on tests, but it qualified me as an authority on *absolutely nothing*. That demands more than intelligence; it requires learning and wisdom. An ordinary person who cultivates his mind will end up far wiser than the savant who fritters away his time on videogames and YouTube.

The type of intelligence measured by standardized testing is an excellent predictor of academic success. But above a certain threshold, it is a very poor predictor of who will really excel. There are too many other factors that contribute toward success, such as emotional intelligence, creativity, and talent. Then there are the physical, personality, and social factors like extroversion, attractiveness, family tradition and culture, athletic ability, height (primarily for men), and sheer dumb luck. Finally, w*ho* you know really does matter, as we saw in the story of Bill Gates. [I rang up short in most of the things on that list].

Superior performance on standardized exams is less than it appears. C. S. Lewis was a genius by any reasonable measure and had a photographic memory of his vast library but struggled to get into Oxford because he was lousy at math. I'd far prefer being able to remember everything I read and to write like Lewis than to solve differential equations in my head.

But people still place great stock in intelligence. A well-known politician once boasted of being "a very stable genius." [I suppose that beats an *unstable* one, all other things being equal]. Is our faith in intelligence warranted? According to British science writer David Robson, probably not. In fact, it may be a liability.[463]

Anecdotal examples abound of brilliant people who believe crazy things. Arthur Conan Doyle, creator of the ruthlessly logical Sherlock Holmes, clung to a naïve but unshakeable faith in spiritualism and fairies. The late Nobel prize winner Kary Mullis recounted his meeting with a luminescent

---

[462] Philippians 3:4
[463] Robson, David. *The Intelligence Trap: Why Smart People Make Dumb Mistakes.* New York: W. W. Norton & Company, 2019.

alien raccoon and actively promoted astrology and AIDS denialism. The name most synonymous with genius — Albert Einstein — saw the hope of mankind in Vladimir Lenin and frittered away the final decades of his life stubbornly rejecting quantum theory. The tendency of Nobel prize winners to go off the rails is so commonplace that science writers coined "Nobel disease" as a term of derision.

Among the higher ranks of the intelligentsia, Robson documents that:

- College graduates are more likely to believe in ESP and "psychic healing."
- People with IQs over 140 are more likely to max out on their credit.
- High-IQ individuals consume more alcohol and are more likely to smoke or take illegal drugs.
- Members of Mensa place more confidence in astrology than does the general public

All I can say is that over a lifetime spanning six decades, I've been tricked many times, and I've been obliged to change my opinions about a lot of things.

By way of explanation, research finds that highly intelligent and educated people are much more confident, and this confidence makes them less likely to doubt their opinions or change their minds. Rather than pursuing truth wherever it leads, smarter people may channel their energy toward arguing and reinforcing their preexisting opinions. Robson enumerates research-based strategies for overcoming the intelligence trap. Not too surprisingly, it begins with intellectual humility. Humility is the bedrock principle for developing a Christian mindset.

Although Robson implies that intelligent people are less humble, the evidence is inconclusive. The Dunning-Kruger phenomenon that we referenced in Chapter 4 predicts that less intelligent people would be overconfident and more intelligent people more mindful of their limitations. But it's difficult to measure intellectual humility in a research setting, and one must be careful to distinguish between intelligence and knowledge. An intelligent person with a large fund of knowledge may be justifiably confident. A genius with a limited fund of knowledge should not be. One thing we know for sure is that intelligence does not protect against cognitive biases, although it does tend to correlate with higher curiosity and higher cognitive reflection ("thinking slow").

Recent research has shown a consistent correlation between intellectual humility and other principles of sound thinking: having a growth mindset, curiosity, open-minded thinking, cognitive reflection, and emotional regulation.[464] In a 2021 paper, researchers found that intellectual humility partially offsets the Dunning-Kruger effect. Low-performing subjects with low measures of intellectual humility showed a greater tendency to overestimate their performance.[465]

There have been increasing calls for greater humility in the scientific community. In 2021, an international team writing for *Nature Human Behavior* called attention to the replication crisis in social, behavioral, and life sciences — and the need for greater humility and transparency about the limitations of research.[466]

An attitude of humility admits how little it knows or understands. It is confident of God's Word and His faithfulness but tentative in its own opinions. The humble mind never imagines it has attained perfect understanding or infallibility. Learn to differentiate between belief and certainty. God's Word never fails, but we do — all the time. Be careful which one you are really trusting.

The late R. C. Sproul was a renowned theologian, thinker, and teacher. Many years ago — I couldn't possibly identify which recording, but it was in the early 2000s — I heard him express hope that when he got to heaven and knew all truth, he would be at least 80% correct in his theology. I could not think of a healthier or humbler attitude. Too many pastors and teachers know far less than Sproul yet are far more certain in their opinions. I've checked several times: "know-it-all" is never listed as a spiritual gift. So why do so many think they have it?

The Christian mind seeks wisdom — a growth mindset.

Christians talk a lot about wisdom. We like to think we have it and tend to want more of it. We hope that with wisdom, we could always make the best life decisions, so there's a certain self-interest at stake. But true wisdom can be costly and unpopular. A favorite passage is James 1:5:

> "If any of you lacks wisdom, let him ask of God, who gives to all liberally and without reproach, and it will be given to him."

This sounds a whole lot like a promise: "ask, and you shall receive." But

---

[464] Krumrei-Mancuso, Elizabeth J., Megan C. Haggard, Jordan P. LaBouff, and Wade C. Rowatt. "Links between intellectual humility and acquiring knowledge." *The Journal of Positive Psychology* 15, no. 2 (2020): 155-170.

[465] Leman, Joseph, Courtney Kurinec, and Wade Rowatt. "Overconfident and unaware: Intellectual humility and the calibration of metacognition." *The Journal of Positive Psychology* (2021): 1-19.

[466] Hoekstra, Rink, and Simine Vazire. "Aspiring to greater intellectual humility in science." *Nature human behaviour* 5, no. 12 (2021): 1602-1607.

there's a qualifier attached:

> "But let him ask in faith, with no doubting, for he who doubts is like a wave of the sea driven and tossed by the wind."[467]

Here's where it gets rather sticky. "Ask in faith, without doubting that I'm going to get it? Then I must claim my prayer has been answered. Hooray! I'm wise!"

No, no, no. The root of the word translated "doubting" is *diakrino* (διακρίνω). It has several meanings: to dispute, to contend, to withdraw from one, to prefer, etc. Common to all is that one who prays for wisdom must have a humble, teachable heart. Wisdom demands humility.

In 1984 I passed my radiology boards and received a lifetime certification from the American Board of Radiology. In subsequent decades, I witnessed the introduction and rapid expansion of clinical MRI, advanced MRI techniques, remarkable progress in the application of CT technology, recognition of new disease conditions, and new insights into the vast spectrum of known disorders. Imagine if I could remember every last fact I read during training — which would be quite an achievement — but simply stopped learning anything new. Today, I would be next to useless as a radiologist. Yet, this is precisely how some approach life in general and their Christian faith in particular. Why? Because of a certain mindset.

The concept of "mindset" was elaborated by Carol Dweck, a social psychologist at Stanford. She defined two types. A fixed mindset assumes intelligence is static and cannot be improved. Those with a fixed mindset tend to avoid challenges, give up easily, ignore criticism, resent the success of others, and ultimately fail to reach their life potential. A growth mindset believes intelligence can be developed, seeks new knowledge, embraces challenges, perseveres through setbacks, learns from criticism, and ultimately attains a higher level of achievement.

Given two individuals with precisely the same IQ, the one with a growth mindset will enjoy far greater success.[468] It is something that can be developed with practice and encouragement. A large national study showed it is highly effective in improving the math performance of underachieving American secondary school students with minimal effort.[469]

I'm not talking about positive thinking: a growth mindset demands action.

---

[467] James 1:6
[468] Dweck, Carol S. *Mindset: The New Psychology of Success.* New York: Ballantine Books, 2008.
[469] Yeager, David S., Paul Hanselman, Gregory M. Walton, Jared S. Murray, Robert Crosnoe, Chandra Muller, Elizabeth Tipton et al. "A national experiment reveals where a growth mindset improves achievement." *Nature* 573, no. 7774 (2019): 364-369.

Nor am I talking about self-esteem. Self-esteem proponents teach the acceptance of limitations, not overcoming them. A growth mindset correlates strongly with intellectual humility, curiosity, and general wisdom. Those with a growth mindset are better able to learn and less encumbered by unsupported dogmatism. If you think about it, every Scriptural admonition to grow in the faith presupposes a growth mindset.

> "A wise man will hear and increase learning, and a man of understanding will attain wise counsel."[470]

> "Study *and* do your best to present yourself to God approved, a workman [tested by trial] who has no reason to be ashamed, accurately handling *and* skillfully teaching the word of truth."[471]

Do you have a growth mindset? You can if you choose to. Your life will be the richer.

The Christian mind learns from others — actively open-minded thinking

Another principle fundamental to sound reasoning is what researchers call actively open-minded thinking (AOT). In general terms, this means admitting you could be wrong, being open to new evidence and opposing arguments, looking for the best case *against* your position, and listening carefully to those with whom you disagree. It, too, is strongly correlated with wisdom and intellectual humility.

It affords a semblance of humility when leaders ostensibly listen to those around them, but this can be very deceptive. Openness does *not* mean listening to people from your personal echo chamber or surrounding yourself with people who think the same as you do.

Research in this realm shows that actively open-minded thinkers are less susceptible to conspiracy theories, misinformation, and disinformation; more content, less depressed, happier in their close relationships, and even live longer.[472] AOT is a proven corrective to the myriad cognitive biases that cloud our judgment, as discussed in Chapter 3.[473]

---

[470] Proverbs 1:5
[471] 2 Timothy 2:15, Amplified
[472] Grossmann, Igor, Jinkyung Na, Michael EW Varnum, Shinobu Kitayama, and Richard E. Nisbett. "A route to well-being: intelligence versus wise reasoning." *Journal of Experimental Psychology: General* 142, no. 3 (2013): 944.
[473] West, Richard F., Maggie E. Toplak, and Keith E. Stanovich. "Heuristics and biases as measures of critical thinking: Associations with cognitive ability and thinking dispositions." *Journal of educational psychology* 100, no. 4 (2008): 930.

Open-mindedness is a basic Scriptural principle:

> "Woe to those who are wise in their own eyes, and prudent in their own sight!"[474]

> "A wise man will hear and increase learning, and a man of understanding will attain wise counsel."[475]

> "For by wise counsel you will wage your own war, and in a multitude of counselors there is safety."[476]

AOT is measured by agreement with statements such as 'Beliefs should always be revised in response to new information or evidence' or 'a person should always consider new possibilities.' As people of faith, we understand there are boundaries to this principle. Some of the standard survey questions would automatically assign lower scores to conservatives or religious people.[477] That might be tolerable if there were similar questions to discern narrow-mindedness in liberals and the irreligious. There aren't.

One can hold fast to the historic principles of the Christian faith and still be open-minded. Most dividing issues are not fundamentals of the faith. Successful Christian apologists apply this principle by carefully examining the arguments of their opponents and considering the weight of their evidence.

Within the boundaries of orthodoxy, open-minded thinking is obligatory. Most conflicts, divisions, and splits emerge in its absence.

As the 1787 Constitutional convention drew to its conclusion, its eventual passage remained very much in doubt. Many delegates were stirred to its final support by the closing speech of Benjamin Franklin, who consciously practiced open-minded thinking throughout most of his adult life. It is good advice:

> "For having lived long, I have experienced many instances of being obliged by better information, or fuller consideration, to change opinions even on important subjects, which I once thought right, but found to be otherwise. It is therefore that the older I grow, the more apt I am to doubt my own judgment, and to pay more respect

---

[474] Isaiah 5:21
[475] Proverbs 1:5
[476] Proverbs 24:6
[477] Stanovich, Keith E., and Maggie E. Toplak. "The need for intellectual diversity in psychological science: Our own studies of actively open-minded thinking as a case study." *Cognition* 187 (2019): 156-166.

to the judgment of others."[478]

The Christian mind is not lazy — cognitive reflection.

Remember Kahneman's two systems of thinking, fast and slow? Cognitive reflection is just a fancy term for thinking slow, avoiding gut reactions, and taking time to consider other possibilities.

Many forces conspire to make us think fast rather than slow. We tend to be lazy, as Kahneman legitimately points out. But we're often busy, and we live in a world of distractions that pull us away from quiet contemplation. In all human history, information has never come so easily, yet it's never been harder to think.

Things really shifted into high gear with the invention of television. Neil Postman (1931-2003) was an American writer and cultural critic, and the author of *Amusing Ourselves to Death* (1985), a study of the cultural consequences of video-based entertainment. The book is perhaps most famous for its preface, in which Postman contrasted the dystopian narratives of *1984* (George Orwell) and *Brave New World* (Aldous Huxley). With preternatural prescience, Postman anticipated the cultural effects of continuous entertainment in the pre-Internet era, concluding that Huxley was closer to the mark:[479]

> "What Orwell feared were those who would ban books. What Huxley feared was that there would be no reason to ban a book, for there would be no one who wanted to read one. Orwell feared those who would deprive us of information. Huxley feared those who would give us so much that we would be reduced to passivity and egoism. Orwell feared that the truth would be concealed from us. Huxley feared the truth would be drowned in a sea of irrelevance. Orwell feared we would become a captive culture. Huxley feared we would become a trivial culture... As Huxley remarked in Brave New World Revisited, the civil libertarians and rationalists who are ever on the alert to oppose tyranny "failed to take into account man's almost infinite appetite for distractions." In 1984, Huxley added, people are controlled by inflicting pain. In Brave New World, they are controlled by inflicting pleasure. In short, Orwell feared that what we hate will ruin us. Huxley feared that what we love will ruin us."

---

[478] "Speech of Benjamin Franklin—The U.S. Constitution Online—USConstitution.Net." Accessed May 26, 2022. https://www.usconstitution.net/franklin.html.
[479] Postman, Neil. *Amusing Ourselves to Death: Public Discourse in the Age of Show Business.* New York: Viking, 1985.

No one who wants to read books? A sea of information and irrelevance? A trivial culture? Controlled by pleasure? Does that not sound like our present age? How is it working for you?

It sure isn't our lack of time. The average American watches television for 2.8 hours per day. [480] Subtract those who don't watch TV at all, and it rises to 3.6 hours per day. That amounts to a lot of vapid, agenda-driven indoctrination. People forget it's totally fictitious. It's not just that the stories are made up. The assumptions behind the stories are made up. Television programming enforces a narrative that exists only in the minds of producers and writers, unencumbered by reality. (On TV, casual sex rarely has consequences. Reality? I think not). It has vastly more impact on public opinion than opposing well-researched books and essays that are read by few.

A traditional belief that wisdom comes with age permeates most societies. Research has shown that is true — to a point. In some studies, wisdom peaks around middle age and then starts to decline. Perhaps, by that time, we think we have everything figured out and stop learning from new experiences. At least, that's how researchers framed it. Besides age, though, education has also been shown to be an important determinant of wisdom. Reporting in *The Journals of Gerontology*, a team found that education promoted the attainment of wisdom and protected against a decline in later years.[481]

Time is a precious and irreplaceable gift we have been charged to diligently steward. Try cutting back on the entertainment. Disengage from social media. Listen, study, and learn, with a teachable heart:

> "He who answers a matter before he hears it, it is folly and shame to him."[482]

> "Study and be eager and do your utmost to present yourself to God approved (tested by trial), a workman who has no cause to be ashamed, correctly analyzing and accurately dividing [rightly handling and skillfully teaching] the Word of Truth."[483]

Take time to think. Our brains need exercise, too.

---

[480] American Time Use Survey, 2019 Data. https://www.bls.gov/tus/a1-2019.pdf Accessed 2/14/2022

[481] Ardelt, Monika, Stephen Pridgen, and Kathryn L. Nutter-Pridgen. "The relation between age and three-dimensional wisdom: Variations by wisdom dimensions and education." *The Journals of Gerontology: Series B* 73, no. 8 (2018): 1339-1349.

[482] Proverbs 18:13

[483] 2 Timothy 2:15, Amplified

The Christian mind checks emotions — emotional awareness and regulation

In Chapter 3, we examined the dominant yet largely invisible role that emotions play in decision-making. This is not uniformly a bad thing, but too frequently, it clouds our judgment leading to bad decisions and bad outcomes. It comes as no surprise, then, that emotional regulation figures prominently in forming a mature and humble Christian mindset.

In simplest terms, this means learning to spot when our decisions are clouded by anger, fear, shame, sadness, or even excessive happiness — and reconsidering our opinions, thoughts, reactions, and plans in that light. In recent years there has been a lot of focus on Emotional Intelligence (EQ), and EQ is nearly synonymous with emotional regulation. The four basic principles of emotional intelligence encompass self-awareness, self-management, social awareness, and relationship management.[484] In fact, emotional intelligence is closely related to humility. The two are not interchangeable, but if one drew a Venn diagram, there would be a lot of overlap.

Paradoxically, the best way to avoid bad decisions is not to suppress your feelings but to become more aware of them. Then you become more conscious of their effects and are more likely to reflect on whether they are helping or holding you back. The next step is differentiation — the ability to distinguish between the many possible emotional states, such as "happy" and "excited" or "guilty" and "ashamed." After we recognize the feelings and identify them correctly, the final step is regulation. One of the key strategies to emotional regulation is self-distancing: making a concerted effort to step outside of yourself and imagine a problem or situation from the standpoint of a disinterested third party.[485]

There is considerable evidence that EQ independently predicts success in academia, the workplace, and relationships. If you are looking for a next step toward maturity after finishing this book, learning and practicing the principles of emotional intelligence would be a perfect place to start.

A worthy first step to reduce emotional distraction is to cut down or eliminate our consumption of television and social media. (Am I repeating myself? Good!) Television news programming has always been driven by advertising revenue, and the old cliché "if it bleeds, it leads" is all too true. Ad-supported news programming exists not primarily to enlighten you but to keep your eyes glued to the screen. Their first tool is to titillate you with sensationalism. Their second is to generate good feelings about your in-

---

[484] Bradberry, Travis & Greaves, Jean. *Emotional Intelligence 2.0*. San Diego: TalentSmart, 2009.
[485] Robson (2019).

group and arouse more anger and contempt toward your political/social opponents. You know it's true.

Social media such as Facebook, Twitter, TikTok, and YouTube are even worse. As elegantly explained in the Netflix documentary *The Social Dilemma*, highly tuned algorithms are designed to hook into your subconscious and keep you engaged as long as possible.[486] This is not accomplished by appealing to your refined intellect.[487]

The Christian mind honors God's word.

The Bible is not and never claims to be the *only* source of truth. God reveals Himself in nature, and through empiric investigation, we learn more each day about the world that He created. The magnificence of our natural universe displays the creative power and transcendent wisdom of God. However, the only source of objective, *propositional* truth about God comes through His own *revealed* Word. Scripture alone holds absolute moral authority over us. God has implanted a moral sense in every human being, but it is not propositional and is easily suppressed or denied. The Bible serves as a fence to define the boundaries of what is morally and theologically sound. Within that fence, there is a lot of freedom to maneuver.

Most Christian traditions accept Scripture as the ultimate rule of both faith and practice. But it is not a simple book, and there are many pitfalls in its use. We often don't appreciate it is such a massive tome. The King James Bible consists of 783,137 words, much more than Tolstoy's *War and Peace* or the entire *Lord of the Rings* trilogy. It contains history, genealogies, poetry, rules for governance, rules for worship, moral instruction, prophecy, and a considerable amount of pure theology. To understand it correctly demands expertise in ancient Hebrew, New Testament Greek, archaeology, history, linguistics, and systematic theology. No one possesses the entire skillset, so even the experts rely upon others.

Yet, some propose that every believer possesses, through the power of the Holy Spirit, the ability to correctly interpret Scripture apart from creeds, commentaries, tradition, or teachers. This is never taught in Scripture, appeals to our basest instinct of pride, and is the cause of much division and chaos. It is one of the reasons there are over 30,000 Christian denominations in the world, each thinking that only they have the correct doctrine. Historian Mark Noll called attention to the fact that leading up to the Civil

---

[486] Orlowski, Jeff, dir. *The Social Dilemma*. Netflix, 2020.

[487] Lewis Mitchell, James Bagrow. "Do social media algorithms erode our ability to make decisions freely? The jury is out." The Conversation, 10/11/2020. https://theconversation.com/do-social-media-algorithms-erode-our-ability-to-make-decisions-freely-the-jury-is-out-140729

War, defenders of slavery were adamant that their view was based upon Scripture.[488] Dr. R. C. Sproul taught a balanced approach:

> "Private interpretation does not give a license for private distortion. Anyone who presumes to interpret the Bible for himself must assume with that right the awesome responsibility of interpreting it correctly."[489]

Anyone feeling led toward a novel interpretation of an ancient passage must proceed with extreme caution and humility. While studying this subject, I often came to see familiar passages in a new and different way. I have endeavored in every instance to check my interpretation against past authorities and usually found a reliable source who had seen the same thing before. If I were the first and only to see it a particular way, I almost certainly would have been wrong.

Scripture often can provide words of comfort and encouragement, but the Bible is not a magical talisman that will accomplish transformation just by holding one.[490] The objective must be to understand what it teaches and proceed to live accordingly. That final step demands individual agency. The apostle James makes it quite clear:

> "But be doers of the word, and not hearers only, deceiving yourselves."[491]

In fact, the entire objective of *this* book is to summon readers to understand and apply the teaching of Scripture.

The Christian mind is discerning.

> "Let no one deceive you with empty words, for because of these things the wrath of God comes upon the sons of disobedience."[492]

In *The Intelligence Trap*, Robson spoke of the importance of an internal "BS detector" (short for "bovine scat," of course. This is a family book). For

---

[488] Mark Noll. (2006). *The Civil War as a Theological Crisis*. University of North Carolina Press

[489] R. C. Sproul. The Word of God in the Hands of Man. Ligonier Ministries, 4/1/2009. https://www.ligonier.org/learn/articles/word-god-hands-man

[490] Some may cite Isaiah 55:11: "So shall My word be that goes forth from My mouth; It shall not return to Me void, but it shall accomplish what I please." However, the context of the preceding verses explicitly alludes to God's sovereign decrees, not written Scripture. Certainly, many people have come to saving faith just by reading the Bible without any apologetics or human intermediary, but a Calvinist like me would explain that as a sovereign act of God imparting saving faith through His chosen instrument. There are many, many more who read the Bible and *still don't* believe.

[491] James 1:22

[492] Ephesians 5:6

those who don't spend much time in these waters, there's a surprising amount of research on bovine scat: why people do it, how they do it, who's good at it, and why people fall for it. In a 2021 preprint that is both entertaining and convicting, a team from The Wisdom and Culture Lab at the University of Waterloo studied a group of 571 volunteers. Subjects were asked to rate the plausibility of randomly generated nonsensical statements ("Mind and matter are subtle and dense vibrations of consciousness.") Though the words were exactly the same, the subjects were much more likely to take it seriously if they were attributed to a respected individual. The upshot seemed to be that if you want someone to believe nonsense, attribute it to the Dalai Lama, not Miley Cyrus.[493] Draw your own conclusions.

Our BS detector can be improved with practice, education, knowledge, and experience. Time invested in serious reading and study serves to sharpen it. People are "believing machines": resist that impulse. If you don't trust the government or mass media, great. Count me among the skeptics, but they're not always wrong, either. Just don't imagine all the other voices out there are any better. They're all human and cut from the same cloth.

> "But reject profane and old wives' fables, and exercise yourself toward godliness."[494]

Then there's the almighty "Wikipedia." It can be a useful reference in straightforward matters, and I cite it frequently, but if there is any controversy over a subject, you can count on a secular progressive bias. In a 2021 interview with *The Times* (London), Wikipedia co-founder Larry Sanger lamented that the operation had been taken over by left-wing ideologues; "I advise against using it, even to conscientious students.... If you don't kowtow to the right people, you won't even be allowed to participate."[495]

The worldwide COVID-19 pandemic of 2019-2022 was one of the most dramatic, life-changing, and polarizing events of the last several decades. It also proved fertile ground for research into human decision-making. A team of researchers from Israel and the UK found that those who rejected vaccination were less inclined to believe well-established facts, more inclined toward "alternative facts," and scored significantly lower in

---

[493] Kara-Yakoubian, Mane, Ethan Andrew Meyers, Konstantyn Sharpinskyi, Anna Dorfman, and Igor Grossmann. "Hidden wisdom or pseudo-profound bullshit? The effect of speaker admirability." (2021). [preprint] 10.31234/osf.io/tpnkw.
[494] I Timothy 4:7
[495] Madeleine Spence. "Larry Sanger: 'I wouldn't trust Wikipedia—and I helped to invent it'". *The Times* 8/1/2021. https://www.thetimes.co.uk/article/larry-sanger-i-wouldnt-trust-wikipedia-and-i-helped-to-invent-it-cflrhmdhx Accessed 2/14/2022

intellectual humility.[496]

Another team of researchers from Texas A&M found a strong correlation between intellectual humility and willingness to be vaccinated — and between lack of humility and anti-vaccination attitudes.[497] This rang true in my personal experience. (The difference could have been much greater, but many who were accepting of vaccination were equally deficient in humility. They just erred in other directions, like school closings or outdoor masking).

The clear connection between anti-vaccination attitudes and intellectual pride was expressed by a converted anti-vaxxer writing for StatNews, Craig Idlebrook: "I take a breath and try to remember that perspective, that feeling of being *so sure I was right and that almost all of modern science was wrong.*"[498] [emphasis added]

This street goes both ways. Intellectual humility is needed from scientists as well. In November 2018, the New York Academy of Sciences held a conference entitled *Science Denial: Lessons and Solutions*. One of the conference organizers, Kari Fischer, recounted having to throw away all her assumptions. She came to understand that the history of science is strewn with past error and failure, that scientists are just as prone to bias, and conflicts of interest are ubiquitous — just to name a few. Without using the term, she issued a call to humility.[499]

It is a stain upon the Church, and a moral failure, when disciples of Christ embrace fantastical conspiracy theories. To some degree, this is understandable. We are curious by nature and programmed by God to look for explanations. The anchoring effect of mass entertainment biases us toward thinking conspiracies are far more common than they really are. And the internet, along with social media, facilitates their dissemination like nothing else in the history of the human race.

But conspiracy theories also fuel our pride. The sense of superiority that comes from being "in the know" can be intoxicating. Like Neo in "The Matrix," proponents imagine themselves escaping the blinders of society by

---

[496] Newman, Devora, Stephan Lewandowsky, and Ruth Mayo. "Believing in nothing and believing in everything: The underlying cognitive paradox of anti-COVID-19 vaccine attitudes." *Personality and Individual Differences* (2022): 111522.

[497] Huynh, Ho P., and Amy R. Senger. "A little shot of humility: Intellectual humility predicts vaccination attitudes and intention to vaccinate against COVID-19." *Journal of Applied Social Psychology* 51, no. 4 (2021): 449-460.

[498] Idlebrook, Craig. "I was once a hardcore anti-vaxxer. Now I try to nudge people to get the Covid-19 vaccine." StatNews, August 29, 2021. https://www.stat-news.com/2021/08/29/former-anti-vaxxer-now-nudge-people-to-get-covid-19-vaccine/

[499] Fischer, Kari. "What you believe about "science denial" may be all wrong." *TheScientist*, February 11, 2019. https://www.the-scientist.com/news-opinion/opinion--what-you-believe-about-science-denial-may-be-all-wrong-65448

taking "the red pill" and becoming the hero of their own pathetic little fiction.

Conspiracy theories justify our prejudices by maligning the innocent. Among all conspiracy theories, the bloodiest, most contemptible, and most enduring must be those surrounding the descendants of Abraham. From being blamed for the bubonic plague in the 14th century, to accusations of conspiring with the enemy in late 19th century France, to the wildest fantasies of an uber-rich and uber-powerful global cabal, the Jews have suffered the most from conspiracy thinking and experienced the deadly power of lies with six million deaths under the Third Reich.

Antisemitism appeals to some of the worst human impulses — to feel superior to those who are different, justify our prejudices, rationalize our own conduct, and absolve ourselves of personal responsibility for failure — all rooted in Pride. Hitler rose to power blaming the Jews for every real and perceived shortcoming of early 20th century Germany, including their loss in World War I.

Those who aspire to be wise and humble must heed the counsel of Scripture by adopting an attitude of healthy skepticism:

> "The simple believes every word, but the prudent considers well his steps."[500]

> "Also do not take to heart everything people say, lest you hear your servant cursing you."[501]

> "... we should no longer be children, tossed to and fro and carried about with every wind of doctrine, by the trickery of men, in the cunning craftiness of deceitful plotting."[502]

However, the skepticism must be inclusive and consistent, not selective. Individuals who disbelieve the government (depending on which party is in power) but trust someone in a viral YouTube video completely miss the point. How many realize that these videos generate a tidy sum of money for the producer, I wonder? Better to be suspicious of both.

Of course, it's insufficient to simply say "trust the experts" because you can find an expert to embrace almost any fringe position imaginable. Because of the Dunning-Kruger phenomenon, people who are least equipped in a subject are least qualified to distinguish between which experts are trustworthy and which are peddling bovine scat. Too many just gravitate

---

[500] Proverbs 14:15
[501] Ecclesiastes 7:21
[502] Ephesians 4:14

toward the "experts" who stoke their emotions and tell them what they want to be true. Most of this could be avoided simply by respecting the consensus of trusted believers qualified in that particular area. Each might err individually, but not all in the same direction. Individual errors tend to cancel out.[503] This has been called "the wisdom of crowds."[504] It's also Biblical:

> "Where *there is* no counsel, the people fall;
> But in the multitude of counselors *there is* safety."[505]

The Christian mind respects tradition.

The great Christian apologist and thinker C. S. Lewis identified a particular foolishness he called "presentism" — the conceit of every generation that it had attained a level of enlightenment and wisdom superior to any that preceded it. This would have been inconceivable before the late Middle Ages. Until then, ancient thought was venerated.

We would be deluded to imagine that we are immune to this fallacy. The dispensationalist interpretation of Revelation was unknown prior to the late 1800s, yet is taken for granted by many contemporary Evangelicals. The Bible always forbade drunkenness, but total abstinence from alcohol was never taught or practiced by the Church before the late 19th century. By the mid-20th century, it had become Holy Writ in some Protestant denominations (though in the early 21st century, it seems to be declining in popularity). The point here is that every generation of believers is subject to some idiosyncratic positions imagined to be traditional Christian beliefs, but that never were.

But tradition can also be mistaken. One can look at the history of medicine and see just how wrong some of those ancient beliefs actually were. The long-held position of geocentrism was based more on Ptolemy than Scripture, but the Old Testament could certainly be read in such a way. The 16th-century reformers denounced Copernicus as a heretic for claiming the earth orbits the sun.[506] Obviously, Luther and Calvin were wrong on that count. The scientific revolution upended some ancient ways of thinking about the physical realm, but as long as a Christian mindset governed

---

[503] Information cascades do happen, but they are uncommon. They also aren't limited to experts. The effect is even stronger among laypeople.

[504] Surowiecki, James. *The Wisdom of Crowds: Why the Many Are Smarter than the Few.* New York: Doubleday, 2004.

[505] Proverbs 11:14

[506] Mathison, Keith. "Luther, Calvin, and Copernicus — A Reformed Approach to Science and Scripture. Ligonier Ministries." June 1, 2012. https://www.ligonier.org/posts/luther-calvin-and-copernicus-reformed-approach-science-and-scripture

Western Civilization, it remained fairly rooted in reality.

Orthodox Christians understand that secular culture has gone totally off the rails in its beliefs and practices regarding human sexuality. If we measure only by that standard, societies of the 18th and 19th centuries were morally superior to present-day America. Yet, in other well-known ways, they were harsher and crueler. Each generation is prone to its own particular follies.

This is why I repeatedly invoke the classic Christian thinkers. In many areas, we are simply too acclimated and comfortable with our contemporary attitudes and lifestyles to recognize a glaring problem. St. Augustine or Jonathan Edwards would instantly recognize the pervasiveness of pride in modern society and the Church.

Someday we will all appear before God. When that day comes, we will all find we were mistaken about a great many things. So why wait? We might as well own up to it now. We can, and we should endeavor to be good stewards with the mind God has given us.

Key points

- The Christian mind is humble
- The Christian mind seeks wisdom
- The Christian mind learns from others
- The Christian mind is not lazy
- The Christian mind is watchful of emotion
- The Christian mind honors God's word.
- The Christian mind is discerning.
- The Christian mind respects tradition.

«14»

The care and feeding of prideful people

Humility in Relationship

It is always easier to see pride in others than in ourselves. Armed with the understanding that not only I but those around me are proud to the core, how does this impact my relationships? How can I be a positive influence on proud people? How do I work with them or for them? How do I teach and disciple them? Is it possible to make judgments without being judgmental?

"Let nothing be done through selfish ambition or conceit, but in lowliness of mind let each esteem others better than himself." [507]

"Yes, all of you be submissive to one another, and be clothed with humility, for 'God resists the proud, but gives grace to the humble.'" [508]

By now, you have undoubtedly diagnosed pride in your spouse, your boss, your coworkers, your children, your pastor, several members of your congregation, and your cat, if you keep one. [Dogs, of course, are instinctively humble creatures]. You may even feel "led" to help them overcome their pride, such as subtly leaving a copy of this book on their desktop with the relevant passages highlighted in bright fluorescent orange. Before you try that approach: Stop! Think about it. First, you are probably right. As we have said, if it is human and has a pulse, it is proud. But second, consider the effect pride has on us: it blinds us to our own faults and rears its ugly head when threatened. Do you really want to poke it?

However, this does not mean that we cannot help others learn to recognize and overcome pride. Scripture reveals several instances where God's servants approached proud people with a successful outcome. By applying

---

[507] Philippians 2:3
[508] 1 Peter 5:5

Biblical principles and understanding the basics of human personality, we can work around pride and even use it to increase our personal effectiveness and relationships with others. With this knowledge comes great danger, however. These same skills can also be used to manipulate and deceive in the pursuit of selfish ends — and that too is recounted in the pages of Scripture.

While it is not the only cause, pride lies at the core of much, if not most, human conflict. Yet, few contemporary books or conferences on marriage, parenting, peacemaking, or anything touching on conflict even raise the issue. It is not that we have been missing some critical but heretofore undiscovered insight, but worse: we have forgotten what our forebears in the faith understood very clearly.

Once we appreciate the pervasiveness and universality of pride, it should illuminate our understanding of what is happening in the world, nations, workplaces, churches, marriages, and families.

The journey begins with recognizing pride's presence within us; only then can we avoid the common habits and inculcate humility. While our primary responsibility is for our own spiritual state and maturity, to stop there would be to abandon our duties to make disciples, to raise our children "in the way [they] should go,"[509] to "reprove, rebuke, and exhort with complete patience and teaching."[510]

Our lives are bound to run more smoothly as *we* grow in humility, but we might still find ourselves surrounded by people who are *not* growing in humility. They may, in fact, be growing in the opposite direction.

Recognizing pride in others is no remarkable feat. It's about as insightful as deducing that water is wet and fire burns. Based on my own study of the subject, I assume everyone I meet has a pride problem. Following the "Jonathan Edwards" principle, I further assume that most do not realize it.

There are two broad areas to examine when considering the impact of pride in our relationships. First, once we understand people are prideful, do we approach relationships and communication differently? Second, when we perceive it as a severe problem in someone, is there a place for intervention?

While there is an abundance of research on the nature of pride, and somewhat less research on the practices of humility, there is very little research-based evidence on how to reduce pride and develop humility in unmotivated individuals. Much of the current literature is merely opinion-based

---

[509] Proverbs 22:6
[510] 2 Timothy 4:2, ESV

advice. However, Scripture has proved a reliable guide so far in our study, and therein we have many examples of how it was addressed.

Section 1: Principles

Lead by example

Humans are relational creatures. Considering how fundamental humility is to our inner lives, of course it extends into all of our relationships. We must begin by embracing humility in all of our interactions, including our peers, those under our authority, and those with power over us. Applying all of the principles in chapters 12 and 13 would be a perfect place to begin.

Sometimes, you just have to kiss the goat.

I am a lifelong fan of Bob Newhart. Throughout the 80s, *Newhart* was the *only* show I watched regularly and consistently. In March of 1990, I had a unique opportunity to sit in the live studio audience for the taping of the third-to-last episode of the entire series. Before the show, Mr. Newhart *himself* came out and gave a stand-up routine for us waiting guests. It was so kind of him, and more than we hoped for. By everyone's accounting, he is a real *mensch*. In the series bearing his name, Newhart played the character of Dick Loudon, a free-lance writer and innkeeper in rural Vermont.

In one episode of *Newhart*, Dick's home office was invaded by a stray goat, wreaking havoc and devouring some of his work.[511] When it happened a second time, Dick called animal control and had the creature arrested. Unfortunately, the goat was a beloved pet of his bumpkin neighbors Larry, Darryl, and Darryl (LD&D). Rather than taking responsibility and apologizing for the trespass, though, the threesome was *deeply wounded* that their beloved creature had been shown such disrespect. (It's a "shame-honor" sort of thing). They proceeded to retaliate against Dick and household with a series of pranks, making life difficult for all at the inn.

The entire community grew angry and frustrated — at Dick. Ultimatums were issued. Dick finally agreed to "apologize" to LD&D and did. But they wouldn't settle for an apology; they demanded restitution. Dick must *kiss* the goat. And with the appropriate displays of disgust, he proceeded to do exactly that. All was well. With the crisis resolved, life returned to normal (at least according to that community's standards).

I found that a touching example of humility. Dick was the injured party. He had every right to stand his ground. But for the good of all, he sacrificed his

---

[511] Brinckerhoff, Burt (Director). (Aired 2/4/1985). "Dick gets Larry's Goat" (Season 3 Episode 57). In *Newhart* CBS (1982-1990)

dignity and right of retribution. I know in my life, I've offered apologies that might not have been heartfelt but were necessary to defuse a situation. Most of you probably have too.

Sometimes, you just have to kiss the goat.

Show respect toward legitimate authorities

Regarding those in authority over us, Proverbs offers time-tested advice: err on the side of deference.

> "Do not exalt yourself in the presence of the king,
> And do not stand in the place of the great;
> For it is better that he say to you,
> 'Come up here,'
> Than that you should be put lower in the presence of the prince,
> Whom your eyes have seen."[512]

Few of us see an audience with kings or princes in our future, but the point is well made. Some people merit a certain deference based on their position, authority, maturity, age, or expertise. There is a fine line, though, between respect and favoritism. The admonition here is to practice humility in their presence, not to afford them special treatment.

Flattery will get you somewhere, but it's wrong.

> *Flattery (noun)*: excessive and insincere praise, given especially to further one's own interests.[513]

Flattery works.

Yes, because people are proud by nature, they hunger for praise and respond with favoritism and positivity toward those who praise them. For the recipient, this can happen subconsciously, even when he is *consciously aware* that he's being flattered.[514] On the plus side, if you can praise someone's character, abilities, or achievements with honesty and sincerity, you are practicing Biblical encouragement. But if it is for selfish reasons, dishonest, or celebrates vice, it is flattery — and a trap. It still works, of course, which is the chief reason people do it. But it's wrong.

---

[512] Proverbs 25:6-7
[513] Lexico Dictionaries | English. "FLATTERY English Definition and Meaning | Lexico.Com." Accessed May 22, 2022. https://www.lexico.com/en/definition/flattery
[514] Chan, Elaine, and Jaideep Sengupta. "Insincere flattery actually works: A dual attitudes perspective." *Journal of Marketing Research* 47, no. 1 (2010): 122-133.

In the Book of Proverbs, Solomon warned:

"A man who flatters his neighbor
Spreads a net for his feet."[515]

A net for *whose* feet? The flatterer or the flatteree? The Hebrew is ambiguous. Probably both. A study in the *Harvard Business Review* found that in the leagues of corporate management, subordinates who flattered their CEOs were *more* likely to harbor resentment and criticize them to journalists compared to the non-flattering employees.[516]

Do not show favoritism

James issued strict admonition against the differential treatment of the wealthy or powerful.[517] This emphasizes a foundational principle of the Gospel that we are all one in Christ and equal in worth. Fawning submission to an important person has the outward appearance of humility, but there are implications. To show undue honor to the rich, successful, or influential tempts them towards sin when what they might need most is to learn humility. Those inclined to show honor to such persons must also check their motives. Could a selfish interest be at work? Are you seeking personal advantage or greater recognition for yourself (or your group) by currying favor?

The habits of favoritism may partly explain the steady stream of narcissists rising to positions of power. Do you want to stop having narcissistic leaders? It isn't that difficult. Just learn to identify them, and stop supporting them.

See every person as a mirror

Since every person is proud to a greater or lesser degree, we would seldom be off-base in judging their attitude or behavior to be influenced by pride. But we are most likely to be aggravated when their pride rubs against our own, so every conflict provides an opportunity for self-reflection. Andrew Murray advised us, "look upon every person who tries or troubles you as a means of grace to humble you."[518]

---

[515] Proverbs 29:5
[516] Keeves, Gareth, James Westphal, and Michael McDonald. "Research: Executives Who Flatter Their CEOs Are More Likely to Criticize Them to the Press." *Harvard Business Review*, April 5, 2017. https://hbr.org/2017/04/research-executives-who-flatter-their-ceos-are-more-likely-to-criticize-them-to-the-press.
[517] James 2:1-7
[518] Murray. p. 85

When people whom I think (well, know) are wrong exhibit dogmatic certainty, their pride annoys me. It was something of a personal breakthrough to realize that the other person was thinking the same thing about me. On social media, I have seen disputes degenerate into a slugfest over who is the "proudest." This is pointless. Better to concede that we are all proud and return to the substance of the issue.

Pride's easy to spot: don't overdo it

Armed with an understanding of human biases, overconfidence, and errors in belief formation, it's pretty easy to deconstruct the beliefs of anyone with whom we disagree. We think we can dismiss their opinions on science, politics, or theology because we've concluded they arose from biases rather than sound reasoning. Red Alert! I'm introducing these principles for personal reflection, *not weapons*. Never forget the "bias blind spot" — we tend to be blind to our own biases.

Another error would be to succumb to Bulverism.[519] As explained by C. S. Lewis:

> "You must show *that* a man is wrong before you start explaining *why* he is wrong. The modern method is to assume without discussion that he is wrong and then distract his attention from this (the only real issue) by busily explaining how he became so silly."

Pointing out someone's biases — real or imagined — never proves they are wrong and you are right. First, you can't really prove they're deceived by their biases. One can be biased and still be right. Second, you're probably just as biased.

It's also easy to see a root of pride in every conflict between parent and child, husband and wife, boss and worker, or pastor and parishioner. It's easy to spot because we all have it. But as we will see in a moment, it's not exactly helpful to point it out on every occasion. We're back to the mirror principle: if you see someone's pride in a particular conflict, ask, "am I doing the same thing?"

Look beyond outward appearances

The first book of Samuel recounts the anointing of David as the future king of Israel. But David did not cut a striking presence. When Samuel came to Bethlehem to the house of Jesse, the elders of the town (and apparently

---

[519] "Bulverism, or, The Foundation of 20th Century Thought" from: Lewis, C.S. *God in the Dock, Essays on Theology and Ethics.* Edited by Walter Hooper. Eerdmans, 1971.

even Samuel) naturally expected Eliab, the eldest, to be the "chosen" one. He just "looked" like a king:

> "So it was, when they came, that he looked at Eliab and said, 'Surely the LORD's anointed *is* before Him!'"[520]

But their perception stood in need of correction:

> "... the LORD said to Samuel, 'Do not look at his appearance or at his physical stature, because I have refused him. For *the* LORD *does* not *see* as man sees; for man looks at the outward appearance, but the LORD looks at the heart.'"[521]

When David later faced Goliath, the warrior was equally unimpressed.[522] (A fatal oversight, in his case).

Our judgment of people based on their outward appearance is not always incorrect but is severely distorted by various biases and reinforced by our unwarranted self-confidence. It is a contributing factor towards racism. For these and many, many other reasons, we must endeavor to be open-minded and humble.

Section 2: Patience.

Hopefully, we have reached a point where old problems may now be seen in a new light. A flaw or sin that we might have seen in the past as bad behavior or false belief we now understand stems from a root of pride. Rather than attacking the issue head-on, maybe going for the source is the better solution.

Be slow to judge: the judgment of charity

Having carefully dissected the expressions of judgmentalism and exposed it as the sin of pride, how do we appropriately respond to perceived sins and failures in those around us? We begin by applying the Golden Rule and treating others as we want others to treat us.

Our experiences do not interpret themselves, and whether we realize it or not, we have considerable latitude in how we frame a given situation. To practice the judgment of charity means to extend to others the benefit of the doubt, allowing that they may have acted out of good intentions or faced mitigating circumstances. Whenever possible, we can choose to

---

[520] I Samuel 16:6
[521] I Samuel 16:7
[522] I Samuel 17:42-43

frame the words and actions of others in a positive rather than negative light. I need to say it again: we're terrible at judging and may be quite wrong. Even if we're right, a genuine recognition of our own depravity makes it far easier to practice patience and forgiveness toward others.

Especially, let us be patient with our brothers and sisters in Christ. As Paul admonished the believers in Rome:

> "Let not him who eats despise him who does not eat, and let not him who does not eat judge him who eats; for God has received him."[523]

> "But why do you judge your brother? Or why do you show contempt for your brother? For we shall all stand before the judgment seat of Christ."[524]

> "Therefore let us not judge one another anymore, but rather resolve this, not to put a stumbling block or a cause to fall in *our* brother's way."[525]

So how do we judge without being judgmental? First and foremost, remember the many pitfalls from Chapter 11:

- We're terrible at diagnosing the motivations and problems of other people
- Despite that, we're far too confident in our assessment of other people
- We are too often tainted with an attitude of superiority
- We gravitate toward legalism
- Too often, self-interests are at stake
- And many, many more.

This might be a good time to go back and review Chapter 11. Now, at least two stages are involved when we perceive a brother sinning. First, we form the judgment in our minds. The second is when (or if) we approach the target. The escalating four-step approach of Matthew 18:15-19 is understood by many as the orthodox Biblical pattern:

- Approach them in private
- Approach them with one or two others
- Take it to the whole congregation
- Disassociate them from the church

---

[523] Romans 14:3
[524] Romans 14:10
[525] Romans 14:13

The principles of this chapter can serve to inform and guide that process — with great humility.

Be quick to forgive

Very few personal conflicts should *ever* lead to the formal process of Matthew 18:15-19. In that context, Jesus was likely referring to ongoing attitudes or behaviors that were harming the sinner, his neighbors, or the assembly. Because the *default* response when someone sins against you (or you perceive that he has) is *not* Matthew 18:15-19 but what immediately follows:

> "Then Peter came to Him and said, "Lord, how often shall my brother sin against me, and I forgive him? Up to seven times?" Jesus said to him, "I do not say to you, up to seven times, but up to seventy times seven."[526]

Our default response, in a word, should be forgiveness — as you have been forgiven.

Let God do the convicting

By now, you surely appreciate that, rightly or wrongly, we will perceive sins in others that they don't see in themselves. On the one hand, we tend to judge unfairly and too severely, but on the other hand, we all have a natural propensity toward self-rationalization. At times, we're all unfair in our judgment of others. But what if we're really not, and the other party is guilty but doesn't see or admit it?

In purely earthly terms, there might seem to be little hope. Left to oneself, the sinner may never come to conviction and repentance. While the Bible is replete with examples and instructions to lead others out of sin, only the Holy Spirit can ultimately bring genuine conviction.

> "And when He has come, He will convict the world of sin, and of righteousness, and of judgment."[527]

Reflect for a moment on the earthly ministry of Christ. Generally, Jesus didn't invest time or energy trying to convince people they were sinners. He regularly offered words of forgiveness and hope to those who already *knew they were*. He could have — but didn't — denounce the crimes of the

---

[526] Matthew 18:21-22
[527] John 16:8

Romans or violent Jewish sects. The primary, almost the only, targets of his denunciations were the self-righteous religious leaders of his day.

Yet throughout the New Testament, there is also a clear mandate to identify and confront sin. Paul, Peter, Jude, and John not only led by example in identifying and denouncing sin but instructed us to imitate them in this regard.[528]

To confront others humbly, then, demands that we first concentrate upon our own sinfulness and only after that the sins of fellow Christian believers while avoiding unbiblical legalism and the many pitfalls of judgmentalism. There is little scriptural support for the incessant deprecation of unbelievers emanating from many pulpits , ministries, and publications. Not that we shouldn't be concerned — especially when there are severe social consequences — but people either will be conscious of their sin or they won't. The Gospel is good news to those who admit their guilt, a mere annoyance to those who will not. Almost nothing you or I say is going to move someone from denying it to admitting it. Again, that is the work of the Holy Spirit.

Section 3: Intervention

So, what if we perceive pride in a situation where it's causing problems, and we decide to intervene? How might one approach the troublemaker?

To date, there is virtually no evidence from the research community on effective interventions against pride, particularly intellectual pride. There is academic interest, but research is really only now getting underway. We can hypothesize some approaches based on Scripture, from the conduct of Jesus and the apostles, and from the many examples of how pride was broken by divine intervention.

Usually, a sinner knows if he's sinning. The adulterer knows if he's cheated or not. The liar knows if she's lying. Anger is hard to hide. Offenders may deny it publicly. They may rationalize it. But in their hearts, they know if they're guilty or innocent. Not so with pride. As we have seen, usually, the proud don't know they're proud, typically don't want to know, and will concentrate their energy on denying it and defending themselves.

But some might be receptive. More mature believers may admit in principle that they are proud and might be receptive to being shown where it is manifest. Some growing Christians will understand the reality of blind spots — those flaws only others can perceive — and be receptive to advice, teaching, or counseling. Perhaps the most receptive of all are those going

---

[528] I Timothy 5:20, 2 Timothy 4:2

through a personal crisis directly because of their pride. That was the case in the Biblical stories of Moses, David, Nebuchadnezzar, Peter, and many others.

Simply improving people's awareness of pride and its expression could put a damper on prideful behavior. Grandstanding, for instance, becomes immediately unacceptable the moment other people see it for what it is. It works because we let it. Stop letting it work.

Even if there is not an ounce of humility in their body, most people seek to avoid the *appearance* of pride. Furthermore, image is much more critical to the proud than the humble. That is not a trivial thing because less outward display of pride would still facilitate better relationships and social cohesion and could stop the cycle of ramping up that causes pride to escalate within social groups. (The "moral communities effect," if you want to delve into this further).

Crisis = Opportunity

The addiction recovery community has a long track record of success that has incorporated pride intervention. It's noteworthy that of the famous "12 Steps" of Alcoholics Anonymous, the first ten are explicitly addressed at remediating pride:[529]

1. We *admitted we were powerless* over alcohol — that our lives had become unmanageable.
2. Came to believe that a Power *greater than ourselves* could restore us to sanity.
3. Made a decision to *turn our will and our lives over to the care of God* as we understood Him.
4. Made a *searching and fearless moral inventory* of ourselves.
5. Admitted to God, to ourselves, and to another human being, the *exact nature of our wrongs.*
6. Were entirely ready to have God remove *all these defects of character.*
7. *Humbly* asked Him to remove our shortcomings.
8. Made a list of all persons we had harmed, and *became willing to make amends* to them all.
9. *Made direct amends* to such people wherever possible, except when to do so would injure them or others.

---

[529] "The Twelve Steps | Alcoholics Anonymous." Accessed May 26, 2022. https://www.aa.org/the-twelve-steps.

10. Continued to take personal inventory and, *when we were wrong, promptly admitted it.*

There is good empirical evidence that twelve-step programs work, so it is at least a reasonable inference that they are effective in mitigating pride.[530] In almost all cases, people enter recovery programs voluntarily. This typically happens at the peak of a crisis, so they are highly motivated. These principles might be of little interest and have little effect upon someone at the height of success. But everyone faces a crisis sooner or later. As seen in Scripture, those are opportunities to address a person's pride. The principles of the twelve-step program can be transferred (and have been) to many other life situations beyond addiction.

What about the person, though, who appears to be on top of the world but clearly has a problem with unrecognized pride? We shouldn't take confrontation off the table. But there are other things worth trying first.

A spoonful of sugar

Most often, direct confrontation is probably not the way to go. This is particularly true when that person possesses power or authority. A full-frontal assault upon a prideful person, or someone in a high position, might only stiffen their resistance or endanger your own situation. Never underestimate the power of a cleverly executed bait and switch.

Because he had several wives, the household of King David consisted of many half-brothers and half-sisters. II Samuel 13 relates how one of David's sons, Amnon, conspired and proceeded to rape his half-sister Tamar. Two years later, Tamar's full brother, Absalom, exacted vengeance through the murder of Amnon. For the next three years, David and Absalom were estranged. Although David desired reconciliation, he took no action to make it happen.[531] Does that not sound like pride?

Eventually, the King's advisor Joab recruited an obscure and unnamed woman from Tekoa in a scheme to bring David around. She presented herself to the king as a meek and helpless widow with only two sons. One was murdered by the other, leaving her with a single heir who was condemned to execution. The widow begged mercy upon him for the sake of herself and her husband. David granted clemency and promised his unconditional support and protection. Then, the actress stepped out of her role:

---

[530] Kelly, John F., Keith Humphreys, and Marica Ferri. "Alcoholics Anonymous and other 12-step programs for alcohol use disorder." *Cochrane Database of Systematic Reviews* 3 (2020).

[531] 2 Samuel 13:39

"So the woman said: 'Why then have you schemed such a thing against the people of God? For the king speaks this thing as one who is guilty, in that the king does not bring his banished one home again. For we will surely die and become like water spilled on the ground, which cannot be gathered up again. Yet God does not take away a life; but He devises means, so that His banished ones are not expelled from Him.'"[532]

But even then, she softens the rebuke with words of praise and admiration:

"The word of my lord the king will now be comforting; for as the angel of God, so is my lord the king in discerning good and evil. And may the Lord your God be with you."[533]

So, in the end, David relented and ordered Joab to bring Absalom back to the king's palace.

Given that this ploy involved open deception, it should probably not be regarded as normative, but there is much wisdom in Joab's approach. First, he sought to lower the temperature by depersonalizing the issue. It wasn't about Absalom but a grieving widow. Second, get the target to admit the moral principle — forgiveness, in this case. Third, apply the target's own declaration of principle to the area of concern, which in this instance was his estrangement from Absalom. There is a pattern here. In Chapter 12 of II Samuel, the prophet Nathan employed a similar strategy to call David to repentance over his adultery with Bathsheba and murder of Uriah.

There are many more principles and strategies for dealing with the sins of others; I leave that for others to elaborate upon.

Confront in love

Lastly, we consider the option of direct confrontation. Is this off the table? Not necessarily. Now, the guiding principle for Christians in all relationships is love:

"If it is possible, as much as depends on you, live peaceably with all men."[534]

---

[532] 2 Samuel 14:13-14
[533] 2 Samuel 14:17
[534] Romans 12:18

"Therefore, as the elect of God, holy and beloved, put on tender mercies, kindness, humility, meekness, longsuffering; bearing with one another, and forgiving one another."[535]

And we are further warned against condemnation:

"Judge not, and you shall not be judged. Condemn not, and you shall not be condemned. Forgive, and you will be forgiven."[536]

Yet we are also commanded to confront sin:

"Those who are sinning rebuke in the presence of all, that the rest also may fear."[537]

"Preach the word! Be ready in season and out of season. Convince, rebuke, exhort, with all longsuffering and teaching."[538]

Love is many things, including gentleness and respect. But its higher purpose is the well-being of the person and the community. The principle of love does not *a priori* preclude forceful confrontation in particular situations. We have numerous examples in Scripture where men set as exemplars resorted to harsh rhetoric [emphasis added]:

- Paul confronting the "Judaizers" — Jewish Christians who wished to impose circumcision and the Mosaic Law upon Gentile converts:

  "O **foolish Galatians**! Who has bewitched you that you should not obey the truth?"[539]

  "I wish that those who are troubling you [by teaching that circumcision is necessary for salvation] would even [go all the way and] **castrate themselves**!"[540]

- Paul writing to the spiritually (and morally) immature Christians at Corinth:

  "And I, brethren, could not speak to you as to spiritual people but as to **carnal**, as to **babes** in Christ. I fed you with milk and not with solid food; for until now you were not able to receive it, and even now you are still not able; for you are still **carnal**."[541]

---

535 Colossians 3:12-13
536 Luke 6:37
537 I Timothy 5:21
538 2 Timothy 4:2
539 Galatians 3:1
540 Galatians 5:12
541 1 Corinthians 3:1-3

This would undoubtedly be construed as condescending by recipients too prideful or immature to accept correction.

- James (brother of Jesus?) to quarreling believers:

  "**Adulterers and adulteresses**! Do you not know that friendship with the world is enmity with God?"[542]

- Jesus addressing the hyper-legalistic and pretentious religious leaders of his culture:

  "But when he saw many of the Pharisees and Sadducees coming to his baptism, he said to them, "**Brood of vipers**! Who warned you to flee from the wrath to come?"[543]

  "Woe to you, scribes and Pharisees, hypocrites! For you are like **whitewashed tombs** which indeed appear beautiful outwardly, but inside are full of **dead men's bones and all uncleanness**."[544]

  "Woe to you, scribes and Pharisees, hypocrites! For you travel land and sea to win one proselyte, and when he is won, you make him twice as much **a son of hell as yourselves**."[545]

There are other instances in Scripture where harsh rhetoric is directed specifically against *false teachers*. For instance:

  "But these, like natural **brute beasts** made to be caught and destroyed, speak evil of the things they do not understand, and will utterly perish in their own corruption. "[546]

  "But these speak evil of whatever they do not know; and whatever they know naturally, like **brute beasts**, in these things they corrupt themselves."[547]

Peter and Jude might have been speaking *about* false teachers rather than *to* them, but we do not know that. Either way, they surely got the message.

Clearly, there is a balance or tension. Whether and how we address the sins of others depends on the severity of the sin, the ages of those involved, the attitude of the sinner, and our relationship to them. These examples do not

---

[542] James 4:4
[543] Matthew 3:7
[544] Matthew 23:27
[545] Matthew 23:15
[546] 2 Peter 2:12
[547] Jude 10

prove it is proper for us to speak harshly, occasionally or ever. They do demonstrate that harsh confrontation is not *in and of itself* unbiblical.

One common element to the harsh approach is that in the examples I've given, the targets were mostly religious leaders with power and influence (the type most likely to be corrupted with pride). They do not set a precedent for discourse with unbelievers or the flock of ordinary believers.

In short, there is no one-size-fits-all approach in Scripture. Perhaps ordinary common sense applies. The more confrontational approach should be limited to situations where much is at stake and only after gentler means have been tried and failed.

There are different purposes behind communicating with someone who is arrogantly clinging to an untruth. It is acceptable and Biblical to speak simply in rebuke. If one's goal is persuasion, softer and more indirect approaches would be more effective. Both techniques might be appropriate within the same relationship, but at different times.

Summary

There are many other areas of life where humility can enhance relationships and success: marriage, parenting, the workplace, and leadership. The opportunities and accumulated wisdom in these areas are rich and vast but far beyond the scope of this work. Probably few, if any, books on marriage, parenting, or leadership address pride to the extent of this study, so take what you've learned here and carry it with you as you read and study other applications.

Key Points:

- Consider how pride can contaminate relationships, both your pride and theirs.
- Be patient: slow to judge, slow to take offense
- Be vigilant: sometimes pride has to be confronted to save a person, a relationship, a church, or an organization.

«15»

Sheep and Goats

Humility in Salvation

Jesus's foretelling of the final judgment challenges each of us with a sober warning: those who think they deserve salvation will be denied it, for salvation is granted only to those who admit they are unworthy. There is no shortage of opinions on what one must do to be saved, or precisely what one must believe to be saved. Whatever one's formulation of the Gospel, the most fundamental element of genuine conversion may be the humble admission that the respondent is, indeed, in desperate need of salvation.

"Humble yourselves in the sight of the Lord, and He will lift you up." [548]

The afterlife

Heaven is a popular place.

Against a current of increasing secularization and declining church involvement, the percentage of Americans who believe in heaven has remained steadily between 70% and 80% across many decades.[549] Among those who believe, over 80% think they have a confirmed reservation.[550]

The promise of an afterlife was often mentioned in the Old Testament (beginning with the oldest of all, the Book of Job) but received much more focus in the New Testament. Jesus often spoke of the world to come and life after death, but personally promised it to rather few.

---

[548] James 4:10
[549] "Few Americans Blame God or Say Faith Has Been Shaken Amid Pandemic, Other Tragedies." *Pew Research Center's Religion & Public Life Project* (blog), November 23, 2021. https://www.pewresearch.org/religion/2021/11/23/few-americans-blame-god-or-say-faith-has-been-shaken-amid-pandemic-other-tragedies/.
[550] "Nine in 10 Believe in Heaven; A quarter Say for Christians Only." ABC News, October 9, 2005. https://abcnews.go.com/images/Politics/994a1Heaven.pdf Accessed 2/5/2022

I am not a theologian, nor do I play one on TV (exciting as that may sound). But as I have studied the issue of pride over many years, it was irresistible to search for any connection between humility and salvation. Thus, the contents of this chapter emerge from my personal reflections upon Scripture, possibly biased by my own decidedly Reformed perspective. But the general principles could be accommodated into whatever faith tradition you prefer.

Over half of professing American Christians believe good works will get you into heaven — even though no historic Christian denomination actually teaches that.[551] It is natural to believe that heaven is a reward for good behavior and hell is just for the naughty (the just-world phenomenon). Hopefully, by now, you appreciate the problem with that line of reasoning. How good am I, really? How good are you? Compared to whom? We can never escape comparing ourselves.

Throughout church history, almost every conceivable interpretation has been promoted by one group or another claiming to provide assurance, or some reasonable expectation, of getting into heaven. Although Jesus explicitly warned most people are headed to hell, that obviously isn't playing well. Only about 2% of Americans see that in their future.[552] That 2% may be more honest and realistic than the plurality of Americans — and the majority of professing Christians — who expect to enter heaven on their own merit.[553]

Humility and Salvation in the Old Testament

Numerous passages in the Old Testament identify the humble as promising candidates for eternal life:

> "The sacrifices of God are a broken spirit,
> A broken and a contrite heart —
> These, O God, You will not despise."[554]

---

[551] "AWVI 2020 Survey: 1 in 3 US Adults Embrace Salvation Through Jesus; More Believe It Can Be 'Earned'—Arizona Christian University," August 4, 2020. https://www.arizonachristian.edu/2020/08/04/1-in-3-us-adults-embrace-salvation-through-jesus-more-believe-it-can-be-earned/ Accessed 2/5/2022

[552] "Survey: Salvation through Christ Attracts Just One in Three Adults;, More Believe It Can Be 'Earned.'" Cultural Research Center, Arizona Christian University, August 4, 2020. https://www.arizonachristian.edu/wp-content/uploads/2020/08/AWVI-2020-Release-08-Perceptions-of-Sin-and-Salvation.pdf Accessed 2/5/2022

[553] Munsil, Tracy. "*AWVI 2020* Survey: 1 in 3 US Adults Embrace Salvation Through Jesus; More Believe It Can Be 'Earned.'" Cultural Research Center, Arizona Christian University, August 4, 2020. https://www.arizonachristian.edu/2020/08/04/1-in-3-us-adults-embrace-salvation-through-jesus-more-believe-it-can-be-earned/

[554] Psalms 51:17

> "For the Lord takes pleasure in His people; He will beautify the **humble** with salvation."[555]

> "Seek the Lord, all you meek of the earth, who have upheld His justice. Seek righteousness, seek **humility**. It may be that you will be hidden in the day of the Lord's anger."[556]

Conversely, the eternal destiny of the proud seems decidedly less promising:

> "For behold, the day is coming, burning like an oven, and all the **proud**, yes, all who do wickedly will be stubble. And the day which is coming shall burn them up."[557]

Consider the enigma of King David. He was an adulterer and a murderer, but pronounced by God to be a man after God's own heart. The ostentatiously righteous Pharisees were denounced by Jesus as liars and hypocrites. How can this be? The difference between David and the Pharisees lies not in their external behavior but in the attitudes of their hearts. David manifested humility and, for that, was blessed by God. He was open to correction, made no attempt to rationalize his transgressions, and was genuine in his repentance.

For insight into the mindset of David, compare him to his predecessor. Students of the Bible will recall that Saul was the first King of Israel, appointed by the prophet Samuel. He started off well but finished poorly and was succeeded by David.

In 1 Samuel 15, Saul was commanded to punish the Amalekites for past treachery, with explicit instructions to kill every living thing.[558] Evidently, Saul didn't have any qualms about killing people but balked at the livestock, and "all that was good."[559]

The prophet Samuel appears on the scene and is greeted by Saul, who boasts of his obedience:

> *Saul*: "Blessed are you of the Lord! I have performed the commandment of the Lord."[560]

---

[555] Psalms 149:4

[556] Zephaniah 2:3

[557] Malachi 4:1

[558] This is another of those narratives that people take issue with because of its seeming cruelty. I can't address that here, but for a good analysis visit Chapter 9, "Didn't God Command Genocide?" in: Samples, Ken. *Christianity Cross-examined.* Covina, CA: Reasons to Believe, 2021.

[559] I Samuel 15:9

[560] I Samuel 15:13

But Samuel wasn't deaf:

> *Samuel:* "What then is this bleating of the sheep in my ears, and the lowing of the oxen which I hear?"

Now let's step aside for a moment. The logical implication in ancient Israel would be the same as today: disobeying God's orders, they kept the good stuff for themselves. But Saul is not going to admit to that. So, he pretends to Samuel, "we kept the best to sacrifice to the Lord!" [561] He lies.

God wanted obedience, not the blood of sheep and oxen. Samuel wasn't buying it:

> *Samuel:* "Now the Lord sent you on a mission, and said, 'Go, and utterly destroy the sinners, the Amalekites, and fight against them until they are consumed.' Why then did you not obey the voice of the Lord? Why did you swoop down on the spoil, and do evil in the sight of the Lord?"[562]

Saul doubles down on his earlier denial, pleading personal innocence while shifting the blame to his wayward followers:

> *Saul* "But I **have obeyed** the voice of the Lord, and gone on the mission on which the Lord sent me...But **the people** took of the plunder, sheep and oxen, the best of the things which should have been utterly destroyed, to sacrifice to the Lord your God in Gilgal."[563] [emphasis added]

Samuel still wasn't buying it. For a third time, he rebukes King Saul:

> *Samuel:* "Has the Lord *as great* delight in burnt offerings and sacrifices,
> As in obeying the voice of the Lord?
> Behold, to obey is better than sacrifice,
> *And* to heed than the fat of rams....
> Because you have rejected the word of the Lord,
> He also has rejected you from *being* king."[564]

Trapped without escape, Saul apologizes, sort of:

> *Saul:* "I have sinned, for I have transgressed the commandment of the Lord and your words, **because I feared the people and**

---

561 I Samuel 15:15, paraphrased
562 I Samuel 15:18-19
563 I Samuel 15:20
564 I Samuel 15:22-23

obeyed their voice."565 [emphasis added]

Saul admits sinning — technically — but this is transparent rationalization. He claimed he was afraid of his followers and only reluctantly acquiesced to their scheme. After the third strike, Samuel pronounces upon Saul the end of his kingship. Saul then resorts to begging, but the trial was over.566 God knew his inner heart, and his time was up.

Contrast Saul with the attitude of King David. Soon after David committed adultery with Bathsheba and arranged the murder of her husband, David is confronted by the prophet Nathan. Nathan tells a parable of a poor man and his baby ewe. His sole possession on earth, the poor man loved it like a daughter. A rich man stole the lamb and fed it to his guests. [Yeah, it's pretty dark]. Responded David:

> "As the Lord lives, the man who has done this shall surely die! And he shall restore fourfold for the lamb, because he did this thing and because he had no pity."567

Then Nathan gets to the point — *You are the man!* — and pronounces judgment. But in this case, there's no rationalizing, blaming, or denial. David responds with humble simplicity:

> "I have sinned against the Lord."568

Two kings, two dramatic acts of disobedience. Saul responds with grandstanding, denial, rationalization, resistance to correction, and blaming — and gets deposed. David just confesses. That is what humility looks like. For David, there would still be consequences — and severe ones — but he was also shown mercy. In this light, it makes sense how David could be a "man after God's own heart" even after all he had done.569

Usually, we aren't going to *deny* our sins in private prayer — at least the ones we recognize — but it doesn't mean we don't blame or rationalize. There's just no one to call us out on the ones we don't admit, even to ourselves. We're not going to be confronted by a living prophet. These principles go beyond our demeanor before God. They should apply to our relationships with one another.

We see quite explicitly that in the Old Testament, God's mercy is directed toward the humble and withdrawn from the prideful. How does this play

---

565 I Samuel 15:24
566 I Samuel 15:30
567 2 Samuel 12:6
568 2 Samuel 12:13
569 Acts 13:22

out under the New Covenant?

Humility and Salvation in Christianity

In the New Testament, there are 55 instances (by my own tally — your mileage may vary) where eternal life is promised on the basis of action by the individual. Care to guess what action that would be? Get baptized? Repent? Confess? Not even close. The number one action, named in 21 of the 55 passages, was "believe." In distant second and third place were "repent" (4 of 55) and "leave" (3 of 55). To someone unfamiliar with the lesson of Chapter 3, this might seem unfair. How can someone force themselves into believing something they thought was untrue? Well, as you now know, beliefs are fluid, to say the least. People are pretty good at finding reasons to believe what they want to believe and to reject what they don't want to believe. Here, the Bible was spot on: certain beliefs are a matter of choice.[570]

I could only find one person in the four accounts of Jesus's earthly ministry who was explicitly told he would go to heaven, the repentant thief hanging on the cross next to Jesus.

> "Then one of the criminals who were hanged blasphemed Him, saying, 'If You are the Christ, save Yourself and us.'
>
> But the other, answering, rebuked him, saying, 'Do you not even fear God, seeing you are under the same condemnation? And we indeed justly, for we receive the due reward of our deeds; but this Man has done nothing wrong.' Then he said to Jesus, 'Lord, remember me when You come into Your kingdom.'
>
> And Jesus said to him, 'Assuredly, I say to you, today you will be with Me in Paradise.'"[571]

If belief is the path to salvation, from that brief exchange, we can deduce at least two things that the redeemed thief confessed:

1. That he was guilty and got what he deserved
2. That Jesus was Lord and had the power to save

The list of necessary beliefs unto salvation might be longer, but I submit it cannot be shorter. This puts a lot of weight on believing in one's own guilt. Can a person be saved who doesn't think he needs to be saved? God can — and will — save whomever He chooses, but prospects did not look

---

[570] Romans 1:18
[571] Luke 23:39-43

auspicious for the rich young ruler.[572]

Take the famous teaching known as the Beatitudes:

> "Blessed are the poor in spirit, for theirs is the kingdom of heaven."[573]

The Greek word translated as "poor" means needy, destitute, or reduced to beggary. The word translated as "spirit" refers to the soul, or rational faculties of the human person. "Poor in spirit" sounds quite a bit like humility to me. It did to John Calvin, who cited Chrysostom:

> "What is meant by the poor in spirit? The humble and contrite in mind."[574]

Moving along, consider the famous description of the final judgment in Matthew 25. Jesus foretells dividing all of humanity into two groups. The sheep (a docile, submissive species) go to heaven. The goats (independent and headstrong) go to everlasting fire.[575] Note what follows. It almost sounds like the sheep are being rewarded for good behavior — that they are saved by their works:

> "When the Son of Man comes in His glory... All the nations will be gathered before Him, and He will separate them one from another, as a shepherd divides his sheep from the goats. And He will set the sheep on His right hand, but the goats on the left. Then the King will say to those on His right hand, 'Come, you blessed of My Father, inherit the kingdom prepared for you from the foundation of the world: for I was hungry and you gave Me food; I was thirsty and you gave Me drink; I was a stranger and you took Me in; I was naked and you clothed Me; I was sick and you visited Me; I was in prison and you came to Me.'

> "Then the righteous will answer Him, saying, 'Lord, when did we see You hungry and feed You, or thirsty and give You drink? When did we see You a stranger and take You in, or naked and clothe You? Or when did we see You sick, or in prison, and come to You?'"

Full stop. Jesus is praising the "sheep" for their good deeds, welcoming them into paradise, and they start to *argue with him?* This tells us little of

---

[572] Matthew 19, Mark 10, Luke 18
[573] Matthew 5:3
[574] "Church Fathers: Homily 15 on Matthew (Chrysostom)." Accessed May 25, 2022. https://www.newadvent.org/fathers/200115.htm.
[575] Pet Keen. "Sheep vs. Goat: What's the Difference?" February 19, 2021. https://pet-keen.com/sheep-vs-goat/.

their actual accomplishments but speaks volumes about their mindset. *They did not feel they deserved the eternal reward.*

OK, how about the other group — the goats? What is their response?

> "Then He will also say to those on the left hand, 'Depart from Me, you cursed, into the everlasting fire prepared for the devil and his angels: for I was hungry and you gave Me no food; I was thirsty and you gave Me no drink; I was a stranger and you did not take Me in, naked and you did not clothe Me, sick and in prison and you did not visit Me.'

> "Then they also will answer Him, saying, 'Lord, when did we see You hungry or thirsty or a stranger or naked or sick or in prison, and did not minister to You?'"

At this point, the "goats" would have been wise to plead for mercy, but they do not. Face to face with the Holy God, their eternity hanging in the balance, they *argue their innocence.* Worse, they fall back upon their own personal merit.

Like any passage of Scripture, this passage has many layers and can be interpreted in many ways, and many different lessons can be mutually consistent. But when I look at this passage, it's pretty hard to ignore the tone of their responses and the mindset that those responses reveal.

The message is twofold. Those who admit their unworthiness will be saved. Those who believe they are worthy are doomed. Just like the thief on the cross and the rich young ruler. If you seek eternal life in communion with God, better start with admitting you don't deserve it. That's not such a huge concession. None of us does. Then throw yourself upon His mercy.

> "His mercy is on those who fear Him from generation to generation."[576]

But there's another layer beneath that attitude. Why do some believe, and others do not? Are the ones who repent and believe inherently more humble, more open-minded, or less wicked at heart? No. That would be the heresy of semipelagianism mentioned in Chapter 6. Scripture teaches clearly[577] — and most major faith traditions agree — that faith itself is a gift of God.[578] We don't even get to claim credit for that. Let's see what six of the oldest and largest have to say:

---

[576] Luke 1:50, from The Song of Mary
[577] Ephesians 2:8-9
[578] There are a few who reject this. They can write their own book on pride and humility.

Baptist:

> "I ask any saved man to look back upon his own conversion, and
> explain how it came about. You turned to Christ, and believed on
> his name: these were your own acts and deeds. But what caused
> you thus to turn? ... Do you attribute this singular renewal to the
> existence of a something better in you than has been yet discov-
> ered in your unconverted neighbor? No, you confess that you
> might have been what he now is if it had not been that there was
> a potent something which touched the spring of your will, enlight-
> ened your understanding, and guided you to the foot of the
> cross."[579]

Catholic:

> "When St. Peter confessed that Jesus is the Christ, the Son of the
> living God, Jesus declared to him that this revelation did not come
> "from flesh and blood," but from "my Father who is in heaven."
> Faith is a gift of God, a supernatural virtue infused by him. "Before
> this faith can be exercised, man must have the grace of God to
> move and assist him; he must have the interior helps of the Holy
> Spirit, who moves the heart and converts it to God, who opens the
> eyes of the mind and 'makes it easy for all to accept and believe
> the truth.'"[580]

Methodist:

> "It was impossible for Lazarus to come forth, till the Lord had
> given him life. And it is equally impossible for us to come out of
> our sins, yea, or to make the least motion toward it, till He who
> hath all power in heaven and earth calls our dead souls into
> life."[581]

Presbyterian:

> "The grace of faith, whereby the elect are enabled to believe to the
> saving of their souls, is the work of the Spirit of Christ in their
> hearts; and is ordinarily wrought by the ministry of the Word: by
> which also, and by the administration of the sacraments, and

---

[579] "C. H. Spurgeon: Spurgeon's Sermons Volume 61: 1915—Christian Classics Ethereal Library." Accessed May 22, 2022. https://ccel.org/ccel/spurgeon/sermons61/ser-
mons61.xl.html.

[580] Catechism of the Catholic Church III:153 http://www.vatican.va/ar-
chive/ENG0015/_PX.HTM

[581] Wesley, John. Sermon 85: "On Working out our Salvation" In: "John Wesley: Sermons on
Several Occasions—Christian Classics Ethereal Library." Accessed May 22, 2022.
https://www.ccel.org/ccel/wesley/sermons.vi.xxxii.html.

prayer, it is increased and strengthened."[582]

Anglican:

> "The condition of Man after the fall of Adam is such, that he cannot turn and prepare himself, by his own natural strength and good works, to faith, and calling upon God: Wherefore we have no power to do good works pleasant and acceptable to God, without the grace of God by Christ preventing us, that we may have a good will, and working with us, when we have that good will."[583]

Lutheran:

> "I believe that I cannot by my own reason or strength believe in Jesus Christ, my Lord, or come to Him; but the Holy Spirit has called me by the Gospel, enlightened me with His gifts, sanctified and kept me in the true faith."[584]

The humble mind is far removed from the proud one in its approach towards God. A humble mind is distinguished by attitudes of conviction, submission, repentance, and gratitude. Submission means honoring God as God and not usurping his authority. Submission means obedience to his commands. A humble mind is grateful, because it does not feel entitled to God's grace, his blessings, or eternal salvation. As all major faith traditions teach, saving faith is a gift of God. An authentic Biblical view of salvation is enveloped in humility.

Moreover, the Biblical view of salvation leaves no room for pride. There is nothing in our character or behavior that separates us from the unbelieving and unredeemed. There is no rational basis for taking credit. The humble mind can be repentant because it is not locked into attitudes of denial and self-rationalization.

On the matter of assurance

The New Testament is clear that some who expect to enter heaven will be turned away at the gate:

> "Not everyone who says to Me, 'Lord, Lord,' shall enter the

---

[582] *Westminster Confession of Faith—Christian Classics Ethereal Library.* Article 14. https://ccel.org/ccel/anonymous/westminster3/westminster3.i.xvi.html. Accessed 25 May 2022.

[583] "Anglicans Online | The Thirty-Nine Articles." Accessed May 22, 2022. http://anglicansonline.org/basics/thirty-nine_articles.html. (Number 10)

[584] "Luther's Small Catechism by Dr. Martin Luther." Accessed May 22, 2022. https://catechism.cph.org/en/creed.html.

kingdom of heaven, but he who does the will of My Father in heaven."[585]

There will be many who correctly believe they are saved, but there will be others who falsely assume that they are saved. The perennial question is, how do you know which one you are?

It is not as simple as it may seem. In a sort of popular contemporary Evangelical formulation, one is saved by praying something called a "prayer of salvation." But the Bible *never* says we are saved by a prayer. Many have prayed one of these prayers whose lives revealed no evidence of regeneration. The usual explanation is that they didn't pray "sincerely." But how do you measure that? Within the Reformed tradition, salvation comes through God's sovereign act of regeneration. But how does one know that one is among the elect?

I don't believe anyone has a perfect, airtight answer to this question, but the Bible lays the fundamentals. This is why in the book of James and many related passages, considerable emphasis is placed on good works and good character as evidence of a changed heart. Good character specifically means exhibiting the fruits of the spirit, and especially the fruit of love.

> "By this all will know that you are My disciples, if you have love for one another."[586]

Reading the biography of Jonathan Edwards, I found that this was a pressing issue in the years prior to the First Great Awakening.[587] The themes of pride and humility are pervasive in the writings of Jonathan Edwards. His father and mentor, Timothy Edwards, is quoted as preaching in 1695:

> "No person that is not truly humbled whatever change is wrought in him is not, can not be, savingly changed or truly converted."[588]

Or, as Jesus taught:

> "Blessed are the meek, for they shall inherit the earth."[589]

In the concluding chapter, we will see that humility is the secret weapon to transforming the world.

---

[585] Matthew 7:21
[586] John 13:25
[587] Marsden, George M. *Jonathan Edwards: A Life*. New Haven, Conn.: Yale University Press, 2003.
[588] Marsden, p58
[589] Matthew 5:5

Key points

- Humility is a core, if not the core, virtue of Christian character.
- Humility is an integral element of saving faith.

« 16 »

"As for me and my house"

Humility in action

Humility respects authority but does not demand universal submission or passivity toward suffering and evil. There are times one must take a stand — alone, if necessary. But when people do that, it's often out of arrogance. How and when can bold action proceed in a spirit of humility?

If God is truly God, not a single particle in the universe acts apart from His will. God is in absolute, sovereign control of past, present, and future. The illusion of pride — that God's plan is contingent upon our efforts — can lead to anxiety and despair. Humility trusts that God is in complete control. His strength is made perfect in our weakness.

"The absence of humility is no doubt the reason why the power of God cannot do its mighty work." [590] — ANDREW MURRAY

".....God doth not need
Either man's work or his own gifts; who best
Bear his mild yoke, they serve him best. His state
Is Kingly: thousands at his bidding speed,
And post o'er land and ocean without rest;
They also serve who only stand and wait." — MILTON[591]

Having spent the better part of this book downplaying our importance, wisdom, ability, and control, it might seem the life of humility would be one of passive indifference and servitude:

---

[590] Murray, p. 49
[591] John Milton. "When I consider how my life is spent." Ca. 1655. (written after he had gone blind)

"You're not that important."
"Always submit to authority."
"How likely is it that you're right and everyone else is wrong?"
"It's not worth trying to make a difference."

However, to generalize such statements to all times and places would be a grievous error, failing to apprehend the immense *power* of humility. God's purposes are seldom attained through worldly means of control but through His own.

Power is fleeting

Since St. Augustine penned *The City of God*, there has been a general agreement that Jesus did not come to establish an earthly dominion. One could argue there have been "Christian nations" in a particular sense, but through most of Western history, church and state have remained separate power bases in an uneasy tension. Sometimes the church was on the ascendancy, as when Pope Gregory VII excommunicated emperor Henry IV (1050-1106) over the investiture controversy. You may have heard the story about how Henry stood three days barefoot in the snow to beg forgiveness. This feeds the popular myth of an all-powerful Catholic church embraced by many secularists. Less well known is that three years later, after his second excommunication, Henry IV led his armies against Rome, forcibly deposing Gregory VII and putting his own man in charge. So much for the "all-powerful" church. Power is fleeting, even for emperors and popes.

Humility is liberating

"My yoke is easy and My burden is light"[592]

Humility frees us from burdens we cannot possibly bear. Let's consider just two.

Humility releases us from the burden of appearing morally perfect.

We invest so much effort trying to maintain the illusion of perfection: speaking and acting in particular ways to impress our peers, justifying our actions to others, rationalizing our actions to ourselves, and experiencing disappointment with ourselves when we can rationalize no longer. It's exhausting. It's also not what Scripture teaches.

---

[592] Matthew 11:30

"If we say that we have no sin, we deceive ourselves, and the truth is not in us. If we confess our sins, He is faithful and just to forgive us our sins and to cleanse us from all unrighteousness."[593]

This begins with the greatest sin. If we say that we have no pride, we deceive ourselves. Personally, I have found that simply admitting it gives me the ability to move forward.

Humility lifts the burden of responsibility for things we cannot control.

"Fear arises when we imagine everything depends on us."
—ELISABETH ELLIOT

When we imagine the future of the church, the nation, or the world depends upon us, we suffer from a control illusion. The biggest problem with the control illusion is not that it's untrue. The real problem is that if it were genuinely true, we'd bear responsibility for the results — and that's an impossible burden to carry. That sense of duty clashes with awareness of our true inadequacy, resulting in perpetual fear and anxiety, or worse, engendering an "ends justify the means" mindset.

Humility acknowledges our own helplessness, thus freeing us from unwarranted guilt and a sense of failure. This is a basic Christian teaching that spans all faith traditions:

"There are times when the burden of need and our own limitations might tempt us to become discouraged... in the end, we are only instruments in the Lord's hands, and this knowledge frees us from the presumption of thinking that we alone are personally responsible for building a better world. In all humility, we will do what we can, and in all humility, we will entrust the rest to the Lord. It is God who governs the world, not we." — POPE BENEDICT XVI[594]

Humility seeks to serve

But this doesn't mean we just "let go and let God." The humility demonstrated by our incarnate Lord was active, not passive. He came to serve, and service is rooted in humility.

Dr. Bill Rhodes serves as a missionary surgeon at Kapsowar Mission Hospital in Kenya. As a young adult, Bill felt called to become a missionary

---

[593] I John 1:8-9
[594] Encyclical Letter, *Deus Caritas Est* (35) December 25, 2006

physician. This necessitated going back to college for pre-med and then gaining admission to medical school. Over many years Bill struggled but persevered, eventually completing his surgical training and going to serve as the only surgeon at Kapsowar.

In academic medicine, where I spent much of my career, individuals are valued according to their achievements. Superior academic performance, research, publication, and savvy political skills render one "worthy" of becoming a department chair or dean. Some people measure human worth in such terms. In the eyes of some academicians, Dr. Rhodes might be seen as an underachiever. But who is more dispensable? If a department chair or dean were to drop dead, ten other candidates would queue up for the honor (and some might even cheer her passing). Not so with Dr. Rhodes. He is irreplaceable.

Humility and courage

> "Choose for yourselves this day whom you will serve, whether the gods which your fathers served that were on the other side of the River, or the gods of the Amorites, in whose land you dwell. But as for me and my house, we will serve the Lord." — Joshua [595]

As a general principle, followers of Christ ought to respect civil and church authorities, obey the laws and submit to church discipline. In Chapter 13, we discussed intellectual humility and the sound principle of respecting the consensus of authorities.

But...

Sometimes authorities are flagrantly immoral. Sometimes the experts are wrong. Sometimes the leaders are domineering bullies.

Is it possible to oppose one or the other without being prideful?

This is not as straightforward as it might seem. Collaborating with abusive authorities or running with the herd is usually safer, easier, and more rewarding in material terms. There you have it. The one who submits may be every bit as self-serving as the one who fancies himself a "lone voice in the wilderness."

Most people are sheep. The normal tendency is to run with the crowd — but not any crowd. *Your* crowd, whatever it happens to be. To stand against the crowd requires not only humility — risking your personal standing —

---

[595] Joshua 24:15

but courage (like humility, an underrated virtue). In such settings, courage starts with a conscious indifference toward the approval and acceptance of others.

Some of my greatest personal heroes stood against authority and against the crowd: Jan Hus, Martin Luther, William Tyndale, John Adams, Dietrich Bonhoeffer. Jesus boldly and consistently opposed the powers of first-century Judaism. A blanket principle of "submit to authorities" in all times and all places simply isn't Biblical.

It's really not that mysterious how to square humility with dissent. The heroes I listed were not acting out of an attitude of superiority or selfish interest but laid down their lives in the service of others. Hus, Tyndale, and Bonhoeffer were martyred. Luther placed himself in mortal peril and might have died but for the protection of a powerful prince. Jesus died to redeem the very ones who condemned him, as many Pharisees became part of the early church.[596]

Sometimes that service means seizing the initiative. In *American Sniper*, Chris Kyle is counseling his boys:

> "There are three types of people in this world: sheep, wolves, and sheepdogs. Some people prefer to believe that evil doesn't exist in this world. Those are the sheep. And then you got predators. They use violence to prey on the weak. Those are the wolves."[597]

But that rare breed devoted to protecting the weak and helpless is the sheepdog. Be a sheepdog, he tells his young sons.

Frank Peretti discerned a similar message in the film classic, *A Few Good Men*.[598] When the trial ended, the two Marines were acquitted of murder but sentenced to a dishonorable discharge:

> "I don't understand," said the younger Marine. "Colonel Jessup said he ordered the code red. What did we do wrong? We did nothing wrong!"

> "Yeah, we did," replied the older and wiser. "We were supposed to fight for people who couldn't fight for themselves. We were supposed to fight for Willie."

---

[596] Acts 15:5
[597] Eastwood, Clint, dir. *American Sniper.* Warner Bros. Pictures, 2014.
[598] Reiner, Rob, dir. *A Few Good Men* Columbia Pictures, 1992.

Wrote Peretti, "the depth of a person's character is not measured by his or her physical strength, but by the depth of his or her nobility. How do we treat those who are weaker?"[599]

It's just my opinion, but in my moral calculus, it is always justifiable to stand up to a bully. It may not always be necessary; it may not always be prudent, and violence must be the absolute last resort, but it's justified. It's immoral *to tolerate* bullying. (As mentioned earlier, ostentatious victimhood is just a form of manipulation that constitutes emotional bullying. It must be challenged, as well).

"What happened to 'turn the other cheek'?" you might ask. It is clear from the context that this refers to personal affronts. I could cite many more verses in both Old and New Testaments commanding us to protect and defend the weak and helpless.

The critical thing, though, is to stand up to bullies without *becoming one*. We do this by ignoring them, resisting them, or defying them. More importantly, we must stop *supporting* them and make it abundantly clear — particularly in the church — that bullying is morally and socially *unacceptable* and will not be tolerated.

It is unconscionable that abuse of women and children should ever occur within the church, but multiple well-publicized scandals have shown that it is both tolerated and prevalent. Some blame it on traditional masculinity. I do not. I blame it on apathy, denial, selfishness, cowardice, and — of course — pride. Where are the protectors? If our congregations cannot be a safe space for women and youth, we may as well shut down the whole operation until we get that one thing right. After the gospel itself, what most distinguished the early church from pagan society was its valuation of women and children. This means more than simply refraining from harassment. It means men treating women as equals, with dignity and respect — as Jesus did.

The future is never bleak

Among pride's great deceptions, perhaps most dangerous of all is the conceit that the world's fate rests in our hands. In the popular mindset, kings, armies, technology, and empires are the driving forces of history. If political and military power are all that count, it would make sense to use them. Nonsense. The humble disciples of Jesus had a far greater impact upon civilization than all the conquerors combined — and their impact was for

---

[599] Peretti, Frank E. *The Wounded Spirit*. Nashville: Word, 2000.

good. All the disciples had was humility, the power of words...and the mighty power of God.

God favors the "losers" of this world.

Back in 1990, super-magnate Ted Turner ruffled the Christian community by declaring Christianity a "religion for losers." (The muddled nuance of his actual intent was drowned in the ensuing indignation). Poor Ted. Maybe we shouldn't have been so hard on Mr. Turner because *he was right*: the shocking truth is that God has a *soft spot* for losers. It's the winners (in the eyes of the world) that have more to fear and the most to lose.[600]

Face it. Cultural trends in the West have not been favorable to Christianity of late, generating a string of titles:

- *That Hideous Strength: How the West Was Lost* — Melvin Tinker, 2018
- *Suicide of the West: How the Rebirth of Tribalism, Populism, Nationalism, and Identity Politics is Destroying American Democracy* — Jonah Goldberg, 2018
- *The Fall of Western Civilization: How Liberalism is Destroying the West from Within* — Robert Gordon, 2018
- *The Benedict Option: A Strategy for Christians in a post-Christian Nation* — Rod Dreher, 2017

The anxiety and suspicion voiced by many Christians borders on clinical paranoia. Only one enemy presents any serious threat, and we will return to him shortly. How can fear and pessimism be so rampant? The imperative "fear not" appears 71 times in the King James translation of the Bible, while "be not afraid" appears an additional 26 times. How often does God have to say something before the command is serious? So why are we so worried? Because we either have forgotten or simply don't believe that God is sovereign and place too much confidence in our own judgments.

We're all notoriously bad at making predictions.

- In the 1960s and 1970s, the Soviet Empire seemed invincible. By the end of the next decade, it had disintegrated.
- Japan was the juggernaut of the 1980s, followed by a decade of economic contraction.

---

[600] In his autobiography, Mr. Turner says he regretted the comment and meant pretty much what I just said: Turner, Ted, and Bill Burke. *Call Me Ted.* New York: Grand Central Pub, 2008. p361

- The 1990s began hopefully, with democracies taking root throughout the world. "The End of History," according to a famous book by Francis Fukuyama. Since the beginning of the new millennium, democracy has been in retreat.
- The Islamification of Europe was the great anxiety of the early 2000s. That's ground to a halt.
- In 2020 and 2021, a series of Pentecostal prophets falsely predicted the triumph of Donald Trump, civil war, then Trump's August 2021 "return" to power. Said the repentant Jeremiah Johnson in late 2021, "they obviously have been humbled." [601]

What do we make of such talk over the perceived decline of Western Christianity? On the one hand, there is nothing inevitable about current trends toward secularism. On the other hand, people in past centuries were probably far less devout than many suppose.

If the great theologians of past generations are correct, the fading of Western Christianity has more to do with failure on the part of the church than the might of its adversaries. I don't know what the next ten years or the next hundred years may bring, nor does anyone else. I do know that God remains in control, and that's all I need.

The absolute sovereignty of God over world affairs is famously expressed in the Westminster Confession:

> "God from all eternity did by the most and holy counsel of His own will, freely and unchangeably ordain whatsoever comes to pass; yet so as thereby neither is God the author of sin; nor is violence offered to the will of the creatures, nor is the liberty or contingency of second causes taken away, but rather established."[602]

However, this is not a doctrine unique to Calvinism. According to theologian Ken Keathley, "All orthodox Christians, across the theological spectrum, affirm that God has an eternal plan and purpose and that he will accomplish his will with precision and success."[603]

This is particularly so concerning earthly rulers:

> "Jesus answered [to Pontius Pilate], "You could have no power at all against Me unless it had been given you from above...."[604]

---

[601] McDade, Stefani. "Prophetic Reckoning". *Christianity Today* July/August 2021, 56-61.
[602] *The Westminster Confession of Faith*, 3:1
[603] Personal communication, December 2021
[604] John 19:11

"...In order that the living may know that the Most High rules in the kingdom of men, gives it to whomever He will, and sets over it the lowest of men."[605]

The sovereignty of God is the critical factor that more pessimistic commentators afford little consideration to. Rulers rise and fall; elections come and go. No one disputes that personal and corporate agency matters. Nevertheless, every world leader is in place only according to the sovereign will of God. As we witnessed in recent history through the collapse of Western Communism, they may appear invincible one day and be gone the next. Eastern Communism will end, too, on the day that God has appointed.

God works through the meek and lowly

In the epic *Lord of the Rings* trilogy, the forces of Sauron were bravely resisted by an army of men, elves, and dwarves assembled under Aragorn. In the heroic defense of Minas Tirith, Sauron's forces were temporarily defeated, but the ultimate threat remained. Though the city was saved, the cost had been high. The army of men was depleted and weary, and fresh legions of Sauron massed at the gates awaiting their orders to advance. In his heroic final stand outside the gates of Mordor, Aragorn's forces were outnumbered a thousand to one. By all outward appearance, Middle Earth was doomed. But the fate of Middle Earth did not reside in horses, armor, and catapults.

As Sauron savored in anticipation of his final triumph, his destruction was but moments away. His defeat came about by no mighty army but by the indomitable persistence of an insignificant pair of Hobbits. Bearing the burden no other creature could have dared or been entrusted with, Sam and Frodo carried the mighty Ring of power to the lava pits of Mount Doom to destroy it forever. At the penultimate moment, the quest nearly failed as Frodo finally succumbed to the power of The Ring. Yet even as Frodo's lapse threatened doom for all, there was an invisible hand at work. In that final pivotal moment, the miserable Gollum reappeared, battled with Frodo for possession of the Ring, and tumbled, Ring in hand, into the fiery lava, destroying the Ring forever and with it Sauron and all his legions.

The theme of the small and weak prevailing over the strong and mighty was uppermost in the mind of Tolkien:

---

[605] Daniel 4:17

"Such is oft the course of deeds that move the wheels of the world: small hands do them because they must, while the eyes of the great are elsewhere."[606]

In his letter to Milton Waldman, Tolkien identified Sam Gamgee, not Frodo, as the "chief hero" of the epic. Sam alone showed himself impervious to the Ring and its lure of absolute power. Tolkien spoke of the power in weakness: "A moral of the whole .... is the obvious one that without the high and noble the simple and vulgar is utterly mean; and without the simple and ordinary the noble and heroic is meaningless."[607] In another letter, Tolkien described his masterpiece as "primarily a study of the ennoblement (or sanctification) of the humble."[608]

But we don't base eternal truths on a work of fiction, even from such a luminary as Tolkien. Is this principle found in Scripture? Indeed, there was a sort of "Sam Gamgee" in the man named Gideon. During the time of the Judges, the Israelites, in a pattern all too common, had done evil in the sight of God, resulting in cruel and severe oppression under the Midianites for seven long years.

After Israel returned to the Lord and cried for relief, God sent an angel to a man named Gideon. Gideon, at the time, was a notably un-valorous farmer hiding from the Midianites by threshing his wheat in a winepress. Suddenly, an angel appears to him, saying, "The Lord is with you, mighty warrior." *Mighty Warrior??* At the moment, Gideon seemed anything but. He understandably took it as a case of mistaken identity. The angel persisted. "'Go in the strength you have, and save Israel out of Midian's hand,' said the Lord. 'But Lord,' Gideon asked, 'how can I save Israel? My clan is the weakest in Manasseh, and I am the least in my family.'" Mighty warrior, indeed! But the Lord answered him, "I will be with you, and you will strike down all the Midianites together."[609]

So, Gideon and his three hundred men entered battle *armed with trumpets, torches, and empty pitchers* (comparable to taking on the Russian army with flashlights and water bottles). The Midianites fell upon one another and fled in terror. For "God has chosen the foolish things of the world to put to shame the wise, and God has chosen the weak things of the world to put to shame the things which are mighty."[610] Gideon was no mighty

---

[606] Tolkien, J. R. R. *The Fellowship of the Ring*. New York: Ballantine Books, 1965 p353. (Spoken by Elrond)

[607] Tolkien, J. R. R., Humphrey Carpenter, and Christopher Tolkien. *The Letters of J.R.R. Tolkien*. Boston: Houghton Mifflin, 1981. (letter 131)

[608] Tolkien, *Letters*, number 181, p232

[609] Judges 6, selected verses

[610] I Corinthians 1:27

warrior, but he had one thing going for him, and that was faithfulness. His courage came not through his own power but an unwavering faith in the Lord. As with all true virtues, such does not emerge from within, but through the Holy Spirit dwelling in us. Gideon was meek, but obedient; God made him brave.

For a more contemporary illustration, think about the "story" problem in "Raiders of the Lost Ark." You didn't know there was a story problem? In the hit TV series "Big Bang Theory," Amy explained to Sheldon:

> Amy: "Indiana Jones plays no role in the outcome of the story. If he weren't in the film, it would turn out exactly the same. The Nazis would have still found the Ark, taken it to the island, opened it up, and all died — just like they did!"[611]

From a cosmic perspective, God was always going to win. Just because they had the Ark, was God somehow obliged to assist them in their evil plan to conquer the world and annihilate His chosen people? Their "only winning move was not to play,"[612] but the Nazis played anyway — and lost spectacularly. This was equally true of the real-life Nazis. God took them down. Sure, He used the Allied armies. But if Hitler had not made some foolish and catastrophic errors, things might have worked out quite differently.

So we could say that Indiana Jones made no difference to the outcome. OK. That's one way of framing it. But let's try framing it a little differently.

As the story unfolded, Henry "Indiana" Jones, Jr. experienced the adventure of a lifetime, demonstrating preternatural courage and perseverance. At the climax, he had a front-row seat to the raw display of God's mighty power. And he ended up with Karen Allen. Not bad at all.

This is a surprisingly Biblical perspective. Think about Jericho: How much difference did Joshua make to the outcome? Gideon? Moses?

I know. You're thinking, "Moses really did something."

Let's talk about Moses.

You know the story. Adopted as a babe, Moses grew up in the court of Pharaoh, where he accumulated great learning and power. This we know from

---

[611] Cendrowski, Mark, dir. "The Raiders Minimization." *The Big Bang Theory*. CBS. Season 7 Episode 4, aired 10/10/2013

[612] Badham, John, dir. *War Games*. Metro-Goldwyn-Mayer/United Artists, 1983.

the testimony of St. Stephen: "Moses was learned in all the wisdom of the Egyptians, and was mighty in words and deeds."[613]

So, one day Moses sees an Egyptian abusing an Israelite and dispenses vigilante-style justice, expecting to be hailed as a hero. Once more, Stephen informs us, "For he supposed that his brethren would have understood that God would deliver them by his hand." To Moses's utter dismay, his people were not in the least impressed. On the verge of being ratted out, he fled for his life to Midian. Here's a question for you: What does God NOT say?

> *"Strong are you, Moses, but you must learn to control your power. Go you must to the land of Dagobah, where you will be trained in the ways of the Ju-di by Master Yodastein."*

If George Lucas had composed the narrative, that's exactly how it would play out. That's how things roll in virtually every popular film. But that's not what happened, was it?

> *"Moses, I'm sending you to herd sheep in Nowheresville for 40 years. There you will learn that it's not about you."*

And Moses returns to face the most *powerful* ruler of the known world as the *humblest man* on the face of the earth.[614]

Perhaps you agree with my take on the story — in principle — but what do we do in practice?

- We attend seminary to master theology and homiletics, but not humility.
- We study apologetics to defend the faith — and become "experts" at detecting the fallacies of others while remaining oblivious to our own.
- We double down on books and courses in leadership — but who's training to become a better servant?
- We pore through the Bible year after year after year — and grow more impressed with our Biblical knowledge and more confident in our opinions.
- We spend weeks, months, or a lifetime studying prophecy — yet completely miss the overarching theme that God is in total control.

---

[613] Acts 7:22
[614] Numbers 12:3

So perhaps we're more like young Moses than we realize. I mean not to oversimplify: expertise still matters. Through his upbringing and service in the court of Pharaoh, Moses acquired skills that would prove indispensable in his subsequent career assignment. He could be forgiven that humility was not part of the curriculum.

First-century Christians didn't set out to take over the world. Jesus reached out to those who were spiritually destitute. There are spiritually hungry people out there today. Are we the sort of people who make them feel welcome? Mostly, no.

The supernatural power of humility

So, having come full circle, we are back to where we started. All natural human thought, discourse, and behavior are corrupted by pride, and pride is a state of opposition to God. It is the root of most conflict. When society descends into tribalism and mutual animosity, there is pride. Where churches are divided, there is pride. When families are estranged, there is pride. Where there is vigorous embrace of falsehood, there is pride. Andrew Murray did not exaggerate: "a lack of humility is the source of every defect and failure."[615]

This realization leads inescapably to one necessary conclusion — if we seek peace, fruitfulness, and success, the only way there is down the hidden pathway of Humility. We've tried everything else. Why not give it a shot?

There is one remaining practice of humility that I have scarcely mentioned thus far — prayer. Properly understood, prayer is the open affirmation of our utter dependence upon God. Unfortunately, too often our prayers are more like instructions than petitions. Rather than trusting His sovereign will over civil governance, we pray for the victory of our chosen candidates from county sheriff to President of the United States, then spend the next ten minutes explaining to God what is at stake if our candidate loses. [Maybe they don't name names in your church, but we all know *who they're talking about*, don't we?] Brothers and sisters, this is not humility, and this is not faith.

When, if ever, do we pray as one for God to break our pride? How often do we pray for the indwelling Spirit to make us humble? When have we prayed for release from *our own* deception?

---

615 Murray, p 17

One of C. S. Lewis's most enduring and popular works is *The Screwtape Letters.* [616] In this serious yet whimsical satire, a senior demon named Screwtape coaches a younger apprentice on ways to undermine the life and faith of a new adult believer. Unfortunately, many just see it as poking fun at liberal thought. There's a good deal of that. But Lewis believed — and so do I — that demonic deception is both real and prevalent.

Well, Uncle Screwtape has been busy of late, and the battle for truth over deceit is a spiritual battle against forces we cannot see, hear, or touch. The Lord's prayer many of us learned — "deliver us from evil" — is better translated as "deliver us from the evil one" (as indeed it is in the NIV and NKJV).[617] In the original Greek, "evil one" (πονηροῦ) is preceded by a definite article "the" (του). The expression is identical to the closing of Ephesians 6:16:

> "above all, taking the shield of faith with which you will be able to quench all the fiery darts *of the wicked one.*"

The biblical accounts of Jesus's engagements with the Pharisees offer a revealing and sobering account of Satanic deception. In the popular imagination, Satan tempts us to disregard the law of God, indulge in wanton pleasures, mock Scripture, and have no regard for the opinions of "religious" people. While all of those serve his purposes quite adequately, he's indifferent regarding what direction we err. After all, what sort of wayward thoughts are more likely to take root in the devout?

The Pharisees were hyper-religious, scrupulously moral, sanctimonious, and highly concerned with appearances. Far from denying the Word of God, they were famous for their rigid, hyperliteral interpretations of God's Word, strict conformity to the Mosaic law, and ostentatious displays of religiosity, with tragic indifference to the virtues of grace, love, kindness, and humility. Jesus called them the children of Satan. There is no shortage of such persons in Christian history or in the Christian present. Satan's chief objective is not to sow false doctrine, but hatred, division, and conflict. He doesn't care what we believe, so long as we are at each other's throats. We make it too easy for him.

In your church, public, and group prayers, how often have people prayed for deliverance from Satan — meaning, above all, deliverance not from

---

[616] Lewis, C. S. *The Screwtape Letters: Letters from a Senior to a Junior Devil.* C. S. Lewis Signature Classics Edition. London: HarperCollins, 2016.
[617] Matthew 6:13, Luke 11:4

illness and troubles but from *deception*? In my experience, hardly ever. Maybe we should be praying the way Jesus taught us?

Nurturing pride in our hearts is like bolting down all the windows and doors but leaving the garage door wide open. It's like a security vulnerability in the operating system through which a hacker can gain complete control of a server. Satan zeroes in on our pride. It worked on Adam and Eve, and it's been working ever since. You think you're immune? Then he has you *exactly* where he wants you. But Edwards knew where true power lay:

> "Nothing sets a person so much out of the devil's reach as humility."[618]

What does the future hold?

Christians, of all people, should be the most expectant and hopeful about the future. Even from a materialistic perspective, our fear is unwarranted. The prevailing secular narratives must eventually collapse under the weight of their many contradictions. There is no unified agenda [Satan doesn't do "unity"], just a *gemisch* of contradictory notions and feuding special interest groups:

- On one side, gender is innate and immutable and to be celebrated; on the other side, it is a fiction imposed by culture and society.
- "Capitalism is evil" — and we want a bigger share of it.
- Transgender individuals must reshape reality to affirm their preferences. Gays who prefer to be straight should accept their lot as fixed for eternity.
- Atheism is on the rise — but astrology's growing faster.
- The moral absolutism of the early 21st century flatly contradicts the moral relativism of the 20th century.
- Secular trends are leading to depopulation, with the looming risk of civilizational collapse.

The pride afflicting the church afflicts humanity across the globe, fueling narcissism, conflict, alienation, economic failure, loneliness, disease, war, and hardship. The worldwide secular culture is *institutionalized* pride. If pride is the root of failure, as I have shown, then Western (and Eastern) secularism *must* eventually fail. The question is, what comes next?

---

[618] Edwards, Jonathan. *Thoughts on the Revival of Religion in New England.* 1740 https://ccel.org/ccel/edwards/works1/works1.ix.v.i.html Accessed 2/14/2022

The Book of Revelation has countless different interpretations, but it concludes with one inescapable message: the Lord prevails. So quit fretting and rejoice in that fact. And be sure you're on the right side — the humble one.

The lost of this world are not our enemies. In our fallen state, all of us remain image-bearers of God. Most people are desperate for peace, harmony, love, friendship, and purpose. Christ has called us to mercy and compassion, not judgment and opposition. To be the "light of the world" demands virtue, but in our pride, we have neglected the virtue of humility. It is something the world desperately needs. It only took a handful of humble Galileans to change the world, yet nothing has been more transformative than the movement they began or boasts more followers today. God will always triumph. He doesn't need us, but He graciously allows us the role of a lifetime.

God seeks humble people through whom He can demonstrate His mighty and irresistible power. No matter your lot in life, you can be that person.

Key points

- Worldly power is fleeting; God remains in absolute sovereign control of world affairs
- God shows His power through the weak and lowly
- Humility is active, not passive
- There is no justification for Christian pessimism: Jesus will triumph over all.

T

V

W

Y

Z